LOURDES

Also by Patrick Marnham

Road to Katmandu
Fantastic Invasion

Patrick Marnham

❧ LOURDES ❧
A Modern Pilgrimage

TEXT COMPLETE AND UNABRIDGED

IMAGE BOOKS
A Division of Doubleday & Company, Inc.
Garden City, New York
1982

Image Book edition published September 1982
by special arrangement with
Coward, McCann & Geoghegan, Inc.

Library of Congress Cataloging in Publication Data

Marnham, Patrick.
  Lourdes: a modern pilgrimage.

  Includes index.
  1. Lourdes (France) 2. Christian pilgrims and
pilgrimages—France—Lourdes. I. Title.
BT653.M348 1982   232.91'7'094478
ISBN 978-0-385-18252-2   AACR2
Library of Congress Catalog Card Number 82-45299

Printed in the United States of America

145052501

For
H. M. M.

❧ Contents ❧

❧ Preface ❧

While this book was being written, religious belief was defined as a form of mental illness in the Soviet Union. And in France the mayor of Vestric-et-Candiac, in the Gard, tried to close a holiday home for the handicapped on the grounds that the pregnant women of his village were alarmed by the sight of such visitors. The pilgrimage to Lourdes is directly opposed to both these forms of intolerance.

The popularity of the pilgrimage increases almost every year and Lourdes now receives between four and five million visitors annually. There are perhaps two reasons for this phenomenon. The first is that the pilgrimage fulfils a need in the lives of those who are seriously ill which is overlooked by modern medical treatment. The sick pilgrims feel better, not in the sense of receiving a cure—that occurs in only a tiny fraction of cases—but in the sense of feeling stronger and happier and more reconciled to their lives.

The other reason is religious. Christianity has been a dominant influence in European history for nearly two thousand years. Today, in decline, it is responding to secular influences such as humanist philanthropy. The anthropologist Mary Douglas has noted the effect of this influence in her book *Natural Symbols*. The new Christian religion is marked by a contempt for external ritual forms; by a private internalizing of religious experience; and by an emphasis on private justification by good works. The result, says Professor Douglas, has been an impoverishment of symbolic perception, a distate for the "magical" element in religion, and the consequent disappearance of the symbolic life of the spirit. Religion is reduced to a branch of ethics.

Lourdes is unusually well placed to take advantage of this tendency. It exercises the religious capacity for ritual in the form of the pilgrimage, and in the elaborate ceremonies of the Domain. At the same time it commemorates a heavenly vision; that is, an instance of the "ideal" form of direct communication, the unmediated understanding which dispenses with the need for symbolism. And the Lourdes pilgrimage, in particular, satisfies the present insistence on good works. Indeed, for the Christian deprived of ritual and driven towards altruism here is the perfect solution: the ritual healing, rather than the actual one, which unites ritual and altruism and so satisfies both public opinion and the spiritual need for symbolism. The pilgrimage to Lourdes is an occasion for the symbolic act of charity, an elaborate form of practical assistance with limited temporal effect.

When reading about Lourdes one should remember the distinction which is always made between "miracles" and "cures." More than five thousand cures have been recorded by the Medical Bureau at Lourdes. A number of these have been thoroughly investigated, and a small proportion, found to be "medically inexplicable," have been forwarded to the appropriate bishop for consideration by a diocesan commission. Of those cures which have been examined by the Church only sixty-four, in over a hundred years, have been proclaimed miraculous. A detailed list is supplied in Appendix III. When referring to any of the proclaimed miracles in the text I have put the miracle list number in brackets after the name of the person cured.

In telling the story of Bernadette, I have relied on the researches of Father René Laurentin, whose six-volume history of the apparitions has recently been condensed and translated into a short work entitled *Bernadette of Lourdes.* I have also found *The Happening at Lourdes* by Alan Neame (1968) consistently helpful. The chronology which follows is partly based on tables supplied in that book and in *Alone of All Her Sex* by Marina Warner.

The rate of exchange at the time of writing was (roughly) 8 French francs to £1.

Among those who assisted me I would like to thank the following, who agreed to read all or part of the text and who made many helpful suggestions: Peter Crane, Dr. St. J. Dowling, Mrs. Winifred Feely, Fr. Crispian Hollis, Marie Kerslake, David Lewis, Malcolm and Annie Massey, Prof. David Morrell, Claude and Mary Pendaries, Pat Porter and John Tangney.

Peter Crane, Councillor of the Hospitality of Our Lady of Lourdes, and three members of the International Medical Committee of Lourdes—Dr. Daniel O'Connell (head of the department of radiotherapy at Charing Cross Hospital, London), Dr. Pierre Lance and Dr. Jean Louis Armand-Laroche—were all patient enough to answer numerous questions.

Dr. John Corcoran, Mr. Charles Gray, FRCS, Sir Ralph Marnham, KCVO, FRCS, and Dr. Elisabeth Whipp, none of whom have any connection with Lourdes, advised me on the meaning of various medical documents.

My thanks are also due to Dr. Théodore Mangiapan, director of the Lourdes Medical Bureau, for his assistance and for his generous permission to quote extensively from the Bureau's records and publications; and to Père Lalaque and Père Ramond of the Lourdes Chaplaincy for the help they gave me. I must also thank M. Jean Buscail of Lourdes for his hospitality and advice; M. Crépin, the headmaster of the Cours Peyramale, Lourdes, for permission to interview some of his pupils; Canon Edmund Mullins; and the Librarian of Downside Abbey, Bath.

Mrs. Winifred Feely, who has worked voluntarily at the Medical Bureau for thirty-one years, was exceptionally helpful over many months, and allowed me to consult her extensive private collection of relevant papers.

Any mistakes of fact which remain, and all the opinions expressed, are entirely my responsibility.

CHRONOLOGY

c400	Temple of Isis at Soissons, France, dedicated to the Holy Virgin
c435	St. Patrick starts the conversion of Ireland
c480	Birth of St. Benedict, founder of western monasticism
563	St. Columba starts the conversion of Scotland
597	St. Augustine starts the conversion of England
638	Fall of Jerusalem to the Moslems
732	Moslems defeated at the Battle of Poitiers
c770	Moslems surrender castle of Lourdes to Charlemagne
c1000	Feast of Conception of the Holy Virgin kept in the West
1003–66	Reign of Edward the Confessor. Holy Virgin appears to a widow of Walsingham, Norfolk
1209	Albigensian crusade devastates Provence
1244	Albigensian crusade ends. Provence pacified
1248	King Henry III of England acquires Lourdes through Simon de Montfort
1251	Holy Virgin appears to St. Simon Stock at Aylesford, Kent, as Our Lady of Mount Carmel
c1295	Duns Scotus defends doctrine of the Immaculate Conception at Oxford against the attacks of the Thomists
1348	The Black Death
1363	Black Prince takes Lourdes Castle for King Edward III of England
1415	Battle of Agincourt
1418	English surrender Lourdes for last time
1431	English burn Joan of Arc
1440	King Henry VI founds colleges at Cambridge and Eton dedicated to the Blessed Virgin Mary
1510	Holy Virgin appears at Garaison in the Pyrenees
1521	Cortez conquers Mexico for the Spanish
1531	Vision of Virgin of Guadalupe, Mexico

"   King Henry VIII assumes leadership of the En-
        glish Church
1538   Shrine at Walsingham destroyed
1634   Maryland, U.S.A., founded for Catholic settlers
"   Father Grandier burned at the stake in Loudun
        for causing diabolic possession in an Ursuline
        convent
1689   St. Margaret-Mary Alacoque sees apparition of
        the Sacred Heart of Jesus at Paray-le-Monial
1708   Feast of the Immaculate Conception declared to
        be a universal holyday of obligation
1773   Jesuits, "the soldiers of the Pope," suppressed by
        Pope Clement XIV
1789   French Revolution
1793   Christian religion abolished in France
1794   Lourdes parish church becomes a powder works
1799   Napoleon Bonaparte to power
1801   Christian religion restored in France
1804   Bonaparte crowned Emperor
1811   Dominique Peyramale born
1830   Apparition of the Miraculous Medal in a Paris
        convent
1844   Bernadette Soubirous born in Lourdes
1846   Holy Virgin appears at La Salette
1848   Archbishop of Paris murdered in June insurrec-
        tion
1852   Second Empire founded in France
1854   Dominique Peyramale becomes parish priest of
        Lourdes
"   Dogma of Immaculate Conception defined by
        Pope Pius IX
1855   Cholera outbreak in Lourdes
1856–57 Famine in Lourdes
1858   Holy Virgin appears to Bernadette in grotto near
        Lourdes, Feb.–July
"   Episcopal investigation into apparitions started,
        July
"   Emperor Napoleon III orders free access to
        Grotto, October

1862	Bishop Laurence of Tarbes authorizes cult of Our Lady of Lourdes
1866	Railway reaches Lourdes
"	Bernadette departs by train for convent in Nevers
"	Garaison fathers arrive and are installed in the Grotto
1869–70	First Vatican Council under Pope Pius IX
1870	Dogma of papal infallibility defined
1871	Paris Commune. Archbishop of Paris murdered again
1872	20,000 mainly royalist pilgrims make national pilgrimage to Lourdes
1876	Grotto separated from parish of Lourdes
"	First Irish pilgrimage to Lourdes
1877	Dominique Peyramale dies in Lourdes
1879	Bernadette dies in convent at Nevers
"	Visions of Holy Virgin at Knock, Co. Mayo
1883	First English pilgrimage to Lourdes
1884	Lourdes Medical Bureau founded
1905	New parish church in Lourdes finally completed
"	Catholic Church disestablished in France
1906	Grotto confiscated from Bishop of Tarbes by French state
1908	50th anniversary of apparitions celebrated. Twenty miracles proclaimed
1910	Ownership of Grotto vested in Lourdes municipality
1917	Holy Virgin appears at Fatima, Portugal
1933	St. Bernadette canonized
1940	Marshal Pétain returns Grotto to Bishop of Tarbes and Lourdes
1947	Medical Bureau modernized. Series of modern miracles starts
1950	Dogma of Assumption of Blessed Virgin Mary defined
1958	Second Vatican Council under Pope John XXIII
"	Putative doctrines of "Mary Redemptrix" and "Mary Mediatrix" abandoned
"	Centenary celebrations at Lourdes

1961–65 Long series of (unrecognized) apparitions of
        Holy Virgin at Garabandal, Spain; strongly
        critical of Catholic innovations
1964   Holy Virgin proclaimed *Mater Ecclesiae*
1969   New *Ordo* of Catholic liturgy published
1977   Archbishop Lefebvre, defender of Tridentine rite,
        disciplined by Vatican
1978   Election of Pope John Paul II
1979   Dr. Hans Kung, progressive Catholic theologian,
        disciplined by Vatican
1981   First papal visit to Lourdes planned

LOURDES

❦ I ❦

What Happened?

> If you are a native of the mountains, you can
> study philosophy or natural history for years
> and do away with the God of old, and yet as
> you feel the *Fohn* wind approach once more
> or hear an avalanche break through the
> thicket, your heart throbs in your breast and
> your thoughts turn to God and to death.
> *Peter Camenzind*, Hermann Hesse

If you climb to the top of the Château Fort, the castle
which dominates Lourdes, and look out over the town the
first thing which catches your eye is the size of the municipal cemetery. It seems to occupy a vast amount of land;
and the roofs and doors of its spacious, stone tombs cluster
together behind their enclosing walls like a doll's city of
the dead. Then you look over your shoulder towards the
other side of town and see that there is a second cemetery,
even larger than the first. Lourdes, which has a population
of about eighteen thousand, appears to be a place to which
people come in large numbers to be buried.

"There are three Lourdes," said the local insurance
agent on being asked about this, "and the cemetery is
nothing to do with it. There is the first town, at the top of
the hill, where most of the original people, the true *Lourdais*, have remained. Then there is the second Lourdes, the
summer town of tradesmen, *les commerçants*, for which
we are always reproached. And the third Lourdes is the
Domain of Our Lady. This is run by the Church and is almost free from commercial influence—much more so than

Jerusalem or Rome. The way the three Lourdes spread out
below the Château Fort shows you the history of this region for the past century."

Looking down from the castle the division between the
high town and the low one is made by the Gave de Pau,
which curls round the foot of the castle rock. On the near
side of the river, the same side as the castle, is the old
quarter which is much like any other Pyrenean town of its
size, a mixture of ancient stone houses and new concrete
ones. With the exception of the medieval castle it is remarkable for nothing in particular—forgetting the cemeteries. But on the far side of the river and below the cliffs
there is a very different sort of place. It seems to have been
built in a hurry and largely in the same style of tall white
buildings, and it would look more comfortable by a Mediterranean beach than by a chilly mountain stream for almost every building is a hotel. A citizen of Lourdes who
was transported from 1858 to the present would recognize
much of the high town; but on the far bank he would be
expecting to see a stony plain, a few water mills and the
rocks, scrub and cliffs which lie all along the river. If anyone had told him then that those few acres of barren
ground were to become some of the most valuable free-
hold in France he would have thought them touched. The
man who owned much of that ground in 1858 was called
Pomès. He might have sold it for a modest price any day
of the week: until that day in February in 1858, when the
notional citizen of Lourdes, peering down from the battlements through the drizzling morning mist, would have seen
three children cross the Gave de Pau by the old bridge out
of the town, and start to walk across Pomès's land to the
foot of a cliff face called Massabielle. There two of the
girls crossed a mill stream to gather firewood and bones,
which they would sell to the rag-and-bone man. But the
third hesitated by the water of this channel, just opposite a
cave or grotto in the cliff. As she bent down to remove her
shoes and stockings before paddling across, she heard a
noise "something like a gust of wind." And the light she
saw when she raised her eyes was, among countless other

consequences, to make the descendants of old Pomès millionaires, and to account for the crowded and opulent tombs in the municipal cemetery.

The idea of pilgrimage is closely related to the idea of heaven. Paradise becomes a place that can be approached by an earthly journey. God has taken some part of earth and made it precious. For any place to be regarded as worthy of pilgrimage it should be removed from all familiar associations. All the pilgrimages of Christianity and Islam have had this belief in common, that by making a journey to a distant place one can acquire grace in the sight of God.

Islam has various places of pilgrimage, with Mecca as the most important. Each day a quarter of the world's population turns towards Mecca in prayer, and in 1977 (during the six weeks of the *Hajj*) it was visited by over a million and a half pilgrims. For Christians, Jerusalem is the most obvious place of pilgrimage. The Christians of Britain also go on pilgrimage to Iona and Walsingham, and those of Ireland to Knock and Lough Derg. But there is one Christian shrine which draws more pilgrims than anywhere else, more even than Jerusalem or Rome. Whatever it is that has survived into modern times of the ancient idea of pilgrimage has flourished most successfully in the pilgrimage to Lourdes. It draws more than three million people each year from all over the world, mainly between the months of May and October. It is still difficult to understand how the girl's vision grew into such an event.

Bernadette of Lourdes was born in 1844, the first child of François Soubirous, who worked the Boly Mill. When she was aged eight her father lost the sight of his left eye from an accident at work. When she was ten her father was turned out of the mill and the family began to grow steadily poorer. A year later cholera broke out in the Bigorre region of the Pyrenees and Bernadette fell ill. She recovered but for the rest of her life she suffered from asthma. While her parents worked, Bernadette looked after her sister and her two small brothers. She also worked for a time as a waitress in a bar owned by an aunt. In 1856,

when Bernadette was aged twelve, her father was unable to
pay the rent, and since the family were without a roof one
of their cousins allowed them to lodge in the *cachot*, a
disused lock-up which had been abandoned by the police
because it was so unhealthy. It was a year of famine in
Lourdes. François Soubirous was arrested for theft but the
charge was dropped for lack of evidence. In the following
year, which was also a famine year, Bernadette went to
live with her former foster-mother in the nearby village of
Bartrès. There she would have food and fresh air, and her
job was to look after a small child and a flock of sheep.
But there was no school in the village. In January 1858,
after seven months at Bartrès, Bernadette decided to return
to Lourdes, to enrol in the free school of the Sisters of
Charity and to prepare for her first communion. One
morning, three weeks after her return, she set out with her
sister and a friend to gather sticks and bones at Massabielle. She was aged fourteen and considered to be sensible but backward in her education and in her physical development.

The series of apparitions which started that morning
continued until July and numbered eighteen. On the first
occasion Bernadette saw a soft glow in the grotto above
a rose bush, and then a beautiful girl appeared, dressed
in white. Bernadette afterwards referred to the girl as
"*Aquero*," meaning "that one" in the local Bigourdan dialect. Feeling frightened on the first occasion, Bernadette
said her rosary. The vision beckoned her. She did not respond and it suddenly disappeared. On her way home Bernadette told her sister what she had seen, and her sister
told her mother. Her mother at once feared that to add to
the family's problems her oldest child was now halluci-
nating. As a precaution she beat the two girls for "telling
stories." Her father, who was in bed that day, said:
"There's never been anything that anyone could say
against our family. You're not going to start something
now." The child was forbidden to go to the grotto again.
Two days later, on Saturday evening, she mentioned the
matter to the priest at confession and he asked if he could

tell the parish priest, Father Peyramale, about it. Father Peyramale was not very interested. On Sunday, after High Mass, the children obtained permission from their father to revisit the grotto. This time they took some holy water with them and the original party of three was accompanied by seven other girls. As Bernadette prayed she saw the second apparition and sprinkled it with the water. *Aquero* smiled. None of the children with her could see anything. Then events were interrupted by Jeanne Abadie, the friend who had also been on the first expedition, who now rolled a large stone down from the top of Massabielle. It crashed close to the grotto. Bernadette remained entranced on her knees, but the other children panicked and ran for help. They found a local miller who returned with them to the grotto and, with the greatest difficulty, carried the oblivious girl back to his mill. He was astonished by her weight, and he said that despite his attempts to distract her she seemed to be smiling at something he could not see. This incident led to the first general interest among the people of Lourdes in events at the grotto. The predominant feeling was disapproval. Bernadette's mother was angry and upset. Next day when Bernadette left school she was rebuked in the street and slapped by a woman she did not know for "putting on comedies." But there was another theory, more sympathetic to Bernadette, that she had seen the soul of a pious girl who had died the year before to the edification of all and who had been a member of the sodality of the Children of Mary. A prosperous woman who sometimes employed Bernadette's mother was interested in this possibility and she arranged to take the child back to the grotto early the next morning. This she did, accompanied by her seamstress and equipped with a pen, paper and an inkstand. It had been decided that *Aquero* should be invited to write her own name. Accordingly when the third apparition began Bernadette was handed the inkstand before she advanced into the cave. To a casual observer the third apparition was not very edifying. While the child knelt in ecstasy her two adult companions nattered at her "to be sure and get the name." At one

point she gestured to them to be quiet. When the vision
was over they asked Bernadette why she had not requested
the name. Bernadette replied that she had asked, but
Aquero had replied "It is not necessary." This was the first
time that *Aquero* had spoken. She had added: "Will you
have the goodness to come here for fifteen days? I don't
promise to make you happy in this world, but in the next."

This was the beginning of what is now known as "the
fortnight of apparitions." In the fifteen days between 18
February and 4 March, Bernadette saw *Aquero* thirteen
times. During this fortnight her audience increased from
two people to eight thousand, and she eventually had to be
escorted to the grotto by armed soldiers. During this time,
too, *Aquero* entrusted her with various secrets which she
never revealed; she discovered a spring in the grotto, a
number of allegedly miraculous cures took place, Father
Peyramale treated her with the deepest suspicion, the police threatened to put her in prison for causing public disorder, and the popular idea grew that Massabielle was a
place chosen by the Mother of God to appear to a peasant
girl of Lourdes.

After the sixth apparition, which had been attended by a
hundred people, Police Commissioner Jacomet took Bernadette to his house in the centre of town and interrogated
her. The interview ended with Jacomet losing his temper.
An angry crowd gathered at his door and Bernadette was
taken home by her father. The commissioner did not know
what to make of her. He decided that she was sincere,
sane, modest, not trying to attract attention, not in it for
the money, not being manipulated by some enterprising
adult, and quite incomprehensible. He forbade her to go to
Massabielle again. On the day following the interrogation
Bernadette ignored the prohibition but saw nothing when
she went to the grotto. At the same time the mayor lifted
the police ban in view of the strength of public opinion in
the child's favour.

During the ninth apparition Bernadette, acting under
Aquero's direction, crawled around the cave and un-
earthed a small spring. She got rather dirty doing this,

which led to a new outburst of mockery, and later that day she was summoned to be interrogated again, this time by the town's imperial prosecutor. This was another failure from the point of view of the authorities. The prosecutor lost the thread of his arguments once he had eliminated all the usual motives and became so flustered that he could not find the hole in his inkwell. Once again a noisy crowd gathered outside, and afterwards Bernadette's humorous account of the meeting caused the town to laugh at the prosecutor and to suggest that he had St. Vitus's dance and that the candles in his house lit up by themselves. Once again, on the day after the interrogation, *Aquero* did not appear to her. But the crowds continued to grow and they contained increasing numbers of educated and sceptical people. Bernadette was interrogated a third time, by the examining magistrate, and the regional commandant of constabulary came over from Tarbes, the county town, to discuss how to control the crowds. During all this time the Church, on the advice of Father Peyramale, kept a discreet distance from the event.

The reserve of the Church authorities was to end after the thirteenth apparition, when *Aquero* told Bernadette to "tell the priests" that people were to come to the grotto in procession and that a chapel was to be built there. On 2 March Bernadette left the crowd of 1,650 people and went to the presbytery with her two aunts, her mother's sisters. Father Peyramale did not receive them well. For the first time he was confronted with the need for a decision. He remembered the aunts because he had expelled them from the Children of Mary when, one after the other, they had become pregnant before marriage—or "Farted at Vespers" in the local phrase. His perplexed anger confused Bernadette, who only remembered part of the message. Finally he told the three of them to get out. Only when she was back in the street did Bernadette realize that she had forgotten about the request to build a chapel. She had only told Father Peyramale about the processions. So she arranged through a friendly sacristan to brave the parish priest's anger again. Father Peyramale's considered re-

sponse was to ask for *Aquero*'s name, and to demand, as a
miraculous sign, that the rose bush in the grotto should
flower at once. At the last apparition of the fortnight, the
fifteenth in total, before a highly expectant crowd of eight
thousand, Bernadette put these requests to the vision but in
return the Lady only smiled. The apparition lasted for
forty-five minutes but when it was over there was a general
feeling of anticlimax. There had been no miraculous signs,
the rose bush had not flowered, and the vision was still
unidentified. In their disappointment the crowds found a
sign where there was none. On her way back to the town
Bernadette embraced a sick girl, Eugénie Troy from
Barèges. The girl removed the bandages round her eyes
and could see. It was rumoured everywhere that a blind
child had been cured, and Father Peyramale went so far as
to report the matter to the Bishop of Tarbes. But his subsequent investigation showed that the girl had never been
blind and that she only wore the bandage because the light
hurt her eyes. She was very ill and continued so after a
temporary improvement effected by her meeting with Bernadette. She died a year later. After the fifteenth apparition, Bernadette returned to school.

So the fortnight ended with the Church uncommitted
and Bernadette apparently at the end of her visions. From
this point on, the story of Lourdes began to pass outside
the control of the girl and into the hands of popular devotion.

That a popular cult at Lourdes did now begin to gather
speed was no tribute to the power of either the authorities
or the local press. As rumours of "a miraculous spring"
revealed by Our Lady spread around the district, Bernadette assured Police Commissioner Jacomet that she did
not believe that she had been responsible for any cures.
The local pharmacist declared that the water from the
mysterious spring was a danger to health. And the papers
mocked the credulity of the poor and suggested that Bernadette should be treated for mental illness. None of this
had any effect on the cultists. Sick people began to come in

greater numbers to the grotto. Candles, statues and money were left there.

Early on the morning of 25 March, the feast of the Annunciation, Bernadette woke up with a strong desire to revisit the grotto. Her parents made her wait until 5 a.m. Though there had been a three-week lull there was still a crowd of about one hundred people waiting for her. During this sixteenth apparition Bernadette put a courteously phrased question to *Aquero*. Three times there was no answer, but the girl persisted because she knew that without an answer there could never be a chapel. The question was: "Mademoiselle, would you be so kind as to tell me who you are, if you please?" The fourth time she asked, *Aquero* "stopped laughing." She opened her clasped hands and extended them towards the ground. Then she joined them again, raised her eyes to the sky and said, as always in Bigourdan, "Que soy era Immaculada Councepciou." Bernadette left at once and proceeded to the presbytery, repeating the meaningless reply all the way. When she reached Father Peyramale she simply said the same words to him, "I am the Immaculate Conception." Peyramale was considerably shocked.

The dogma of the Immaculate Conception of the Blessed Virgin Mary was of some political importance to nineteenth-century Catholicism. Duns Scotus (1265–1308), the Scottish Franciscan who was trained at Oxford, was one of the early partisans of the doctrine and defended it against the attacks of St. Thomas Aquinas and the Dominicans. But it was not marked by a universal holyday of obligation until 1708 and it was not finally promulgated until 1854, four years before the apparitions. That Christ was conceived by the Holy Ghost, and was therefore conceived "immaculately" without the stain of original sin, was well understood by theologians and half-wits alike. But the doctrine of the Immaculate Conception extended this state of purity to the moment of conception of Christ's mother. Since Mary was conceived by St. Joachim, and since *he* was marked by the original sin of Adam and Eve, the doctrine of the Immaculate Conception of Mary was to most

people as unapproachable as the idea of the Trinity itself.
It was certainly well beyond the understanding of the
millers of Lourdes, and quite outside the mental grasp of
Bernadette. Nevertheless, enthusiasm for the baffling new
dogma was an important part of the French clergy's attempts to lead a nineteenth-century religious revival. Bernadette could hardly have provided Father Peyramale with
a more welcome, or a more unexpected, name. It was not
until that evening, at the home of Monsieur Estrade, a tax
inspector who had been one of the first educated people to
be convinced by her story, that she was to learn what the
words meant. But from that day forth Father Peyramale
was convinced that these were genuine apparitions of the
Mother of God.

Two weeks later, on 7 April, which was Easter Wednes-
day, Bernadette went to the grotto before dawn. One of
her friends had seen her at confession the previous evening
and had guessed what she was going to do. A thousand
people were gathered for this, which was to be the last
public apparition. Among the crowd was a sceptical doctor, Pierre Dozous. While she was in ecstasy on this occasion Bernadette held a long candle, and she had cupped
her hands around the stem. As the candle burnt lower the
flame began to burn right through her loosely clasped
fingers. The crowd cried out that she was burning. Dr.
Dozous warned them to leave her alone and timed this
event at ten minutes. As soon as the ecstasy was over he
examined her hands and found that they were quite
unaffected. The doctor was convinced on the spot,* the
first in a long line of medical men to be attracted by the
events at Lourdes. It was also on this day that souvenir
sellers were first reported to be working among the crowds.

There was to be one more apparition. On 16 July, by
which time the grotto had been barricaded by the authorities and Bernadette had spent some days away from the
town, she was once again drawn back to Massabielle. It
was the Feast of Our Lady of Mount Carmel. In the eve-

* Medical science can now suggest a natural explanation for this
phenomenon.

ning, accompanied by an aunt and two friends, she followed the course of the river on the far bank until she was opposite the grotto. There were several cultists already there with lighted candles, rather as there are every night of every year today. Bernadette was wearing a hood and she was unrecognized. She knelt down and for the last time experienced the same vision of her "beautiful Lady." She said afterwards that it seemed to her as though she was no farther from the grotto than she had ever been. When the apparition ended she returned home quietly. It was to be the last extraordinary experience of her life. Two years later, almost to the day, she left home and went to live in the local hospice of the Sisters of Nevers. And in 1866, at the age of 22, she left Lourdes for ever and entered the Sisters' convent in the town of Nevers, half-way across France. She remained a nun until she died in 1879 after several long and painful illnesses, aged 35.

With the end of the public life of Bernadette, the public life of the grotto really begins. The first episode was a vigorous battle between the authorities and the early cultists as to what should be permitted there. As soon as the spring was uncovered, on 25 February, local craftsmen started to channel out a tank which was then equipped with outlet pipes; and a board for holding candles was also provided. This work was given free. The worshippers then inserted money into the crevices of the grotto, and this was eventually collected by the sacristan and taken to Father Peyramale. Rosaries were said by the devout every day, and by July a total of fifty people claimed to have experienced visions of the Virgin. The cult very soon began to get out of hand. Early in May the Prefect in Tarbes declared that "anyone claiming to see visions will be arrested and taken to hospital." The visions stopped. At the same time the police commissioner confiscated all the devotional objects which had been left in the grotto on the grounds that it was an unauthorized place of worship. In June the area was barricaded off, only for the barricades to be demolished by the angry faithful. They were demolished and

re-erected three times in the course of a month. Finally the
Bishop of Tarbes interceded on the side of the police and
the barricades stayed up.

While all this was going on the fame of the shrine
spread throughout France and from the first it was described as a place of miraculous cures. One of the earliest
of these "cures" was that of the Prince Imperial, the two-
year-old son and heir of the Emperor Napoleon III, who
contracted a dangerous sunstroke in the July heat of Biarritz. The imperial infant's governess travelled the ninety
miles to Lourdes by road, interviewed Father Peyramale
and Bernadette (who had experienced her last vision
twelve days earlier), and then went to the grotto where she
asked the policeman who was supposed to arrest cultists to
fill her bottle from the spring. Subsequently the two-year-
old prince was sprinkled with the water and delivered from
sunstroke and the threat of meningitis.* In September Father Peyramale, who remained a staunch supporter of Bernadette's story, arranged for the Soubirous family to be
moved from the lock-up to a healthier house. In October
the Emperor directed that the barricades be removed from
the grotto. In November a commission of inquiry appointed by the Bishop of Tarbes opened its hearings.

Once the barricades were down there was nothing to im-
pede the growth of popular devotion. The bishop's commission took four years to complete its work, but from the
first its members were deeply impressed by Bernadette's
sincerity, authority and clarity of mind. Pending the
bishop's decision, no ceremonies could take place at the
grotto, but the numbers making the pilgrimage there for
private prayer steadily increased. So did the numbers of
sick pilgrims claiming to be cured. Three decisive steps,
which transformed Lourdes from a place of temporary and
largely local interest into the greatest shrine in Europe, followed. In 1862 Monseigneur Laurence, Bishop of Tarbes,
recognized the apparitions. His *mandat* stated: "We judge
that Mary Immaculate, Mother of God, really appeared to

* He lived on till he was twenty-one, when he was speared to
death in the British interest during the Zulu wars.

Bernadette Soubirous on 11 February, 1858, and on subsequent days, eighteen times in all. . . . The faithful are justified in believing this to be certain. . . . We authorize the cult of the Our Lady of the Grotto of Lourdes in our diocese . . . [and] in conformity with the wishes of the Blessed Virgin, expressed more than once in the course of the apparitions, we propose to build a shrine on the land of the Grotto, which has now been acquired by the Bishops of Tarbes." The same document proclaimed seven of the cures which had taken place at the Grotto in 1858 to be "miraculous."

In 1866, the bishop asked the Garaison Fathers, an order of full-time revivalists who were based at a nearby shrine, to move to Lourdes. And finally, in the same year, Achille Fould, a Jewish financier and former Minister of Finance, intervened decisively to secure the future of the enterprise. M. Fould had recently purchased an estate near Lourdes and he intended to develop it. The Southern Railway Company was about to extend the line from Tarbes to Pau. M. Fould had sufficient influence to persuade them to make a detour of thirteen miles south, via Lourdes and his estate. So within ten years of the apparitions the cult had been authorized and professionalized; and the formerly remote little town had been linked to the rest of Europe.

In his mandate, Mgr. Laurence said that the name of Our Lady of Lourdes should be added "to the blessed names of Our Lady of Garaison, of Poëylanun, of Héas and of Piétat." These four places, all nearby, had also in earlier times been associated with cults of the Virgin Mary. What happened in Lourdes in 1858 was not therefore a completely novel event to the *Lourdais*. The essential points of the Lourdes story were that a vision of a Lady experienced by a young shepherdess led to a cult, a chapel, processions and a spring which was credited with miraculous powers. Every feature of this story had been proposed before, and some had been proposed several times. In his book *Pilgrimages in the Pyrenees and Landes*, written in 1870, Denis Lawlor lists the following Marian shrines in the region, apart from the four referred to by Mgr. Laurence: "Our Lady of Bétharram, Our Lady of Sarrance, Our Lady of Bourisp, Our Lady of Médous, Our Lady of Nestes and Our Lady of Buglose." To many *Lourdais*, to Father Peyramale, for instance, "Our Lady of Lourdes" must have seemed uncannily familiar. Lawlor also lists as regional centres of pilgrimage the churches of St. Savin, St. Aventin d'Aquitaine, St. Bertrand de Comminges and St. Vincent. This amounts to fourteen established centres of pilgrimage close to Lourdes in a casual list compiled by one foreign visitor. Garaison, the home of the professional revivalists, was not even the most famous shrine in the region before the apparitions at Lourdes. That was Bétharram, which the imperial governess would actually have driven through on her quest for the new *diva*. But Bétharram was established in about 1475, when a youthful shepherd saw a vision of the Lady who asked for a chapel to be erected there, and by 1858 its inspiration was on the wane. The story of Garaison started in 1510, when the Lady appeared to a young shepherdess, Agnes de Sagazan, who also reported a request for a chapel. In 1864, two years before they moved into Lourdes, the Garaison Fathers were successful in persuading the bishop, Mgr. Laurence, to petition Pope Pius IX to authorize a ceremony at which the statue of the Virgin of Garaison was crowned. It was held in September of that year in the presence of the Archbishop of Toulouse, Bishop Laurence of Tarbes, five other bishops, one hundred priests and twelve thousand of the faithful, who sang the special Garaison hymn. It is an interesting sidelight on the strength of Pyrenean devotion to the Lady that Mgr. Laurence did not hesitate to encourage a rival shrine only two years after he had authorized the cult at Lourdes.

There were good reasons why the people of the Pyrenees should have developed these distinctive interests. It is said of the inhabited valleys of this region that "they are separated from each other like the teeth of a comb." The Pyrenees lie in the Languedoc (the area where, in the Middle Ages, people spoke the language of "oc" or "yes"; as opposed to the Langue d'Oil, the language of "oui" or "yes" which developed into modern French). This linguistic empire was broken down into regional *patois;* and in the county of Bigorre, where the *patois* was Bigourdan, the inhabitants of each valley were further divided by different dialects, which frequently required skilled translation. But although language and geography to some extent isolated Bigorre from the rest of Europe it had not always been as politically and socially isolated as it had become in 1858. Richard Coeur de Lion had Bigourdan as his first language, not by reason of birth—he was born in Oxford—but of upbringing; he was raised in his mother's Duchy of Aquitaine. He never spent a complete year of his life in England and it is doubtful whether he ever spoke English. It was quite possible, in those days of "benighted" and inward-looking communities, for the King of England to be, essentially, a man of Bigorre. *Occitan,* the tongue of "oc," was considered by Dante as a possible choice for the *Divine Comedy.* The Black Prince spent so much time and energy subduing and holding the Château Fort in the fourteenth century that he is still "the most hated Englishman in Bigorre," and children are still frightened into good behaviour by the threat of his return. And Henri of Navarre, the greatest, the only Protestant and the most licentious king of France, had Béarnais, the *Occitan patois* of the next county to Bigorre, as his first tongue—even in the sixteenth century. In other words, though Lourdes in 1858 seemed a remote antechamber to modern Europe, it had not always been so. And the town's sophisticates who originally laughed at the Lady for addressing Bernadette in Bigourdan would have been more sophisticated if they had known more of their own history, and had placed more value on their own cultural heritage.

Besides their familiarity with visions, the people of Bigorre, like many European mountain dwellers, were also thoroughly familiar with the notion of healing springs. There are still seven thriving "thermal centres" in the department of the High Pyrenees, which attracted fifty-six per cent of the total number of French thermal curists in

1977; and at Cauterets for instance there are rival modern
baths which continue to specialize in the treatment of
asthma and throat complaints—or "oto-rhino-laryngol-
ogie" as it is now unreassuringly termed. It is one
of the more intriguing and lesser known details of the
story of Bernadette that she was actually taken to try for
an asthma cure at the fashionable spa of Cauterets between the seventeenth and eighteenth apparitions. That is,
just at the time when the fame of Lourdes was spreading
right across France, when its water was declared to be
wholesome, when the mayor was planning to open a mineral spa there and make the town's fortune scientifically,
and when the unscientific were broadcasting the information that at Lourdes the blind could see, cripples could
walk and the consumptive could be made whole, just at
that time the small originator of all this fuss preferred to
try the curative powers of a village in the next valley.

Four of the cures which were shortly to be proclaimed
as genuine and miraculous had already been effected, and
Bernadette had herself met at least two truthful and sincere people who claimed cures, but she did not seek her
own cure at Lourdes. The devout explanation is that the
Lady had already told her that she would not make her
happy in this world, but the simpler reason is that Bernadette did not herself believe in the cures of Lourdes.

Apart from the little girl with the bandaged eyes,
Eugénie Troy, whose true condition was discovered in the
middle of March, Bernadette had visited the former mayor
of Adé, who had been healed at the Grotto. And she had
also been taken to a nearby farm where a boy of nine
whose mouth would not close had asked to see her. During
her visits he became normal and was able to eat (and he
did eventually recover from his condition). Nonetheless
when she was asked by an English tourist, R. S. Standen,
about the miracles in April 1859, she replied: "There's no
truth in all that." And when two other visitors asked her if
she knew anything of any cures she said: "I have been
told that there have been miracles, but . . . I have not
seen them." She explicitly denied contributing to any of

them, and for her own case Bernadette preferred thermalism.

This then was the country, and these were the people, that Father Peyramale had to deal with in his attempts to direct the astonishing religious revival which sometimes threatened to swamp his parish in the wake of Bernadette's experience. The extent of his original authority in the matter can be gauged by the fact that on his prohibition (as rural dean) not a single priest witnessed any of the apparitions, except for a visiting abbé who was on holiday at the time of the twelfth apparition, and who did not know of the dean's ban. Once convinced, by the Lady's name, Peyramale kept his deep feelings to himself, but it must have seemed to him a most extraordinary gift of God that this thing should have happened in his parish. His support for Bernadette never wavered for the rest of his life—which was to last almost as long as that of the sickly child he was protecting. His first action on her behalf was on 4 June, the day after the feast of Corpus Christi, when Bernadette made her first communion. Peyramale discovered that the prefect in Tarbes intended to commit Bernadette herself to an asylum. He told the authorities that he would absolutely oppose any such plan and it was dropped at once. In the story of the apparitions, as opposed to the story of the pilgrimages, Father Peyramale is, apart from the child, by far the most important character. Without his support the whole incident would have been seen as a passing childish fancy, leading to a brief outbreak of communal hysteria, and long since been forgotten. The priest was a striking figure, educated better than most other parish priests with deep-set bright eyes, a beaky nose, a short temper and a generous heart. As the pilgrimages grew, Father Peyramale naturally looked on this as a great opportunity for his parish. Unfortunately for him, the diocesan authorities did not share this view. Four years after the mandate, by which time Father Peyramale had opened the chapel above the Grotto which was eventually to serve as the crypt of the upper basilica (thereby fulfilling the instructions issued

by the Mother of God), Mgr. Laurence installed four
Garaison Fathers in Lourdes with their own superior to run
the mission to the pilgrims.

The Garaison Fathers, led by Father Sempé, regarded
themselves as specialists in the preservation of the moment
of vision. They were not prepared to share their work with
amateurs and it was not long before they began to disagree
with Father Peyramale. The Lady had asked that a chapel
should be built and that people should come in procession.
But the Garaison Fathers were prepared to go much farther
than that. They envisaged a park and a parade ground surrounding the Grotto, which would form an enclosed "domain of Our Lady." To the original crypt they added first
the basilica, then an elaborate altar behind high railings by
the Grotto itself. And they next constructed a fourth sanctuary, the *Rosaire,* in front of the basilica and at a more
approachable level from the parade ground between the
Grotto and the town. Father Sempé's schemes consumed
more and more of the offerings made by the pilgrims, and
his parade ground and novel services took up more and
more of the pilgrims' time. Father Peyramale very much
resented the fact that processions from the parish church
to the Grotto became less and less frequent. As long as
Mgr. Laurence was alive his position was generally secure.
But the old bishop died in 1870. For all Peyramale's intelligence, strength of character and even holiness he was neither a businessman nor a diocesan politician. He had the
perception to support Bernadette in her original claims,
and the faith to believe in them and to fight for them, but
he had no conception of where it might all lead. He never
imagined that the small town which formed the limit of his
responsibilities was to become the largest pilgrimage centre
in the world. By 1875 the parish and the Domain had been
officially separated. Peyramale and Sempé were no longer
on speaking terms. No money was to pass from one to the
other and no pilgrims need do so either. Peyramale's obsti-
nate and courageous response was to lay a foundation
stone for a new parish church in the centre of the old
town. It was to succeed the old St. Peter's and was to be

dedicated to the Sacred Heart. He died in 1877 with an enormous debt, and with building work on his church abandoned before the roof was installed. It was not completed until 1905.

Meanwhile, down in the Domain, Father Sempé's inspired plans were going from strength to strength. From 1858 to 1863 pilgrims arrived individually or in small unofficial groups. Then in 1864 Mgr. Laurence led a diocesan pilgrimage of eight thousand people to Lourdes. In 1866 the railway arrived and pilgrims started to come from all over France. In 1867 the Basque diocese of Bayonne made a pilgrimage. In 1871 Paris was in the hands of the Commune, the archbishop was murdered and anti-Catholic riots broke out elsewhere. At Nantes railway station a mob attacked pilgrims as they were returning from Lourdes. This incident led to an appeal for a Catholic show of strength, and in 1872 a national rally was held at Lourdes presided over by nine bishops and numbering twenty thousand people. This event placed Lourdes in a very political context. The Third Republic was three years old and religious demonstrations were widely regarded as pro-royalist. But, however much the religious authorities might regret this confusion, the political association seems to have been the making of Lourdes as a centre of first national and then international pilgrimage. The first organized foreign pilgrimages came in 1873, from Canada and Belgium. In 1874 one from the United States joined them. In 1875 the first pilgrimages arrived from Poland, Italy and Germany. In 1876 Spain and Ireland joined in. In 1877 (the year of Father Peyramale's death) Portugal and Switzerland sent contingents; by which time the annual French National pilgrimage had started, with twelve hundred pilgrims and two hundred sick. Other early arrivals were Brazil (1879), Hungary and the Argentine (1881), Holland (1882), England and Sardinia (1883), Rumania (1885), Bolivia (1887), Venezuela (1890) and Austria (1895). By 1892, thirty-five years after the apparitions, the French National had grown to approximately its present size, that is to a total of thirty

thousand pilgrims, including one thousand sick. Note that
during all this time, while the reputation of Lourdes as a
place of cures and conversions spread round the world, the
Church proclaimed no further miracles.

The process by which Lourdes was transformed from a
child's vision into a major religious centre was a mixture
of revivalism, professional stage management, folk medicine, right-wing politics, simple faith, railway engineering
and ancient traditions. The last were not always spiritual.
In 1062, the Count of Bigorre placed his lands under the
protection of Our Lady, and when Jerusalem fell to the
First Crusade in 1099 *"Notre Dame de Bigorre"* was
among the war cries which were heard outside its walls.*
But in the following century the people of the Languedoc
(including Bigorre) adopted with the greatest enthusiasm
the Albigensian heresy, an anti-papal belief which divided
Christendom; and so found another opportunity to separate themselves from the French-speaking north. Early in
the thirteenth century a crusade against the Albigensian
heresy was launched by Pope Innocent III, and Bigorre
was put to the sword. Lourdes fell to Simon de Montfort,
and the town became an English possession. The Inquisition was unleashed, burning even the bones of those who
had died before their heretical beliefs could be discovered.
In the words of the *Shorter Cambridge Medieval History,*
these methods "left behind a generation orthodox in doctrine but no lovers of the clergy."

   A vision of God is a form of direct spiritual experience
which dispenses with the need for clerical mediation. During the Age of Belief, Lourdes lay on one of the main pilgrim roads of southern France, the road from Arles to
Compostella. The people of the county and of the town
would have had every reason to yearn for the unmediated
vision and for the distant place which had been touched by
God. Their immediate enthusiasm in 1858 for the cult of
Massabielle could draw on well-nourished roots.

* *The Happening at Lourdes* by Alan Neame.

❦ II ❦

The Journey

Lord Jesu Christ that madest me
And boughtest me on rode-tree . . .
Do with me Lord as pleaseth thee
Amen Jesu. For thy pitye.
from a *Prayer* of King Henry VI

A pilgrimage demands an effort of those who join it. It is
not unlike stepping into a cold bath. On the one hand
there is the usual world. On the other hand there is this
small badge, thoughtfully provided by the Catholic Association, which announces that its bearer is a pilgrim. That is
to say, the wearer of this badge is a pilgrim to Lourdes,
and the figure-in-the-centre-is-a-representation-of-the-
Crowned-Virgin? It all seemed to take rather a long time
to explain.

For the Catholic Association Annual, the pilgrims as-
semble in Southwark just as Chaucer's Canterbury pilgrims
did six hundred years ago. Canterbury was then the
greatest centre of English pilgrimage; but the greatest
centre of Christian pilgrimage, Santiago de Compostella in
northern Spain, drew many onwards across the Channel. It
occurred to me that some of the English pilgrims to Canterbury and Compostella who set out from Southwark may
have passed through Lourdes, but investigation showed
this to be unlikely. Most English pilgrims to Compostella
sailed to northern Spain or to Bordeaux, and even those

who landed on the Normandy coast would hardly have entered Bigorre in their journey through France to the
Pyrenean gateway at St.-Jean-Pied-de-Port. In any event,
our starting point turned out to be the steps not of the
Tabard Inn, which was demolished in 1875, but of St.
George's Cathedral, half-a-mile to the west. And further
investigation showed that it was fixed with more reference
to the office of our travel agent, Tangney Tours Ltd. of
Catford, than the footsteps of Geoffrey Chaucer. And we
were going to Dover by "luxury" coach. A glance at the
railway timetable was all that was necessary to return the
mind to the modern world. If one took the *train* to Dover
and joined up there, one would not need to wear the
badge. There would be no point in wearing it on the train.
That is what is known as moral cowardice, and that is
what I did.

The train journey sped by. It seemed only moments out
of Victoria when the sign at Canterbury East was en-
couraging one to "alight here for the Cathedral." And
there behind the station was the shrine which it took
Chaucer's pilgrims five days to reach. There lay the head-
quarters of Christianity in England, the scene of St.
Thomas's martyrdom. The August sun was baking its grey
roof and softening its grey walls. Perhaps, by concentrating on its splendour, one might by-pass the need for
spiritual preparation which a pilgrimage demands. How
many people knew that Thomas Beckett was very fond of
horses? Was it even true? Would he have approved of the
Donkey Shelter? The modern, non-pilgrimaging world in-
truded, slightly frantically again. Perhaps *The Times* could
be of assistance. And, yes, that morning *The Times* had
discovered the extraordinary fact that "Britons have not
given up religion." There had been an opinion poll, and
ninety-four per cent of the population denied that they
were agnostics or atheists. We one thousand pilgrims,
bound for southern France, were quite in order after all.
Another story listed the resorts in southern France where
one could now take "a topless" holiday. I turned to the
Cathedral again.

Chaucer's pilgrims were in quest of spiritual benefits so clearly conceived as to be almost material. The indulgences which they acquired were more functional to them than souvenirs. You could sell them again. Pardoners sold them all the time. If the list of Lourdes indulgences which were available in 1958 was still current, one would need a calculator to discover how much of one's time in Purgatory had been remitted by a pilgrimage. "Indulgence of the Holy Staircase, nine years for each step ascended on one's knees, four times a year: Partial indulgence of seven years and seven quarantines each time a pilgrim assists at any ceremony of his pilgrimage. . . ." They were all set out in the old guide books. Were they still one of the available rewards? The train lurched forward again, and Canterbury Cathedral, with its turnstiles, and audio-historical guides and finger-lickin', rubberneckin', near-topless tourists, descended over the horizon. And I remembered another curious fact, that Thomas Beckett's skull, unlike the rest of him, was taken to Eton in the fifteenth century, to bolster King Henry VI's new educational foundation. Pilgrims had gone to Eton too; they had gone "by plumps, with candles and images of wax in their hands." When they departed, having been cured, as they believed, by the intercession of the saintly Henry, they left behind them their sticks and crutches and wax images of eyes or hands or feet, the formerly stricken bodily parts. Would we on our way to Lourdes band together in such desperate enthusiasm? How did you describe votive offerings to the Customs and Excise? As Dover approached the rational world tugged harder. Growing more ingenious in its attempts not to be overthrown it had suggested a new idea; I would not like my fellow pilgrims. I would be able to recognize them by their unpleasing appearance. They would be devout and enthusiastic and unattractive.

This proved not to be the case. The departure hall at Dover was packed with tourists and it was only after some time that I noticed that many of them were wearing badges. None appeared to be suffering, instead they were cheerful and sensible. If something important separated

them from the modern world they were keeping it to themselves. The last arguments against badges and in favour of
an easily defensible anonymity were overcome. With the
badge on, one changed sides. One was presumed to be
Catholic, to be concerned for the sick, to be preoccupied
with the state of one's immortal soul. Oddly, no one else
seemed to notice this. Still, wearing a badge undoubtedly
made a difference. In an instant I found that I had now
started to despise the tourists. Instead of looking down on
the devout as simple-minded, I was pitying the pleasure-
seekers for their triviality. They had become the inferior
species. An open mind on this subject, the possibility of
some form of harmony between those in search of a holiday and those in search of spiritual peace was no nearer.
The medieval indulgences might have gone, but so had the
pleasure of a matter-of-factness in the quest for grace.
"The town of London," wrote Daniel Defoe, "is a kind
of large Forest of wild beasts where most of us range
about at a venture, and mutually destructive of one another . . ." Perhaps that was what accounted for these for-
tifications? Whichever world one occupied one had to arm
oneself with contempt for its opposite.

Standing outside the Gents in the departure lounge was
a good-looking young man who was wearing a badge. As I
emerged a woman with him, seeing my badge, asked me to
take him in. He was called David. David said nothing. His
expression was intelligent, there was perhaps a slightly
watchful look in his eyes. Once inside he disappeared in
the normal manner into a cubicle. It seemed rather odd
that a complete stranger should be asked to accompany
this silent but thoughtful David on his mundane errand.
After a period of silence David emerged from his cubicle
with his flies open and gestured for a towel. This he used
without washing his hands. Reminded first by word, then
by gesture, of the business of washing he went to the basin
and started to spit. He managed this without taking the
cigarette from his mouth. Other people came and went
while I pondered what to do with his flies. He looked so

normal, I could hardly set about them without explanation. The badge had posed its first problem.

Eventually David regained the company of his mother, who had come to see him off. He had, she told me, been perfectly healthy until two years earlier when he had suffered brain damage from a virus infection. The technical description of his condition was "post-encephalitic dementia." His only visible symptoms were a slightly absent manner and a preoccupied expression, as though he had forgotten something but could not remember what. He had actually forgotten virtually everything. He could not use language, he had to be helped in the simplest tasks. He recognized his mother, and he would grow to remember people he saw every day. He made friends very easily and generally demonstrated huge affection. His mental condition was that of a baby of about eighteen months. He was likely to enjoy the pilgrimage very much indeed. While sitting with his mother he was given some crisps, became excited, spluttered the food about and waved his arms. His mother caught his wrists and held them. He bent down to her lap and kissed her hands. His mother seemed overwhelmed with happiness by this gesture. When the time came for him to leave he proved to have the normal physical strength of any man of twenty-five and bent to lift his large suitcase with ease. The boat was in. For the first time the whole party were to be assembled together.

The pilgrimage business is closely related to the regular holiday industry. It is largely in the hands of travel agents. The fact that your customers are not described as tourists apparently poses no very significant changes, though there are some. A few years back one of the leading Lourdes specialists was trying to sell his business. "It's a lovely line," he told one prospective purchaser. "No trouble with the customers. Last year I took a plane load out and found the hotel was double-booked. Nothing. Every bed in town was sold. Could have been a disaster. Some of the punters were elderly and they were all tired. What did they say? 'Oh, don't worry,' they said. 'We'll do an All-Night Vigil.' And the whole lot spent the night in church. Pray-

ing! Would you get that in Torremolinos? It's a lovely
business." That story represents the eccentric aspect of
Lourdes travel agency. A more routine problem was dealt
with by John Tangney over a meditative off-season drink
in the Hotel Astoria. "People often ask me," he said,
" 'How *could* you make a profit out of sending people to
Lourdes?' Well, I've thought about it a bit, and I've decided it must be . . . because I charge less than everyone
else." This joke did not go down very well with the rather
sanctimonious young priest whom it was intended to
arouse, but the priest was making his first trip.

Lourdes business has to be drummed up just like any
other form of travel. Some agents go in for the
straightforward advertisement of services and prices.
Others are more evocative. A travel supplement in the
Catholic Herald starts: "All Christians are essentially pilgrims. The whole of our life is one long journey towards
God. The Risen Lord invites us to Himself . . . 'I come
from the Father and now I am going to the Father.' "
There then follow details of booking arrangements. St.
Christopher Tours, one of the specialist companies, minced
its words just as finely. A colour brochure offered pilgrimages to Lourdes, Fatima, Lisieux, San Sebastian (the
fashionable seaside centre) and the Holy Land (via El
Al). For Lourdes there were Budget, Weekend or Mid-
week pilgrimages. "We are confident," said Managing Director G. Roy Peters in his Pilgrimage Message, "that
from somewhere within all these variations every Pilgrim
can now answer the call of Our Lady to the Grotto." Later
Mr. Peters admitted that rising costs had caused him to become "concerned that many intending pilgrims are finding
it more difficult to answer the call of Our Blessed Lady to
come in procession to the cleft in the rock at Massabielle
where she appeared to a little peasant girl named Bernadette. We are convinced that in order to answer Mary's
call, many pilgrims would be quite willing to forgo some
of the softer comforts of the better-class hotels and, in the
spirit of true penance that Our Lady asked for, be content
with plainer but adequately comfortable accommodation in

the one-star Hôtel Miramont." (Eight days by air, half-board and shared rooms £112–1978 prices.) No penitent could say that he had not been warned.*

The Catholic Association used to cross the Channel by British Rail ferry but in 1976 British Rail wrote to them declining to take a pilgrimage unless it chartered an entire boat. "We do not wish to depart from our policy," the letter said, "whereby stretchers and unsightly sick pilgrims are conveyed by special train and ships. While it is physically possible to carry sick persons in passenger accommodation it could cause embarrassment to other passengers. We could only consider relaxing the rule if the service selected was known to be extremely lightly used. . . ."

It is not that the sick are just unsightly to the modern mind, they are also untidy to the official one. In 1977 the Department of Health and Social Security withheld an invalidity allowance of £10 a week from sixty sick pilgrims living in Portsmouth who went to Lourdes, because the regulations stated that they had to be indisposed for twenty-eight consecutive weeks, all of which time had to be spent in the United Kingdom. The fact that some of the claimants had been ill since they were born, and had never been abroad before, was not relevant. Essex County Council's Education Department once tried to stop a nine-year-old spastic boy from travelling to Lourdes with his mother since the officials could see no benefit to be gained from the journey. In the face of such obstacles the common determination of the pilgrims is considerably strengthened. "There is no difference between men, in intelligence or race, so profound as the difference between the sick and the well," wrote Scott Fitzgerald in *The Great Gatsby*. As our party, wheeling, escorting or carrying its ninety-four sick, descended onto the car deck of the P. & O. Ferry, one felt that part of the idea of Lourdes was to refute this widely accepted proposition.

I was sitting in the upper lounge while dusk fell and the boat slipped out of the harbour, when I heard the first talk

* St. Christopher Tours went out of business in the middle of the 1979 pilgrimage season for financial reasons.

of miracles. I had been looking at a government poster
which showed a truly revolting dog slavering at the mouth.
It was an anti-rabies poster, and the slogan beneath the
dog read: "This could bite children." The government, it
seemed to me, had got the psychological effect of this
poster all wrong. No one, on being confronted with that
disgusting dog would think "this could bite children." If
they thought at all they would think, "This could bite *me.*"
The attempt to combine fear with sentimentality was a
failure because it was bogus. Sitting beneath this horrifying
creature there was an elderly nurse in full-dress uniform
who was surrounded by a group of women who were apparently enjoying a reunion. The nurse turned out to be
not the head nurse of the pilgrimage but the proprietor of
an old people's home. Several of her residents were with
her and one was telling the rest of the group about her recovery in health. She asked if the others remembered how
ill she had been the previous year. Now she was feeling so
much better that she was no longer permitted to travel
with the sick. The forbidden topic had been broached at
last.

The modern Lourdes pilgrims are insistent that they do
not go in search of a cure, but the subject of miracles
tends to recur nonetheless. And wherever two or three
British pilgrims are gathered together the story of John
Traynor will sooner or later be told. John Traynor was the
nearest any British or Irish invalid got to being proclaimed
a Lourdes miracle. He was also one of the most remarkable of all the Lourdes cures. In 1914 Traynor, an Irishman aged thirty-two, was mobilized with the Royal Naval
Reserve and was wounded in the head in October in the
battle of Antwerp. He was unconscious for five weeks but
eventually recovered consciousness after an operation. He
was posted to Egypt, where he was wounded again, but he
recovered to volunteer for the Gallipoli landings in April
1915. After two weeks of fighting he was caught in ma-
chine-gun fire during a bayonet charge. Again he was
wounded in the head; two bullets passed through the right

side of his chest and another crossed the chest and right upper arm and lodged under his right collarbone, cutting the brachial plexus, the nerves of the shoulder and upper arm. His right arm was completely paralysed. Four operations were carried out to suture the nerves but all failed. He also began to suffer from epilepsy. The surgeons in Liverpool finally advised that his arm be amputated. Traynor refused this, but was nonetheless awarded a hundred per cent War Pension. His epilepsy grew worse, he became doubly incontinent, both legs were partly paralysed and, in April 1920, his skull was trepanned, and a silver plate was inserted into it to protect his brain. His condition continued to grow worse. He was confined to a wheelchair, and he had to be lifted in and out of bed every day. For three more years he was in the condition of an incurable invalid living at home in conditions of considerable poverty. Finally, in July 1923, arrangements were made to admit him to the Mossley Hill Home for Incurables.

But earlier that month a neighbour told John Traynor about the Liverpool diocesan pilgrimage to Lourdes. Traynor gave his last gold sovereign as a down-payment and persuaded his wife to pawn whatever she had left to raise the balance of £12. The priests in charge of the pilgrimage tried to dissuade him on the grounds that he would "probably die on the way and bring trouble and grief to everyone." His doctor refused to give him a certificate of fitness to travel. The Ministry of Pensions protested very strongly about his intentions. The newspapers began to carry stories about his wild scheme. At the station Traynor arrived too late for the first train and another attempt was made to dissuade him. But he insisted and was placed in the second train. During the journey his condition grew worse and at three stops in France enquiries were made for a local hospital so that he could be put off in an apparently dying condition. Each time there was no hospital nearby. After arriving at the *Asile* Hospital in Lourdes he suffered a bad epileptic fit during which

he started to bleed from the mouth. He was then examined
by the three pilgrimage doctors who stated the following:

                                                24 July 1923
Epilepsy: The fits during the journey have been recorded. Paralysis: involving the median, musculo-
spinal and ulnar nerves with typical "main en griffe"
deformity and wasting of all the muscles of the right
upper limb, wasting of the right pectoral and axillary
muscles. There was a trephine hole 2 cm diameter in
the right parietal area, pulsation of the brain was palpable and the area was covered by a metal plate.
There was loss of sensation and of voluntary movement in the lower limbs. There was incontinence of
urine and faeces.
            Signed, Doctors Azurdia, Finn and Marley.

On the afternoon of 26 July Traynor spent his last few
shillings on some medals which were hawked around the
wards of the *Asile*, intending to take them home as a present for his wife. Then he was wheeled down to the baths.
During the bath his legs started to thrash around and the
*brancardiers** assumed that he was starting another epileptic
fit. He himself tried to get to his feet, feeling that he could
do so easily, but instead he was held down. When he was
lifted from the bath he felt so weak and tired that he cried.
He was then taken to the procession of the Blessed Sacrament where all the sick are assembled every afternoon in
front of the basilicas. As the Archbishop of Rheims passed
in front of him carrying the monstrance Traynor realized
that, for the first time since the Battle of Gallipoli, eight
years before, he could move his right arm. He moved it so
vigorously that it burst from its fastenings. Then he tried
to rise from his stretcher. Once again the *brancardiers* held
him down and this time they gave him a sedative injection
in the belief that he had become hysterical. But when they
got him back to the *Asile* he was able to walk seven steps

* A *brancardier* is a volunteer stretcher-bearer.

(according to the doctors "with difficulty") and his reflexes were restored. He was given another injection and a *brancardier* was instructed to watch him throughout the night. Early next morning Traynor climbed out of bed and rushed out of the ward, brushing aside those who were watching him. He then ran barefoot, pursued by two *brancardiers*, from the *Asile* to the Grotto, a distance of several hundred yards over gravel. He remained praying at the Grotto for about twenty minutes while a crowd gathered. Then he returned to his ward, washed and dressed. All this time he was in a confused mental state, aware that he had experienced an extraordinary recovery but with no clear recollection of his previous condition. Throughout the morning news spread around the town and an enormous crowd gathered in front of the *Asile*. Traynor was surprised and irritated by the crowds and puzzled by the constant enquiries after his health. The Liverpool pilgrimage was due to leave on the following morning, but before it did so Traynor was examined again. He was found to have a normal gait and to have recovered the sensation in his legs. His right arm was usable. There had been no more epileptic fits, and the opening in his skull was considerably smaller. Only on the train back through France, when he was questioned by the Archbishop of Liverpool, Mgr. Keating, did he realize the full extent of what had happened to him.

When the Liverpool pilgrimage regained Lime Street Station there were what the *Liverpool Post* described as "extraordinary scenes." The train had to be stopped outside the station while the crowds were calmed by the Archbishop, but even then Traynor was only able to reach his home with the help of policemen wielding truncheons. It was the supreme moment of the British pilgrimage to Lourdes.

Subsequent investigation showed that Traynor retained no trace of epilepsy or paralysis. His right arm was restored to normal use and appearance, except for a minor deformity of the muscles of the right hand. Where there had formerly been a hole in the skull there was only a

slight' depression. He went into the haulage business and
was able to work with two-hundred-pound sacks of coal.
He went to Lourdes every year until the war as a *brancardier* and eventually died of a strangulated hernia in 1943,
just before his sixty-first birthday. Four years after his cure
the Medical Bureau declared that it could not be due to
any natural process, "because of the certain knowledge of
the pre-existing lesions which had not responded to surgical treatment, because of the suddenness of the cure and
lack of convalescence and because the cure persisted." The
medical report was sent to the Archbishop of Liverpool in
the normal way but it seems to have disappeared into the
archives of the diocese without trace; enquirers today are
told that it never arrived. When Traynor informed the
Ministry of Pensions that he was no longer entitled to receive his pension, he was told that there was no machinery
to discontinue a hundred per cent pension which had been
granted on the grounds that he was "an incurable and
powerless epileptic."

Although Traynor's case was never proclaimed to be a
miracle it is still one of the most famous of all Lourdes
cures, chiefly on account of the surgical confirmation of
the injury to the nerves and the extraordinary speed of recovery. The fact that it was never proclaimed seems to be
generally regarded among pilgrims as an administrative
mischance rather than a criticism of its miraculous character. Nevertheless, cases as dramatic as Traynor's are extremely rare, and very few of the sick pilgrims on our boat
that evening would have stated that they were going in
hopes of a cure. In that at least they showed a marked
difference from their medieval predecessors.

Among the sick pilgrims on the boat was Michael. Michael
was in a state which required him to be kept lying flat for
most of the time. He was also extremely heavy. As a result
he travelled not on the passenger deck with the other sick
but in the solitary splendour of his own ambulance on the
car deck.

Michael had been to Lourdes twenty-one times already.

"Before I went to Lourdes, my life wasn't worth living,"
he said. "I felt suicidal. When you're first hurt you think
only of yourself. Now, after what I've seen there, I can
carry on. And every time I go there it's like going the first
time again." Michael is a burly man about fifty years old.
At the time of his accident he was a foreman engineer in
London. Then his motor bike crashed in the Harrow Road,
and ever since he has been paralysed from the waist down,
and in constant pain. He first went to Lourdes in 1956, at
which time he could only sit up for about an hour at a
time. Now he says he can sit up for most of the day.

"The second time I was there a blind chap called
George Anderson was cured. He wrote his name and address in the missal I had given my wife when we were
married. The night he was cured he didn't close his eyes at
all. I was beside him in the ward and I watched him lying
awake. He told me that he was afraid to close his eyes that
first night in case when he opened them in the morning he
couldn't see.

"People, especially non-Catholics, think I go to Lourdes
to be cured. I never did go there for that. How could God
pick me out from among so many? Every time I've been
there it's been for the same reason; to find peace of mind.
Once you go into the Domain, you're out of this world. I
just go to Lourdes as a pilgrim, and to learn how to carry
on. You get some great blessings just from that."

With Michael on the pilgrimage were his wife and his
son, also called Michael. His wife was formerly a nurse,
now she spends the time looking after her husband and her
son. For young Michael suffers from muscular dystrophy
and is partly paralysed. But he can still play the guitar.
They say he would have been very musical if he had been
well.

When old Michael first went to Lourdes, the return fare
for the sick was £18. By 1980 this had risen to £99.
Apart from the miracles the next question he expected to
be asked was about the commercialization. He thought
most of the criticism on that score came from the visitors
or casual tourists rather than from the devout pilgrims

who did not seem to be bothered by it at all. "People like
to take back some souvenirs. It's natural to want to, and
the shops are useful enough. Still, it'll be a shock when
you first see the place. It *is* exploited too much. But the
clergy try to keep it under control, they're very against it.
You used to be able to buy a crucifix with the water in it
but the clergy put a stop to that. The water can never be
sold." He seemed to regret the disappearance of these
crucifixes.

Back at home, in Shepherd's Bush, Michael and his wife
always kept a half-gallon jar of Lourdes water which he
used in time of trouble. Even when he kept it for several
years he said that it was remarkable how fresh it always
tasted. Michael was a pilgrim in the Traynor tradition.
You felt that if he were to experience a similar cure he
would show as little astonishment about it.

One of the sick pilgrims who had been carried up the two
flights of stairs from the car deck to the ship's bar was
Eddy; he was not a Catholic and he had never been to
Lourdes. Eddy was twenty-eight. Six years earlier, just
after he was married and while he was working in the Post
Office in North London, he had contracted multiple
sclerosis. He was by now almost completely paralysed, and
was confined to a wheelchair. He could swallow but he
could not lift a cup unaided. He could just about nod. He
could slur a few words so that his mother could understand. His vision was blurred. He could raise his head for
short periods and then turn it slightly. His hearing and understanding were unimpaired. He could manage a smile
and a few other expressions. He could lift an arm out of
the blanket to gesture goodbye. He lived at home in a
small council flat in Camden with his three younger
brothers and his parents. His father was a cab driver.

In conversation before the pilgrimage assembled, Eddy's
parents discussed Lourdes in vaguely religious terms, but
religion was probably a new subject in their home. The
idea of sending Eddy there was suggested to them by the
nuns at the Catholic hospice who sometimes took Eddy in

for a week or so to give his mother a rest. At first when Eddy became ill he lived with his wife and young daughter in a flat for the handicapped in Basingstoke. Then he moved back to London.

"His mother doesn't like me to say it, but Eddy's wife kicked him out," said his father. "Don't talk like that," said his mother at once. Eddy gave an impression of amusement while listening to his father talk. It seemed to be a performance he was well-accustomed to. There were several thoughts or phrases that occurred again and again. "Why us?" "We're going to keep going, aren't we boy?" "You're better than you were." His father was heavily preoccupied with the difficulties of getting a more suitable flat and of finding a nurse when there was a crisis. When he talked about the expense of looking after his son he added: "Don't get me wrong. I *want* him to keep the heating on." But the flat was damp at the best of times and quite unsuitable for nursing Eddy. Both parents mentioned a recent report of new progress in research into the disease. His father also mentioned miracles as soon as he mentioned Lourdes. "If Eddy could just walk that would be all right with me. When you come back off that train, Eddy, you're going to walk off."

By his own account the problems of dealing with Camden Council's social welfare department were considerable. Eddy had been discharged from hospital some time previously. There was nothing more that medical science could do to combat the progress of his condition. The hospice, which specialized in the care of the chronically sick, at least offered more hope. One of the regular pilgrims had raised the money for his fare, and so Eddy's parents had agreed to let him go. "I'm going to tell you about the last social worker the council sent round," said his father. "Eddy won't mind. He's heard it before."

"Well, this chap, I call him a social worker although he couldn't have been very experienced, just walked in here one day and said he wanted to talk to Eddy alone. And when he thought he was alone with Eddy he said, 'You know you'll be dead in two years, don't you?' What sort of

a thing is that to say to him? Eddy was very upset. Weren't
you, boy? I told them not to bother to call round again if
that's what they've come to say."

Although the flat is both damp and overcrowded the
council have been unable to find a more suitable place for
them to move to. So Eddy has to be nursed in the company of his three young brothers, and their dog. In their
high spirits and muscular noisiness, these boys provided a
vivid reminder of what Eddy had once been.

When discussing the pilgrimage Eddy's parents had
noted the practical points. There was the fact that the
wheelchair had to be insured because it belonged to the
National Health Service and regulations stated that it
could only leave the country at the patient's risk. They'd
also been warned by the nuns that Lourdes was a thieves'
paradise, and so various precautions were discussed as to
where Eddy might keep his money. They had some colour
pictures of Lourdes and were able to point out the hospital
where Eddy would be staying. His mother who thought he
smoked too much still kept on giving him cigarettes. That
and the cups of coffee were about all she could do apart
from talking to him. His eyes could not always follow the
television pictures. It was hard to know what his own
thoughts were about going without his parents. He might
have been glad just to be giving his mother a rest. Though
his understanding was normal he could not communicate
his views on this extended journey to a country he had
never previously visited, to which he was committed in the
care of strangers.

At Boulogne, in the early darkness of an August night, the
pilgrimage made its way down to the car deck and then,
led by Michael's ambulance, walked up the ramps onto the
quay and onto the train. It took one and a half hours for
the sick to be transferred from their chairs or stretchers
into the three ambulance cars, and for their eight hundred
healthy companions to find reserved berths. With everyone
aboard, the long train, which had been drawn up on four
platforms, was assembled and ready to move off. Every

carriage, including the ambulance section, was wired for sound; and at 1 a.m., as we drew out of the docks, the loudspeakers opened up with the first ceremony of the pilgrimage, a decade of the Rosary, the First Joyful Mystery. Outside on the quay another boat had arrived, and as the ambulance train rattled out, with its passengers saying their Hail Mary's, it passed a long column of mainly youthful travellers humping their luggage beneath the lights towards the distant and sleeping town.

One of the particular things about the pilgrimage to Lourdes is said to be that people who are unbearable anywhere else become very pleasant there. The pilgrims, thrown together in groups of six, usually strangers, trying to settle for the night in a space where two people would be short of room, had an early chance to test this theory. Watching an exceptionally awkward sleeping companion, a man who fussed over his case and retrieved it from the most inaccessible corner of the carriage, a man who smoked a pipe in this cat box and who woke everyone up to tell them that he had cut his finger and then refused to have it plastered, a man who fiddled with the lights throughout the night and was always standing in the doorway when someone else wanted to pass through it, condemned to spend the night with such a man and aware that one would have to return eventually in the same company, one could look forward to observing the operation of this Lourdes effect.

There are a limited number of things to do on a train, even a pilgrimage train. This one seemed to keep hospital hours. Quite early in the morning, at which time the sick had already been refreshed, the loudspeaker opened up again with more prayers. The rather croaky responses were lubricated by tea served by the pilgrimage handmaids, already dressed in their blue nurse's uniforms. During the night the train had passed through either Rouen or Paris and was now between Tours and Poitiers. It was a brilliant day. For miles on either side of the track there were wheat or maize fields, ripening in the clear light of the south. Soon we would be entering La Vendée, traditionally the

Catholic and royalist province, which contained some of
the richest architectural remains of the pilgrimage to
Compostella, and from which came the celebrated Lourdes
hymn.

Among my fellow travellers there were several who proposed themselves as persons of interest. There was a frail
nun who sometimes needed a wheelchair and who was
seen off at Dover by another nun of the same order. With
complete unconcern for the frantic surroundings of the departure hall she had asked her healthy sister to pray for
her while she was at the shrine. She surely must be in
search of a cure. There was an Indian woman in a sari
who was carrying a baby. Both were extremely healthy.
But whereas so many other people were burdened with the
sick or with their medical supplies she was burdened with
nappies and tufty tails and milk formula. It seemed a kind
of fussiness in her, in such company, to be so hygienically
concerned with her infant. One found oneself wondering,
absurdly, why a perfectly *healthy* three-month-old baby
could not look after itself. There was another sick pilgrim,
a young crippled woman on crutches who was not travelling in the ambulance car but was lodged in a couchette.
As she struggled aboard at Boulogne she confronted a
healthy woman who instinctively flinched and then recovered to say oversolicitously, "Take it slowly, dear." "I
can't do anything else," replied the sick woman coldly.
And then unexpectedly added, "Hold me, I'm feeling
drunk."

Back in the ambulance section David had been put in
the charge of an oldish bishop who was finding it hard
going. Stimulated by the more than usually confusing impressions of the journey, and by the great number of new
friends it offered, David had spent the last hour walking
up and down the train quite quickly. Everywhere he went
he had to be followed since he was quite capable of opening a door and stepping out. The bishop who accompanied
him was feeling the pace, but since the only alternative
was strapping David into his bunk, and since David was a
privileged member of this pilgrimage and one of those

whom the healthy were intending to serve, there was no
question of restraining him more than absolutely necessary. Occasionally the bishop was able to hold his hand,
but generally David was too far ahead of him. He made
his happiness evident by murmuring continually and by
approaching anyone he saw, with every sign of striking up
a sensible conversation.

French railways have been able to maintain and install a
full fleet of modern ambulance cars entirely as a result of
the Lourdes pilgrimage. In 1978, 486,344 pilgrims arrived
at Lourdes station in 709 special trains, almost all of
which included two or three ambulance coaches. (British
Rail used ambulance cars in the war but these became obsolete in 1972, by which time almost their only users were
the half-dozen or so Lourdes trains hired by the big British
pilgrimages.) The new French coaches are arranged so
that the berths face fore and aft. On one side there are
pairs of berths one above the other, then there is a central
gangway and then on the other side a line of single berths
with a narrower gangway beyond that, so that those re-
quiring heavy nursing can be lifted from both sides.
Throughout the journey the sick in each of the three cars
were attended by a duty nurse, by a team of *brancardiers*
and handmaids and by one of the pilgrimage's three doctors. There were nine nurses and 120 volunteer helpers in
all.

Among the sick was Canon Wainwright, an experienced
Lourdes pilgrim, who was not sick but who, since he was
aged ninety-two, had been advised to sleep in the ambulance. He sat on his bunk in the sunshine reading his
breviary until, somewhere outside Bordeaux, he was interrupted by a younger priest. "Good-morning, Canon!"
"What? Oh good-morning." "Are you praying for sinners?" "What?" "I said are you praying for sinners?" "Oh.
Well, yes." "Well I'll be all right then," said the young
priest, and left the old Canon to get on with his job. In his
autobiography, *A Sort of Life*, Graham Greene recalls
how, when Antonia White was attending the funeral of her
father, she met an old priest who tried to persuade her to

return to the Church. "Well then, Father," she said, "re-mind me of the arguments for the existence of God." Eventually he admitted to her, "I knew them once, but I have forgotten them." Canon Wainwright sitting on the edge of his cot, saying his breviary in the sunshine and surrounded by the dying, could hardly have been expected to recall them either. At the end of his working life he was down to essentials—trying to reduce the future ranks of the damned.

His companions in the ambulance coach included twelve cases of heart disease, twelve of multiple sclerosis, eleven who had suffered strokes, nine with cancer, eight with epilepsy, seven who were mentally subnormal, and so on. The list of diagnoses read like an index of obscure and untreatable diseases. There was Huntington's Chorea, Raynaud's Phenomenon, Addison's disease, Wilson's disease, and motor neurone disease. There were sixteen cases of rheumatoid or osteo-arthritis. Other pilgrims suffered from polio, blindness, cystic fibrosis, brain tumour, spina bifida and hydrocephalus. Some had drawn an unbelievable assortment of marked cards. One woman had hypertension, heart disease, degenerative joint disease and was blind in one eye. She had recovered from cervical cancer twenty years before. Another had transverse spinal cord syndrome, facial hemiparesis and depression. A man had leucopenia, rectal prolapse, urethral stricture, spastic colon, hypoglycaemia and diverticulosis. These were not the sort of records likely to be listed by *Guinness*. These record holders were more likely to be set aside from the world for the remainder of their lives. People were not supposed to get these diseases in the age of scientific medicine. The newspapers reassured us about this every day. But the sick pilgrims were not included in this universal promise. They were, in Zola's words, "abandoned by science." As such, they were a more select group than would have been included in that phrase fifty years ago. And as God's domain has diminished and that of science has increased a corresponding wish has grown up to render incurable illness invisible. The spectacle of the assembled sick pilgrims of a

large Lourdes pilgrimage is a chilling reminder of how
very far scientific understanding is from being complete.
And the shock evoked by the sight is a sign of our
diminished ability to accept the idea of suffering, once it
has been suggested to us that suffering is no longer inevitable.

But the old canon was concerned with those who might
be abandoned by God, rather than by science, and to pass
the time while we rattled on through the heat of the Midi I
turned to a description of the Faith which preceded the
current streamlined and tearproof version, and with which
he must have been more familiar. Antonia White's novel
Frost in May is concerned with some of the Catholic prac-
tices of 1908 which were extant until recently. Here are
the notes which one of her characters, a schoolgirl, makes
during her convent retreat.

> Pride first and deadliest of sins. Heresies all due to
> pride. Setting oneself up against God's divine revela-
> tion in the Church. Even children have difficulties
> about religion . . . Vanity, self-indulgence, etc. lead
> to doubting God's law. Hence importance of
> mortification. Mortal sin makes the soul loathsome in
> the sight of God. Saints could detect horrible stench
> in presence of sinners. Soul dead to God . . . Venial
> sins punished in purgatory, a place as terrible as hell,
> but not eternal. Souls in purgatory cannot help them-
> selves. Only prayers on earth can shorten their suffer-
> ings. *Better to be afflicted with the most appalling dis-
> ease than to commit one mortal sin. Disease a faint
> type of sin . . .*

Sometimes this girl,

> lay awake at night worrying miserably over the
> damned. For months she would forget all about them,
> then an account of a horrible accident or a sermon
> like this would remind her of them. She would pray
> frantically for them, forgetting that it was useless. In

spite of this she would go so far as to beg Our Lady
to do something for them, clinging to some vague leg-
end about their being allowed one day's respite in ten
thousand years. Sometimes, she even doubted that
their punishments were eternal, only to remember,
horrified, that the eternity of hell was an article of
faith, and that to doubt it endangered her own soul.
Indeed the eternity of hell was another proof of God's
goodness, since the theologians agreed that *annihi-
lation would be a worse punishment than endless ages
of fiery pain.*

Extraordinary to think that the high-spirited, tea-bearing
handmaids on our train must have missed such rigours,
and the traditions of two thousand years, by the skin of
their teeth.

Looking around my companions in the compartment, I
wondered what each of their motives for joining the pilgrimage might be. They were not there primarily to help
the sick, for they were not *brancardiers,* and I wondered
whether any of them were penitents. It was hardly the sort
of thing one could ask. That the disciplines of *Frost in
May* had lasted well into the 1960s I knew from the case
of one young girl whose account of her penitential pilgrimage I had been told before I left.

At that time [she said], I was a nurse in a London
teaching hospital. After I had conceived, but before I
knew I was pregnant, I was caught climbing out of
the nurses' home at night and I was dismissed. So
then I got a job as an air hostess. Shortly after that I
started to be sick in the morning. My doctor was a
friend of my mother and he knew we were Catholic
and that my mother would disapprove of an abortion
so he told me that I was suffering from altitude
sickness. He wouldn't tell me that I was actually pregnant until it was too late to do anything about it. Of
course I was very naïve. I was twenty-two at the time.
Neither of my parents was much help when they were

told. My father had very grand ideas about himself
and was mortified by my pregnancy, mainly because
he feared that his friends at the office might find out.
So when I became visibly pregnant I was sent to stay
on a housing estate in north London and I was not allowed to take a bus across London in case anyone I
knew saw me. I remember after I'd had the baby how
the ward sister said to all those waiting to come in,
"Would all the husbands and Miss —'s visitor (that
was my boy friend) come in and see their babies
now." Then the priest came to see me and told me to
give the child to an adoption society. My mother arranged *that* too. My baby was taken in a taxi to another county and although I tried I couldn't get her
back. And after all that I was sent to Lourdes as a
penance for my sinful behaviour. It's extraordinary
how much has been changed by the pill.

A pilgrimage priest who heard this story in 1978 was duly
horrified by it. In his view it would take a mad penitent or
a mad confessor to arrange for anyone to go to Lourdes as
a penance, because of the expense. Nonetheless, a fair proportion of the pilgrims are penitents in the more general
sense. And the sad student nurse might have been com-
forted to know that there is a thirteenth-century record of
two English women, Mabel de Boclande and the mother of
John Mayde, who were both sent to Compostella; in the
first case for committing adultery and in the second for
fornication with a godson.* Other pilgrims, usually men of
power, went as a public demonstration of piety, others still
as part of an obsessive attempt to collect indulgences.
Some went to soothe a feeling of restlessness or from a
sense of adventure. And some simply went for a holiday.
Chaucer's Wife of Bath had been to Boulogne (or
Bologna), Cologne, Rome, and Jerusalem three times, as
well as to Santiago.

After a brief stop at Bordeaux to load on bread for

* *The Pilgrimage to Santiago*, Edwin Mullins.

lunch the train branched left and eventually, towards 4 o'clock, began to run up the green rocky valley of the Gave de Pau. Here the pilgrims started to crowd the windows for their first glimpse of the town. The Grotto could not be better placed for the view presented by this arrival. There running parallel to the track is the river, and parallel to the river is a panorama of all the significant places in the story. There are the baths, then the blaze of candles, then the Grotto itself at the foot of the dark mass of Massabielle, then the wall of the first basilica and the wide ramps leading up to it, all in full view from the carriages. As the train approached, our loudspeaker announced the Lourdes hymn, which for old Michael lying on his side in the ambulance and not really able to see the Domain, always marks the moment of arrival.

The Lourdes hymn was first heard in Lourdes in May 1873, and became immediately popular. It is sung every night in the torchlight procession and is a theme tune for every pilgrimage. It starts with the words:

> Immaculate Mary
> Our hearts are on fire . . .

and continues on this level of simplicity, sweetness and fervour to a maximum of sixty verses—every one of which, given the length of the major processions, is sometimes needed. It is a slight tune, in some danger of becoming a lisping dirge, but it has the "strange appeal" of cheap music. Given out from the radio car, by half-a-dozen strong male voices, as the woods closed around the train and the river swept past beneath the carriage windows, it created a moment of unrehearsed theatre. The pilgrims sang the hymn softly, even those lines which refer to England as "Mary's dowry," which have to be dropped in the Domain, presumably because they wouldn't go at all with the Irish. And as the Grotto came into sight one could see that the town was covered with a heat haze. The tall wooden crosses on the distant hills were indistinct in the soft light. The train slowed down before the station and

people living by the line looked up on hearing the singing,
giving the impression of expectancy, though they must
have heard the tune ten thousand times already. On the
long platform those who had gone ahead to make arrangements were waiting to greet us. They stood in the heat in
their panama hats and cotton jackets, plump, moustached,
redfaced English figures, and took up the singing as they
heard the quiet sound without any of the self-conscious-
ness normally aroused by such demonstrations. And it
no longer seemed so odd to be sitting in a French railway
carriage singing hymns with various strangers. The man
with the pipe was no longer in the doorway, even though it
was perfectly clear that everyone else wanted to use it.
"The Lourdes effect" had started and the singing grew in
strength.

❧ III ❧

The High Town

A miracle is no argument to one who is deliberately, and on principle, an atheist.
Cardinal Newman

To get from the station to the hotel quarter of Lourdes in
the high season one has to pass through a Carnival of
Piety. The streets are generally blocked with traffic and as
the coach trickles down the hill from the old high town to
the new low one there is every opportunity to take in the
full horror of the event.

At first sight one seems to be moving down an arcade of
garish souvenir shops. Then one realizes that these shops
are not selling little dolls in national costume, or scarves
painted with the regional arms, or cheap jewellery; they
are all selling "objects of piety." The strings of beads turn
into rosaries, thousands and thousands of rosaries of every
size, colour and price. The mannequins turn into Virgins; baby virgins, haggard virgins, flashing virgins—("Our
Mama with the lights on," as one Brazilian pilgrim put it).
There are virgins in a snow storm, virgins in a television
set, little cutie-doll bug-eyed half-witted virgins praying on
velveteen mats; virgins in make-up, virgins in modern
dress and the world-renowned hollow, plastic virgins
whose crowns unscrew to turn into bottle stoppers. There

are Virgins in Grottos, and there are virgins in grottos
mounted on varnished Dutch clogs, an international two-
horrors-in-one. If the wind got up you could be deafened
by the tinkling cascades of medals which glitter and dangle
in luxuriant clumps in shop after shop. When I finally
summoned the courage to examine them, I found that half
the medals bore the figure of Mary, and the other half the
signs of the Zodiac. But you never got Mary on one side
and Virgo on the other; that would be sacrilegious.

"When considering the perennial question of the rosary
shops," said the insurance agent, morosely, "remember
why there are so many of them. It is not possible for so
many people to make a living out of trading in cheap
goods unless they are supplying an enormous demand."
And he looked both gloomy and righteous. But he was not
given an opportunity to mount his defence until later; and
so my first impressions, as the coach moved towards the
hotel, piled up without mediation. Surely, I thought, as the
bus squeezed down this Ali Baba's tunnel of twinkling rubbish, surely it can't all be like this?

To understand how this emporium came to be spawned on
Lourdes one has to follow the early progress of the Domain. It is a story of separation, of parish and Domain, of
Domain and town, and finally of the separation within the
town, between the *commerçants* around the Domain and
the original local businessmen.

It is interesting to speculate on what would have happened to the town of Lourdes if parish and Domain had
not quarrelled. It is possible that all the development
which has gone into the new town would simply have
taken place in the old one, destroying such of its character
as still remains, and would then have spread out into what
has now become the new town anyway. But, remembering
the powerful rivalry which marked the birth of the new
town, it is hard to suppose that nothing would have been
different without it. Zola, describing the atmosphere of the
1890s, wrote, of a Lourdes barber, that "you could divine
within him all the slowly accumulated overflowing spite

with which the old town regarded the new town—that
town which had sprung up so quickly on the other side of
the castle, that rich city with houses as big as palaces
whither flowed all the life, all the luxury, all the money of
Lourdes, so that it was incessantly growing larger and
wealthier, whilst its elder sister, the poor, antique town of
the mountains, with its narrow, grass-grown, deserted
streets, seemed near the point of death . . . Custom only
flowed to the shops which were near the Grotto, and only
the poorer pilgrims were willing to lodge so far away; so
that the unequal conditions of the struggle intensified the
rupture and turned the high town and the low town into
two irreconcilable enemies, who preyed upon one another
amidst continual intrigues." Remembering this long slow
poisoning of relations, the vulgar low town begins to seem
like the high town's revenge on the Domain for having
granted it less than its due share of glory.

From the first, the old town saw the development of the
Domain as a threat to its own interests. There was of
course in those days no "new town" near the Grotto at all.
All the available lodgings and shops were in the town and
so was the railway station. It was inevitable that the great
majority of pilgrims should, by passing through the town,
benefit its inhabitants. Then when Abbé Peyramale quarrelled with Père Sempé the town found that it too began to
suffer. The Domain began to assume its present form as a
self-contained processional area in 1875, the year when the
procession from the parish church was stopped. By 1877,
the year of Abbé Peyramale's death, the statue of the
Crowned Virgin, which forms the centrepiece of the processional esplanade, was in position. And in the same year
the Garaison fathers secured a great triumph over the
town by arranging for a brand new road, called the Boulevard de la Grotte, to be built over the bed of the Lapacca
torrent, so enabling the pilgrims to pass from the railway
station to the Domain without entering the town at all. Instead, hotels and shops began to spring up along the new
boulevard, forming the nucleus of what has since become
the new town, below the hill. In 1877, too, the *Asile* hospi-

tal was opened in the Domain, so even the sick pilgrims,
who had until then been lodged in the Seven Sorrows Hospital just outside the high town by the old bridge, now had
the choice of passing their stay entirely within the area
controlled by the Garaison order.

For the devout of the high town the possibility of an imposing new parish church to rival the sanctuaries of the
Domain was their chief consolation for this snub. But after
Peyramale's death work came to a halt and the unfinished
structure began to deteriorate. When Zola visited it in
1892 there was still no roof and after fifteen years of ne-
glect it resembled the ruin of a sacked monastery more
than a building in construction. But, unknown to Zola,
even while he inspected it the tide was turning. The year
before, a group of Peyramale's admirers had commis-
sioned two expensive stained glass windows from a leading
manufacturer in Bordeaux. These can be seen today at the
west end of the nave. Each shows an unmistakable likeness
of the priest with the saint. In the north window the Abbé
is standing in his study and is saying his famous line,
which marked the first moment of his curiosity—"Ask this
Lady her name." In the south window he and the tiny,
broad-backed little saint, now fetchingly recostumed in an
alternative peasant outfit, have been joined by *Aquero* who
gives her stupendous answer, "I am the Immaculate Conception." This south window is usually rather harder to
study, since it is above the recess which is used by the
town's undertakers for the lying-in of corpses. And the
church still buries enough of the Lourdais for a brisk flow
of mourners to be passing around the coffin on most days.

That the new church was dedicated to the Sacred Heart
also suggests a challenge to the Domain. Devotion to the
Sacred Heart of Jesus had been made universally acceptable by the seventeenth-century visions of another French
girl-saint, Margaret-Mary Alacoque. And the Eucharistic
movement, which was launched early in the twentieth century at about the time of the church's dedication, in an
effort to correct the Marian tendencies of the day, found
its inspiration in this idea. But the clearest record of the

battle lies in the crypt. Fixed to Father Peyramale's tomb
there are two tablets which state that Marie Dominique
Peyramale was "a great servant of Our Lady of Lourdes,"
and add the lines from Matthew v:10: "Blessed are they
that suffer persecution for justice' sake . . ." This eloquent
rebuke rings out through the silence even today.

The year 1905, when the parish church was finally completed, was also, by a strange chance, the year when the
Catholic Church was disestablished in France. In 1903 the
Garaison fathers had been suppressed by the state, and in
1906 the humiliation of the Domain was completed when
the entire property was confiscated from the bishop and its
ownership vested in the municipality of Lourdes. In the
face of this common enemy, parish and Domain were at
last able to compose their differences. These events also
marked the opening of the modern era of Lourdes, when it
became a place of more importance to the Universal
Church than to French Catholic politics. The fiftieth anniversary celebration of 1908 was followed by an international onslaught which concentrated the united attention of
the townspeople on the serious business of making money.
It is a curious fact that there have been no miraculous
cures at all among the people of Lourdes since 1858, but
the local saying has it that their devotion has been replaced
by prosperity; they have been blessed in other ways. Since
the reunion of the town, no one has remained aloof. Even
Bernadette's family opened its souvenir shops and partici-
pated in the construction of a luxury hotel. The Lourdais
were offered a rare opportunity to exploit the spiritual de-
spair of the twentieth century, and in accepting it, and
building the low town, they have provided us with a monu-
ment worthy of our age.

The advantage of the division into high and low towns is
that it has enabled the old Lourdes to retain some of its
character, and to provide a convenient retreat for those
weary of the profitable arena across the river. The high
town, through which our coach had passed before descending the hill, is much like other small towns anywhere;

it buys and sells and counts its change. At the end of the season, the souvenir shops in the pilgrim quarter put up their steel shutters, and overnight on the last Sunday in October they remove the heads from the parking meters. The Lac de Lourdes, a local beauty spot, is deserted except for its swans thawing out amid the upturned rowing boats. And in Bartrès the village church sinks into an appropriate if rather damp somnolence. All the hotels on the left bank are locked, their staffs are paid off until the early spring redecoration, and the proprietorial families move into comfortable homes in other parts of the country, or retire to their villas in the West Indies. There is a great deal of profit in servicing other people's spiritual needs.

Out of season, the town at the top of the hill reasserts its position in the modern world. If there is a scandal it may well be about an abortion clinic, although in Lourdes there is always the chance that the doctor who ran it has christened it "the Notre Dame." The rest of the town's doctors are able to relax their seasonal vigilance. They have so arranged matters with the pilgrimages that, despite the presence of so many visiting physicians, their own practice is actually increased. There is a strict protocol about this. The pilgrimage doctors have to agree not to treat anyone, even if they are requested to, even if they are fellow pilgrims, and even if they are lodged in the adjoining hotel room, unless the sufferer is a registered sick pilgrim on their own pilgrimage. The determined guardian of this protective protocol on behalf of the doctors of France is the director of the Medical Bureau of the Domain, Dr. Théodore Mangiapan, who includes stern warnings about it in his Bulletin. Dr. Mangiapan, of course, has to bear the whole burden of complaint if the convention is breached, and points out that very few visiting doctors are even licensed to practise medicine in France. He gets to the hub of this ethical objection with great speed. "Above all," he implores, "never ask for or accept a fee for services rendered within your pilgrimage."

In winter the cinemas start to include blue movies in their programmes. And if a perambulating Grotto chaplain who is outraged by the poster for *Couvent en Chaleur* tears it down, he will be fortunate not to be prosecuted for malicious damage. The regional news magazine will carry well-informed stories about local personalities, of a scandalous and diverting nature. The response of the town, over-excited by such up-to-date celebrity, will be to flood the office of the inoffensive local paper with anonymous but delicious reports about the neighbours. Appalled, the editor of the local paper will be forced to insert a notice in his own columns requesting his readers to stop calling *him* with these details, as he, contrary to general belief, has nothing to do with the magazine series and wishes to resume the use of his telephone.

Lourdes lies in a county, Bigorre, which retains its individuality. The *Bigourdan* dialect is so varied today that peasant women from adjacent valleys who meet at a common market town can still find each other loquaciously incomprehensible. The life of Lourdes in winter is based on the traditional wealth of the area, on good cooking, pigeon shooting and the passion for rugby football. It was no accident that when the north and centre of France took to association football the south should have looked for something different. The cultural line from Bordeaux to Lyons still exists, and those living south of it count their half as the virtuous land. The south-west is the region of rugby, and of all the towns of the south-west none is prouder of its football team than Lourdes. In one miraculous year every member of the French national team but one was from Lourdes. And if they were asked what their town was famous for, many Lourdais would reply "football"; and then add "hotels."

"La vie lourdaise" has its own solemn rituals. On the first Sunday of September, the feast of St. Giles of Béziers, perhaps, or the eve of the Nativity of Our Lady, the wood pigeon season opens. Anyone who has a gun joins in. There are the preparations of the evening before, the buying of cartridges, the smell of the leather, the drinking among the hunters. Then comes the departure before dawn from the silent town and the climb to the highest pine

woods, just below the rock ridges of the Pyrenean foot-
hills. A decoy is placed in a likely tree, and the hunters
conceal themselves and wait for "les bleus," the first flash
of blue feathers. The pigeons migrate each year over the
Pyrenees to Spain, and as soon as the annual passage is
under way the munitions factories in Tarbes, where many
Lourdais work, can count on a thirty per cent increase in
the sickness rate. Success in the hunt is a matter of great
importance. "Pray for me at the Grotto," said a leading
sportsman of Argelès to Peter Crane, one of the officials of
the Domain. "Ask the Holy Virgin to restore my aim. I
have shot nothing all week." And when, two weeks later,
Monsieur Crane encountered him again, standing at a bar,
buying drinks for half the town, and literally dripping with
the blood of his bag, which he had strung round his neck
and waist, the sportsman's first thought was to thank his
friend and Our Lady for the successful intervention.

In March there is an increase in nocturnal visits to the
Domain by local schoolboys, who believe with great fervour that there is in the Gave de Pau, just downstream
from the Grotto, where the overflow of the miraculous
spring flows into the river, a very deep pool in which the
trout reach an amazing size and delicacy. Here the fish
congregate knowing that, even during the season, fishing is
not allowed in the Domain. A secular explanation is that
their size is due more to the dressings which float downstream from the *Asile* than to the spring. This remains a
matter for whispered dispute, as the pupils stand up to
their necks in the river, casting about in the dark.

As for the rugby, Lourdes is proud to have invented the
style of play known as champagne rugby, *rugby lourdais*.
When asked to name a famous personality of the town,
dead or alive, apart from the saint, most of the children in
two senior classes of the school could think of no one. But
every single one of those who did reply wrote "Jean Prat,"
the finest footballer France ever produced whose bar "Le
Winger" on the outskirts of town was a place of pilgrimage for visiting Welsh bishops for years. As in Wales,
French rugby is sufficiently bound up with nationalism to

be played at all levels by people of all classes. The Lourdais think of Wales as a mountainous area famous for its
sheep and trout rivers. And one Welsh pilgrim talking of
the remarkable strength possessed by the local *brancardiers*
said, "You should see the legs on them. All that lifting and
pushing. It must be great training for the rugby." Gripped
by their mutual enthusiasm, the Welsh and the Lourdais
gaze at each other, and see an approvable resemblance.

The Lourdais are also proud of their cuisine. They point
out that the local death rate from heart disease is, at forty-
eight per cent, seven per cent higher than the national average, which is officially stated to be due to the excessive
richness of the local diet. There is no sign that the health
services are making any impact in this matter on the local
chefs. In the rue de la Grotte, there is a small family *char-
cuterie*. Into its back yard sacks of blood, giblets, offal and
various other animal organs are carried every day from a
juggernaut lorry, there to be transmogrified by the *charcu-
tier*'s art into the tempting contents of the trays in the window. As one gazes at these delicacies, it is a surprise to recall that this was the street down which Bernadette passed
to see her first vision.

In those days the Soubirous family would seldom have had
the money to spend in the pork butcher's. Bernadette's
small brother was once found eating the candle wax that
had dripped onto the church floor, an adventurous snack
that is piously ascribed to the family's poverty in the years
of famine. But outside the Domain and the low town such
reminders of the story of Bernadette are few and far between. Like so many other places in Europe with spectacular scenery and a falling agricultural population, the department of the High Pyrenees has become a tourist resort.
In economic reports the pilgrimage industry is classed as
"tourism," together with winter sports, spa-bathing and
camping. "Lourdes is not a health-resort, a spa or the
touristic crossroads of the Pyrenees" said the 1960 *Guide
to the Grotto,* defiantly. But it has been contradicted by
events. The Club *Méditerranée* has opened a hotel in Su-

perbagnères, formerly a mountain village, now a ski resort. Cauterets, the spa which Bernadette visited between the seventeenth and eighteenth apparitions, is also now a winter resort and I drove there, curious to see what this would have done to it.

Cauterets occupies "a superb position," to that extent I could make no criticism of the brochure. The mountains do not move; Julius Caesar, who is reputed to have taken the cure, would have found much that was familiar. And it has of course been "exploited" by travel agents for over a hundred years. To revert to the *brochurese* of the previous century, "a picturesque mountain torrent foams through the town centre and the settlement is notable for its elegant avenues and delicate wrought-iron arcades." And for its delicate over-wrought visitors, who walked in the Esplanade des Oeufs (or Egg Parade) for just long enough to inflate their rotting lungs to withstand the next sanitary plunge. Today, both esplanade and torrent are still in place, as are the two bathing establishments named César and Le Rocher; but they, and the rest of the town, "modern resort in the heart of the national park" though it be, are now in a state of profitable mouldiness.

It might have surprised nineteenth-century rationalists such as Zola if they could have looked ahead to February 1979 and seen the progress of Cauterets and Lourdes, comparing the future development of the latest in fashionable medical practice with the sorry revival of peasant superstition. Cauterets's torrent is choked with non-biodegradable packaging from the shelves of the Monoprix, and the Esplanade des Oeufs, once the focal point of elegance, now leads only to a shoddy line of souvenir stalls. The Casino has become a bowling alley, and in winter *les curistes*, suffering from catarrh or tuberculosis, are replaced by morose groups of *après-skieurs*, more suited to an Esplanade des Oafs, mooching from wimpey bar to amusement arcade in their day-glo tubular safety clothing.

The obvious place in Cauterets to look for traces of Bernadette is the church. Here there is a statue of the Virgin about one foot high in plain stone, the simplicity of which

comes as a blessed relief after the encrustations of
Lourdes. It stands on a red draped plinth beneath a glass
case, and there is a notice beneath it in faded handwritten
ink which says: "In the year of Our Lord 1858 between
the 17th and 18th apparitions, the little Lourdaise, the
humble seer of Massabielle, Bernadette Soubirous, who
had come to Cauterets to cure her health, recited her rosary before this statue of the Virgin." And on the saint's
feast day there was a small tray of candles burning, and
two bowls of flowers in position. The peace of this simple
shrine, with its offerings and its unassuming statue attended by candles in the deserted church was far more impressive than much of the flummery and fuss of the great
Domain of Our Lady in the valley below. There was a certain local pride in the memorial as well. "When 'the little
seer from Lourdes' wished to cure her health she came to
Cauterets, and when she came she found that we and our
ancient statue were ready for her."

Outside the church there is the usual war memorial, at
which once a year the state holds a remembrance service.
The veterans line up in medals and suits. The fire brigade
turns out in ceremonial dress. And the service consists of
two municipal officials, both in suit and tricolor sash, reading out the roll of honour. As one reads out each name
and rank—"Boulanger, Pierre, Caporal"—the other cries
"Mort pour la France." It is a moving occasion, but the
reverence due to even this secular ritual has begun to die.
On the Cauterets war memorial, where the names are as
usual arranged in strict alphabetical order, some irreverent
hand has taken the opportunity of a gap beneath the name

LACABANNE, Jacques, Capitaine

to scrawl, in correct alphabetical form,

L'ARMÉE Tue!!

To reach Cauterets from Lourdes, Bernadette would have
taken the road which passes St. Savin, by then a small village but formerly the site of a Benedictine abbey which
was the centre of both the economic and spiritual life of

Bigorre. Even today one can see how this might have been. The church is placed on the sharp rim of hills above a long curving valley, where it would have been defensible from all directions. Inside the massive walls of the building there is a wooden crucifixion, carved in Catalonia in the thirteenth century, and a curious old organ. Its painted wooden screen is rather rickety now, but it still includes a line of infernal masks, the eyes and mouths of which were designed to open and shut with the organ stops, causing the damned visible anguish as the celestial music swelled. The Church which installed that creaking, lopsided and still beautiful instrument was not afraid to temper devotion with humour. But the satirical organ has now been superseded by a neat little electric keyboard.

To safeguard its interests, including the profits from the thermal water at Cauterets, the Benedictine abbey was fortified, and fealty was owed to it by all the people of the long valley. The church apart, there is little left of it today. The rest of the monastery has been knocked down or converted into the *mairie*. There is a municipal lavatory in the cloisters and motorbike tracks on the lawns, and no one in the village could be found to give even an approximate date for the monastery's dissolution. But in this faded church, before the tomb of a forgotten saint, one can still see the point of the religion which lived before Lourdes. Enough of its memory survived to direct Cardinal Pacelli (later Pius XII) here in 1935. There is, unusually for "tourist" churches, a notice forbidding photography; and another reading. "This is a place of prayer, respect the silence." Only the birds in the lantern ignore it, until the doors open to admit a stray file of day-glo skiing tubes from Cauterets who have been driven away from the Egg Parade by boredom with the over-familiar, and who lack even a guide book to dispel the boredom with the unfamiliar that descends on them in the abbey church of St. Savin. To them, as to the villagers, the meaning of the terrific building is as lost as the history of the *cagot* baptismal font just inside the church entrance.

Active local preoccupations, though ancient, are more

profane. Many of the mountain communities around
Lourdes are noted for their continuing tradition of smug-
gling. One Englishman who was considering buying a
mountain puppy decided to decline the offer because of his
country's rabies laws. "Pah," said the prospective seller.
"That is nothing. Buy the little dog and leave it with me.
In less than a month you collect it in England. It will be
carried over the Pyrenees to Spain and will go to one of
the northern Spanish ports. In England there is a place
called Ply-moothe. It will be waiting for you there."

The ambivalence of Lourdes to its past is typified by a
large oil painting which stands in the hallway of *l'Hôtel de
Ville*. This painting, which extends along the wall of a narrow corridor facing a staircase, is, in the site chosen for it,
almost impossible to view. One can climb the stairs, or descend them, one can try to stand away, one can walk along
the corridor and crane back from the correct distance but
at the incorrect angle, one can stand absolutely anywhere
but one cannot properly see it. On the other hand one cannot Not see it either. Once you have passed the reception
desk in the foyer of the Town Hall, there it is, lowering at
you in its dramatic way, all highlights and gestures. Its
subject is the Pilgrimage to the Grotto.

A bishop in a mitre is standing among a number of mor-
tally sick people. The costumes place the picture in the late
nineteenth-century school of narrative art. The group is arranged in front of the Grotto. The bishop seems to be in a
fury. The sick seem to be very sick indeed. One of them
could well be dead. The bishop is thundering on the gates
of heaven. He entreats, he insists on, a cure. The pilgrims,
by some artistic inattention, seem almost more concerned
about the bishop's blood pressure than about the fate of
the sick. Dotted around the group are solicitous or heart-
broken helpers. Here is the romantic conception of nineteenth-century Lourdes, a vivid statement of the original
purposes of the place. A rejection of science, a rejection of
the imperfect ecclesiastical institution—with its endless hierarchy leading up from individual soul to priest, bishop,

pope and God—and its replacement by the direct experience of divine power, and by a passionate return to the
certainties of the medieval shrine, the place apart.
But here too is the febrile anxiety of that attempt. A re-
alization of the desperation in the faith that nourished it,
and a hint of the fear among the sick that the mere spectacle of their condition will be insufficient to alter it. And
here too, exposed by the placing of the picture, is the mud-
dle into which this inexperienced little town was thrown by
these events. On the one hand it is a very striking picture,
and although painted in a rather unfashionable style it
does represent an interesting relic of the town's recent history. No event has taken place in Tarbes or Pau or even
Toulouse which could justify a memorial of equivalent op-
ulence. It is certainly not something to be bundled away in
a cellar. On the other hand . . . it is not exactly the sort of
picture one would wish to draw attention to. This bishop,
for instance, in his, you know, Mitre, well . . . that is certainly not how the secular town, the concern of *l'Hôtel de
Ville*, would wish to present itself. So, place it, extraordinary compromise, in a prominent position from which it
is almost impossible to see it—from where it can flood the
corner of the eye, and thunder through the *back* of the
mind, as one might choose to place a fact which is too
large for comfort. And that is exactly what they have
done.
   The temporal preoccupations of the town have also been
accurately reflected over the years in the weekly newspaper, *L'Essor Bigourdan*, "the organ of Pyrenean democ-
racy." In 1950 the *annus mirabilis* for the rugby team,
not the shrine, the headline over a sports article read,
"Jean Prat and the consistency of his form—a study in
Enigma." Even in those days Jean Prat owned "Le
Winger" bar, the popularity of which does not seem to
have infringed his amateur status. Numerous other head-
lines mentioning "Our Lady of Lourdes" referred to a
football team. There was regular coverage of developments
in the world of *Esperanto*, and a column headed "Socialist
Voice." (When the present editor, M. Bouyssonnie, was

asked about this feature he expressed considerable surprise. *"L'Essor,"* he said firmly, "is not a socialist paper.")
During the 1950s there was comparatively little coverage
of the Domain. The death of the Countess Bianca de Beck
was, however, noted in the *necrologie* column, and it was
remembered that she had been famous for her prophecies,
including a prophecy of the hour of her own death. In
1950 the ninety-second anniversary of the apparitions
drew a small commemoration. And it is interesting that the
presence of Cardinal Spellman was reported in Cannes. He
was returning from a pilgrimage to Rome in Holy Year
but he did not make a diversion to Lourdes.

In 1952 an appeal from the bishop, Pierre Marie Théas,
on the subject of Lourdes's housing conditions, was reported. The bishop pitched his appeal at an effectively low
level by pointing out that the interests of the whole town
were at stake, since "tourists" could be counted on to report back what they had seen. That winter Bishop Théas
fell ill and, echoing Bernadette, he chose to seek his cure
elsewhere. He convalesced for four months at the Marian
shrine of Hal in Belgium.

The parish priests of Lourdes are well aware of the town's
spiritual apathy. Lourdes is a parish of nearly twenty thousand people which has ten parish priests, about the average
ratio for France. It claims a thirty per cent proportion of
practising Catholic adults, which is higher than the national average but not higher than the average for small
country towns. It is a matter of particular concern that
since 1954 the number of divorces per one hundred mar-
riages has risen from seven to twenty-one.

Every year in February, at the time of the two Lourdes
feasts, there is a procession from the parish church to the
Grotto, the only time when the original processional route
is now used. This has come to be called the "hotelier's pilgrimage." It is also the time when the annual conference
of travel agents is held, and they too join the procession.
At one time there was a day of pilgrimage for all the shop
assistants of Lourdes, but this seems to have expired; the

shops do not now close for a single day of the season, and
the February procession is the nearest there is to a replacement. It is led by four of the nuns of Nevers carrying a
casket containing the relics of the saint. In 1958, the centenary of the apparitions, forty thousand Bigourdans
joined in this celebration, a massive gathering that
heralded a record season, when the number of visitors rose
from 1.8 to 4.8 million (a total which has only been
regained very recently). But in 1979, on the saint's own
centenary, the pilgrims of the region numbered only ten
thousand. That is a reasonable measure of the way things
have gone with the people of Lourdes and the High
Pyrenees in the twenty-one intervening years. In 1979 the
parish used the occasion to organize a mission to its own
town, and in particular to the hoteliers and *commerçants*,
instructing them in the elementary facts of the story of
Bernadette, and explaining to them the purpose of the
modern pilgrimage. One sermon was entitled "What is
going on at the Grotto nowadays." It was rather like the
authorities in Majorca giving the island's hoteliers a lecture
on the purpose of the modern Mediterranean beach.

A Grotto chaplain who was asked about present relations between the Domain and the parish said that the
chaplains had nothing to do with the parish. There were
no baptisms, weddings or funerals in the Domain and
therefore there was no problem about relations between
the two. The only parish occasion which sometimes takes
place in the Grotto is when a bride and groom, after a
wedding, walk to the Grotto with their families so that the
bride can leave her bouquet there.

There are also occasional first communion ceremonies
for sick children. But the idea that merely by avoiding the
work of the parish the chaplains are bound to avoid all
causes of friction seems naïve. Of course there is no neces-
sity for friction, particularly as both parish priests and
chaplains are now drawn from the diocese, but history
shows that friction has been frequent in the past.

The presbytery, which is in the centre of the old town,
looks out on a fine statue of Father Peyramale that was

erected in 1928 and sculpted by the Duchess of Uzès. For
the priests of the parish the sixteen hundred *commerçants*
who, in the words of the modern *Official Guide,* "should,
according to some, be chased from the temple," are their
flock. "Among them are many Christians who . . . try to
understand that it is possible to work for Christ and his
Church just as well behind a till, a stove or a counter as in
the Grotto . . . Christ does not only walk the path of the
shrines. He also visits the town . . ." Prompted by the
parish the "inhabitants of Lourdes" recently distributed a
leaflet to the pilgrims which read: "It is true that we live
by the work you bring us. But our aim is not to make a
profit out of you . . . If you bear this in mind it will help
us. And our contacts, the dialogue between us, will be
more authentic and more Christian." Presbytery and chaplaincy remain opposed to that extent at least.

For the clergy, recent times have seen as much of a decline in Lourdes as elsewhere in France. The parish of
Lourdes is important and its priest is still French, which is
not invariably the case. The Vicar of Belley, in north-east
France, for instance, is Father Finegan; and the annual
pilgrimage from the diocese of Agen is also led by an
Irishman. In 1965, there were thirty-five thousand French
priests of working age, that is, under sixty-five. In 1975
this had fallen to twenty-seven thousand. By 1988 the
number is expected to fall to fewer than eighteen thousand. So many priests have married and left the clergy that
six thousand have formed an association called, rather op-
timistically, *Prêtres en Foyer.* And the rising number of
laicized priests in France has occurred at a time when the
rate of departures from the Catholic clergy in other parts
of the world is diminishing. Only 136 priests were ordained in France in 1976, and only ninety-nine in 1977.
The diocese of Tarbes and Lourdes has closed its junior
seminary and now has about twelve boys in high school os-
tensibly preparing for the priesthood. But in 1977 there
were only three entrants to the diocesan seminary, and in
1978 none. Tarbes and Lourdes, in fact, has done nothing

out of the ordinary to assist the notorious weakness of the French priesthood and the French Church. Without a junior seminary, those boys from Lourdes who are intending to enter the priesthood first attend the town's Catholic school, the Cours Peyramale, named after the heroic priest. So I obtained permission to visit two of the senior classes there and ask them some questions.

Until 1942, when the Cours Peyramale was founded, the children of Lourdes had to go to the diocesan town of Tarbes for a secondary education. Today they have the choice of the Catholic secondary school or a new state *lycée,* but until the latter was opened almost everyone in the town went to the Cours Peyramale. An entire generation grew up there and shared the same teachers and the same memories; for that period it was one of the most important links of Lourdes.

The pupils at the Cours Peyramale are assisted by the state if their parents cannot afford the fees, and it is noticeable how those parents who are prosperous hoteliers are forever claiming assistance on the grounds that they have just been repairing the roof, while those who are poor are always trying to squeeze into the superior class of unassisted parents by paying their own way somehow; members of both groups, by pretending to be what they are not, ensuring that they will remain what they have always been for another generation. Here is another historical echo. Commissioner Jacomet noted at the time of the apparitions that, in the amounts of money left in the Grotto, "the richest offerings come from the poorer people."

Of two classes I questioned at the school, nineteen out of twenty-one pupils in the younger class said that they believed in the miraculous cures, whereas only ten out of twenty-four of the older class said that they believed. Seven out of those ten stubborn believers (in a class which was evenly divided between boys and girls) were girls. Eighteen of the total of twenty-nine believers were girls, for what that is worth. None of the forty-five pupils asked were able to give a reasonable approximation of the number of proclaimed miracles, although the latest mira-

cle, that of a Frenchman, had been published six months
earlier.

It may be noted that the traditional highlights of "la vie
lourdaise," rugby, shooting and fishing, offer very little for
a girl. Of the forty-five pupils at the Cours Peyramale
whom I asked whether or not they wished to live in
Lourdes after they had left school, half the girls said "no"
but only a quarter of the boys. In the older of the two
groups the proportion of the girls wishing to leave had
risen to three-quarters. The girls of Lourdes talk impa-
tiently of the small town and of the restrictions imposed by
their family and friends. They feel the full force of a community which intends to renew itself through them and
they struggle against it, holding out for jobs, sometimes in
commerce like their parents, but more often hoping to be
teachers or social workers or nurses or doctors. And they
are determined to travel—"to America," "to China," "to
Tahiti." And generally they stay in Lourdes, and marry
there, and continue the commerce handed on by their
families.

That the town now has two secondary schools is an indication of the way in which it has grown. In 1858 its population was about four thousand; in 1928 it was eight thousand; today it is 18,096. This increase of 225 per cent is
completely out of proportion to the rest of France (which
has grown by forty-five per cent in that time), and even
more so to the rest of the Department of the High
Pyrenees. In 1850 the region contained 250,000, which
was 0.7 per cent of the French population; today it contains 225,000, which is 0.43 per cent of the national total.
Whatever it is that has happened to this one town has distorted the economy of the entire region. Lourdes now has
more hotels (402) than any other town in France, save
Paris and Nice. But the population of Paris is 9,250,000,
and that of Nice is 346,620. In the official categories
Lourdes does not even rank as a town of "medium size"; it
is a "petite ville."

While the railway played an important part in the development of Lourdes as an international centre, not even the

largest station in provincial France has been adequate to handle the present pilgrim traffic. For that task this "small town" has needed an international airport. This is placed midway between Tarbes and Lourdes and was originally an offshoot of the Pyrenean arms industry. In 1938 a factory for fighter planes was opened near Tarbes and a small grass runway was brought into use. During the occupation the German Luftwaffe used this as a base for attacking the Atlantic convoys. The R.A.F. then bombed it into closure. After the war the airport was taken over by the Chamber of Commerce in Tarbes and for the first time it was put to civilian use. In 1950 it even acquired a control tower, made of wood. The passenger traffic built up to around twenty thousand, most of it pilgrims who formed a very small proportion of the 1.5 to 2 million pilgrims then coming to Lourdes each year. But by 1958, the centenary year, someone in the Chamber of Commerce saw an opportunity and prepared a new terminal building and additional taxiing areas, and the number of passengers jumped to 120,000. Despite the fact that the runways at Tarbes airport lie north to south, which is not popular with pilots in foggy conditions due to the well-established east-west direction of the Pyrenees, the airport grew steadily from then on. But even today it is not really the thriving regional airport which its position as tenth busiest in France would suggest. Because, once again, nine-tenths of its commercial traffic takes place between April and October. Indeed it must be unique among French airports in that it receives more passengers from Ireland than from any other country, including France. In 1978 the airport received 318,000 passengers, mostly pilgrims, against the railway's total of 486,000 registered pilgrims.

Apart from the pilgrims the most important users of the airport are the military flights. But they cannot keep it busy. And in winter it is as deserted as the abbey church of St. Savin, with its thirty-six-bed sick bay and its enormous freight lifts (which can load twenty wheelchairs at once) lying idle for six months at a time. Not even the arrival of the daily internal flight from Paris, led by an Air-

Inter stewardess dressed up as a mixture of a Jaffa orange
cake and a Tudor banquet minstrel, can bring the extensive terminal to life in February.

The effects of this seasonal distortion are to be seen in
the region's employment figures. Agriculture, which occupied thirty-five per cent of the male population in 1954,
now occupies sixteen per cent. There has been the usual
drift to the towns and the usual unemployment in consequence. There are now one hundred and fifty potential applicants for every office job, and seventy-five for every
commercial vacancy. Industry has expanded to some extent, particularly the arms and aeronautical factories; but
fifty per cent of the employment in the High Pyrenees is
still in tourism or the other service industries. The department is noted for the number of its hotel and café workers
(due to the Domain), the number of its clergy (due to
the Domain) and the numbers working in the arms factories; but there are fifty-four hotel workers and clergymen
for every forty-nine air and arms workers. And it is particularly difficult for those aged less than twenty-five to find
jobs.

If you do well in Lourdes, you can do very well. The price
of the smallest detached house is the same as in Paris.
There is a serious shortage of accommodation, and the
typical lease is able to include a catch-all clause on tenants'
obligations which requires them to behave at all times as
"good members of the bourgeoisie." But in 1978 there was
a local calamity which affected even the prosperous
members of the community.

Traditionally the man of the mountains is said to keep
his considerable pile of savings under his bed in gold
pieces. In Lourdes this method has been replaced by the
small private bank with only one branch. The biggest
shock to hit the town for many years occurred on 4 December that year when the town's bank, the Banque Lacaze, closed its doors overnight. As the local paper reported, it was a thunderbolt. "People of Lourdes . . ." it
cried, "stick together!" The insurance agent explained

what had happened. "It could be a disaster for many," he said. "Already the other banks, the big ones, are lending less. And since this is an agricultural region with some tourism, but mostly just the pilgrimage, people have not spread their money around. There is no local investment. Just re-investment in the business. A few people play with the Stock Exchange, others put it in the trunk, and most of the rest used the Banque Lacaze."

In a way the bank was itself a victim of the town's growing prosperity. It had been one of the ten biggest private banks in France but it had been defeated by the problem of what to do with the great seasonal glut of deposits made by its investors, the *commerçants*. Somehow the bank had to put this money to use in such a way that it could pay out slightly higher interest than its competitors, the national banks. So restricted were the opportunities in this mis-shapen economy, that much of the money had to be lent out to builders who were engaged in providing houses for the prosperous, or in expanding the facilities of the pilgrim trade. The bank was imprudent in choosing its clients, it tended to get the applicants who had been turned down by the bigger banks, and the result was that it was too generous with its loans. The winter in any case is not the best time for the construction industry, work is held up by the weather, clients are slow to pay, builders fall behind with their repayments, but the bank, naturally, had to continue paying out its interest to depositors. And finally it had to close.

Its principal creditors (those who had deposits) employed a total of 1,145 people. Prominent among them was the candle factory, Ciergerie Lourdaise (with a workforce of 112). The insurance agent (who was neither creditor nor debtor) was confident that, since there was no justice, the bank's creditors, the prosperous *commerçants* who were apparently out of pocket, would survive comfortably; whereas the bank's debtors, the small builders and those just starting up in business, would be in serious trouble by the time the receiver had finished with them. People always said of the Banque Lacaze that it occupied a splendid site. Oddly enough the central corner in question had formerly been occupied by the *Café Français*. The *Français* was the old gathering point for the sophisticates of the town, the people who, in the Lourdes story, poured scorn on Bernadette and her delusions. "Sceptical men," it is said, "used to gather there to laugh at her." And it was probably there that someone first proposed that the little simpleton should be confined in an asylum.

The names of the champions of that controversy are forgotten today. But they may still be inspected in the two cemeteries, where the division between high and low towns continues, to some extent, unhealed. In the original graveyard, overlooking the back of Massabielle, there are numerous stones engraved with the name Soubirous, or Théas, or Viron, the policeman who photographed the saint, or Abadie, the child who interrupted the second apparition. And there is a very handsome temple erected to the family Pomès. Behind its roof extends the spire of the basilica, which marks the far boundary of the lucrative plot between.

But it is the second, larger cemetery that contains all the pilgrim graves. Many of the bigger pilgrimages have bought a communal plot bounded by a long stone wall waiting for the names. The British and the Irish have been placed side by side, the Irish cross towering over the rest of the row. Beneath it says, "Priez pour le repos des âmes des Irlandais Morts en pèlerins à Lourdes." Both British and Irish graves go back to the 1930s and it is not only the sick who die there. One stone reads, "In loving memory of Michael J. Brophy, Brancardier, Dublin Pilgrimage. Died in the service of Our Lady, 9 September 1972. R.I.P." *Brancardiers,* as is well-known to pilgrimage doctors, often overdo it.

Among the tablets on the British grave is one to Sister Bonaventura, who died on the Welsh pilgrimage on 27 July 1976. On the day she died the whole pilgrimage turned out to accompany her coffin. Anyone who had a uniform wore it and the town came to a halt as the procession of about one thousand Welsh pilgrims passed through. But her tablet simply records her name, her pilgrimage and the date of her death. Beside it another wreath commemorates a pilgrim who died with "le Group Stevenage." These graves, which seem so far from home, are visited every year when the appropriate pilgrimage returns. It is one of the oddities of the pilgrimage business that the booking conditions issued to pilgrims include instructions about burial in Lourdes. Those issued by the Catholic Association read as follows: "In the event of the death of a Pilgrim on the journey to or in Lourdes the Requiem and Burial will take place there. The Catholic Association Pilgrimage Trust has a vault for this purpose in the Lourdes cemetery and a visit is made each year during the pilgrimage by the Director, or someone appointed by him, together with other officials, and prayers are offered for the departed Souls."

There is one corner of Lourdes which is completely unaffected by seasonal fluctuations. The view of this place from St. Michael's bridge at the end of the Domain is arresting. From there one can look back along the flow of the Gave and over the foaming white barrage of the weir to a simple and well-proportioned grey building that was once well found on a bend in the river, sufficiently far up the bank to be safe from the floods. At first sight, it seems to be a small fortress. Its windows have been replaced by barred vents which scarcely pierce the high blind walls. It has the air of an institution, perhaps of the town prison.

In fact it is the convent of the Poor Clares, an enclosed community, so it is indeed a fortress. But though it now stands in one of the noisiest parts of town, the rue de la Grotte, the convent chapel retains its peace. The Blessed Sacrament is reserved in a covered chalice, a light burns above the altar, there is holy water in the font. The old rituals of the Church, designed to break the ungodly personality of the street, are still in use. There is mass every day at 5:30 p.m. And, on the allotted hours of the conventual day, under the rule laid down by St. Clare in the thirteenth

century, the doors open behind a tall grille, which is itself
behind the altar, and anyone in the public part of the
divided chapel can hear the community singing the office.
In the porch, just off the street, the notices say "Silence," and then, "Here mass is said every day for the
200,000 faithful who face the agony of death or who will
die this day." Prayer is the only work of these nuns. There
is a bell above the roof which is rung when *les Clarisses*
need food, for the order has always lived by alms alone.
But it is said in Lourdes that their Poor Clares have never
had to ring the bell for food. And visiting the convent
chapel one sometimes finds several prosperous ladies of the
town gathered round the grille in the hall, the scent of furs
and silk scarves mingling oddly with the smell of the fresh
loaves and vegetables that they have carried in.

Seen from the distance of the bridge, the convent illus-
trates exactly what has happened to Lourdes. When it was
built, some years after the apparitions, it would have stood
alone on the high bank overshadowed only by the trees
and castle rock. The contemplative order was drawn there
by the fame of the shrine, and it established its small grey
battlements by the stream which passes the Grotto. The
sisters retired within and started to pray. They have prayed
for a hundred years, during which time the convent has
become completely surrounded by the other idea. Towering behind it, on all three landed sides, there has sprung
up the stone confectionery of commerce. Newcomers,
transfixed in their bus seats by their first encounter with
the souvenir shops, do not notice the convent at all. It has
become all but invisible, lost to sight like a slab of rock on
an overgrown cliff face, camouflaged by the low town's
success in accommodating the cult. It is a commerce which
also nurtures the Poor Clares, and which actually offers in
a café only one hundred yards from the convent walls a
digestif called "CHIMAY—la vraie Trappiste."

❧ IV ❧

The Low Town

Do you remember an Inn,
Miranda?
Do you remember an Inn? . . .
And the fleas that tease in the High Pyrenees . . .
Tarantella, Hilaire Belloc

From a terrace overlooking the river, on the opposite bank
to the convent, one has a fine view of both Lourdes. Sitting
there, lulled by the noise of the weir and the cool green
flow of the stream, one can imagine oneself in any small
southern French town. There are palm trees and chestnuts
and firs and vines growing on the bank, and there are curious daytime bats, small, two-tone, dark grey and copper,
fluttering into the blinding sun shafts that pierce the soft
green refuge of these ill-assorted trees. The hotel names on
the far bank, the old side, lend some dignity to the skyline.
Over there are the Imperial Hôtel, the Hôtel de France,
the Grand Hôtel d'Espagne, the Hôtel Versailles. They
look very correct, like the republican tricolor flying above
the castle. But on the near side of the bank the hotel
names give a slightly crazy look to the proceedings. The
hotels are called Golgotha, St. François d'Assise, St. Daniel et du Centenaire, Star of the Morning (in Latin), Vatican, the Angelic, the Angelus, Calvary, Maltese Cross,
Nazareth, Our Lady of . . . (here follow 26 varieties),
the Sacred Heart, the Hotel of St. Theresa of the Child
Jesus, the Hotel of the Child Jesus of Prague; and so on to

the total of 402 hotels which can offer 16,000 rooms and
32,000 beds. When there is a rush on, the total number of
prostrate visiting bodies may well reach 45,000.

Sipping a pastis on this terrace the morning after the arrival of our pilgrimage, and looking along the river, I realized that the terrace, being characteristically French, was
on this bank an anachronism. On the other side of the
bridge one was in France. On this side one was . . . hard
to say. At a nearby table of English priests and one English archbishop I noticed a flash of gold. But it was not
the cross of archiepiscopal authority—the archbishop did
not wear one. It was a yellow plastic duck worn by the
youngest priest present, who was introduced (possibly for
his psychic qualities) as "Radar." Then on the packed
bridge which links France with this celestial island there
was a flash of purple on the skull. But again it was not a
bishop. It was a photo-pedlar in a jockey cap. Perhaps the
higher clergy become disillusioned with their ancient finery
on the pilgrimage to Lourdes? There are cafés in many
parts of the world which might even be impressed with a
canon, but in Lourdes an archbishop passes without evok-
ing a genuflection. *Possibly* a cardinal would make some
impression, but with these waiters one could not be certain.

And it was while sitting at this border post of Holy Disney land, and looking down the line of riverbank cottages,
that my eye was caught by a sudden bag of rubbish hurled
by an improvident hand over the Gave de Pau to splash
into the current. Then another hand from a neighbouring
cottage, more frugal than the first, hurtled a jug of once-
served town water through the window, surely *her* window, neatly clearing the nylon bridal nightgown which was
drying on the heated line, to spatter itself over the hydran-
geas and zonal pelargoniums planted in military order in
the crumbly dust of the bank. It would seem, after another
glance into the cool flowing Gave, that the first hand, *Madame l'Imprévoyance*, was the more characteristic of Bigorre. The river, the chosen river which washes the bank

of the Grotto, is in effect a sluice. The rubbish from the town floats beneath the bridge and over the weir, the trout battling through it in search of the deceitful upstream worm, and the wagtails paddling past it on the shallow stones. And then the rubbish bobs under the windows of the *Asile* hospital, where it is joined by the soiled dressings which certain medical attendants of the sick pilgrims have become accustomed to dumping out of the window. From there, considerably enriched, it bobs on past the basilica, past the Grotto, past the deep trout pool and the outlet of the sacred spring and the statue to Saint Queen Margaret of Scotland. And the Gave de Sluice, having swept past all these with its burden of garbage, sweeps on into the real France beyond the moonstruck peninsula; past the stricken shrine of Bétharram, past Pau with the ghosts of its forty thousand Victorian English mountaineers and its five Anglican *temples;* and so on to the Atlantic oil slicks and rationalism.

When we had finally reached our hotels on the previous evening, we had found the remaining members of the Catholic Association pilgrimage waiting for us. They were the three hundred members of the party who had chosen, for an extra £22, to fly out rather than come by train. Air travel is advertised as "the modern pilgrim's way," but there is no doubt that those who choose it miss much of the essential experience. Our fellow pilgrims who joined us in the dining-room were no exception. They were particularly cross, with some reason; but as they explained why, they only gave us a disappointing reminder of the world of telegrams and anger which we had managed to discard at Dover.

Their least, although in our view it should have been their chief, complaint was that on the plane there had been no hymns. "The bishop was on board," said one darkly, "but I expect he was too busy with the duty-free." They were quite right. The plane had been chartered for the Catholic Association and there should have been hymns. That is one of the things that bishops are for. Then, their plane had been delayed by a strike and so they had lost a day in Lourdes. But since they were getting an extra day over the rail party anyway they received little sympathy on those grounds. Then (this was clearly going to take most of dinner), they were getting no refund for this loss, although the hotel had sold their rooms to others for their missing night. We sipped our soup and nodded. Then, their plane had been too small to fly direct to Lourdes and so it had had to descend for refuelling. This had made their flight long and uncomfortable. Our thoughts went back to the couchette and then to the ambulance cars. Then . . . there had been no lunch when they arrived! Oh dear, we thought, we should have saved them some of our bread from Bordeaux. As they continued the eyes of their initially sympathetic audience glazed over, for we were unwilling to be transported on this wave of airport-induced righteous indignation straight back to the departure lounge. Something drastic was needed if we were to recover from this attack of bile. And just at that moment our waiter entered bearing news. "You 'ave a Pop!" Sensation. "EEz EEtalian." Comprehension. "EEz called—Paul John." Nearly right. The dining-room emptied at once and everyone converged on the Domain.

And the day of arrival had ended with dusk falling on the candlelight procession as it started down the esplanade. By the statue of the Crowned Virgin, in the centre of the esplanade, an old Frenchman wearing a balloon beret and clutching his beads stood oblivious to the thousands of people processing around him and, gazing up at the face of the statue, quavered the words of the Lourdes hymn at the top of his discordant voice. Nearby two chic Francophone-Africans watched him in mild disbelief. Almost alone among the pilgrims there that night they preferred to sing the hymn in Latin.

For the majority of pilgrims who were not concerned with the hourly care of the sick there was, during the week of the pilgrimage, plenty of time available to explore the religious sideshows. One of the most popular of these is

the Miraculous Medal show, which occupies a prime site
near the *cachot*, the dwelling from which the saint set out
to visit the grotto. The old lock-up is now a small museum
and chapel run by the Sisters of Nevers and, although it is
still simple in appearance, one has to make an imaginative
effort to realize how filthy it must have been in 1858. It is
obviously a place of valid and authorized interest to
Lourdes pilgrims, but the Miraculous Medal show is a
more speculative enterprise. I asked one of the Grotto
chaplains about it and he said that the Church had no connection with it and did not encourage others. "We don't
like too many of these enterprises," he said. "Some of
them are little more than disguised businesses." But the
Miraculous Medal show was actually inaugurated by
Bishop Théas in person in 1959, the year following the extraordinary pilgrimage boom of the centenary.

The similarity between the story of the Miraculous
Medal and the story of Lourdes is quite close. In 1830,
twenty-eight years before the apparitions of Bernadette, a
nun called Catherine Labouré, who was living in a convent
of the Sisters of Charity (of St. Vincent de Paul) in the
rue du Bac in Paris, had several visions of the Virgin. She
was wakened by her guardian angel, who appeared as a
little golden-haired boy, and summoned to the chapel of
the convent in the middle of the night. There she saw a vision of the Virgin. Across the Lady's shoulders in letters of
gold was written, "Oh Mary, *conceived without sin,* pray
for us who have recourse to thee." And a voice told Sister
Catherine to strike a medal reproducing this scene and this
message. The visions of Catherine were eventually approved and were taken to be divine encouragement for the
doctrine of the Immaculate Conception.* Within a few
years, millions of the medals had been struck, and in 1842
the conversion occurred of Alphonse Ratisbonne, a stead-
fast Jew, who had agreed to wear the medal to humour a

* At that time the doctrine was deadlocked in the Vatican and
Archbishop Ferreti was praying for a sign from heaven to clinch
it. In 1854 it was to be Giovanni Ferreti, as Pius IX, who defined
the dogma of the Immaculate Conception.

devout friend and who was seduced by a Marian vision.
The wearing of the medal, advertised at the Miraculous
Medal show as "the only medal worn by the Pope," has
always been associated with miracles and with the acquisi-
tion of grace—particularly so since the conversion of M.
Ratisbonne. Another consequence of the new cult was the
formation of a group called "the Children of Mary."

The points of coincidence between this story and that of
Lourdes are so numerous as almost to make the Miraculous Medal a sort of first draft of the Lourdes story.
Lourdes does not just echo Pyrenean myths and legends
but also the approved practice of visionaries in other parts
of nineteenth-century France; and since both experiences
were entirely dependent on the approval of the Church for
their institutionalization there must have been an element
of choice in this.

Both girls came from an illiterate peasant background.
The importance of both visions, one prophetic, the other
confirmatory, to the doctrine of the Immaculate Conception and to the personal faith of Pius IX, is obvious. Both
visionaries were left with a supernatural talisman, for Bernadette the water, for Catherine the medal, which it was
believed could work great good. At Lourdes too there was
the conversion of a Jew, in this case the famous case of
the Jewess Nina Kin who was cured of a withered leg, became a Catholic, converted her family and then lived a
holy life as a nun. Bernadette herself may have been familiar with the story of the Miraculous Medal in 1858, since
she had two aunts who were for a time Children of Mary.
After the apparitions she too joined the Children of Mary,
wore the Miraculous Medal and, according to publicity at
the Show, prayed twice a day in the approved position
with her arms outstretched. Dressing her in the uniform of
the Children of Mary was one of the better ways of dis-
guising her attendance at a big ceremony after she became
famous.

Naturally, at the Miraculous Medal show, or Diorama,
some of these similarities are emphasized. The Diorama,
which is only twenty years old, is held in a small theatre.

At the beginning of the show this is plunged into complete darkness. Then a series of static waxwork scenes are lit up one by one. These illustrate Sister St. Catherine Labouré's story. The commentary is given in different languages by prior arrangement. This is an extraordinarily modest technical accomplishment, and must have disappointed many thousands of mechanically minded pilgrims over the years. But perhaps the Diorama is coming into its own at last. So rapid have been the advances in the world of propaganda techniques, that the antique technology of this Diorama is itself by now an assistance to a feeling of otherworldliness.

A rival attraction, the Padre Pio show, is rather more of a hard-sell. It has a particular goal, which is the canonization of Padre Pio, a Capuchin friar who died in southern Italy in 1968 with a reputation for great holiness. That he bore the stigmata for fifty years is beyond dispute. But he is also reported to have had powers of bilocation, that is he was seen and spoken with in two places at once. At this point the mild interest of the non-believer begins to shade off into polite and total scepticism, but among those who testified to the phenomenon there are included several people who do not normally take any interest at all in such matters. Presumably, unless the cultists of Padre Pio are going to claim that he had two bodies, which might cause a very general loss of interest, the phenomenon of bilocation is somewhat akin to hallucinations or a form of temporal apparition.

Padre Pio's powers of miraculous healing were so great and so well-documented that, during his lifetime, a prominent American heart specialist, Dr. Paul Dudley White, wanted to establish a world centre for the study of psychosomatic medicine in the little town of San Giovanni Rotondo. That was not done; instead a thriving pilgrimage centre has been established and the movement for Padre Pio's beatification has grown to such an extent that during the season the bureau in Lourdes is able to support a fulltime priest and a nun. The bureau stands in the rue des

Petits Fossés, again conveniently close to the *cachot,* and distributes information about the holy man. All leaflets carry the assurance that the cause is absolutely faithful to the teachings of the Church and the Holy Father, a necessary precaution in a town which attracts so many unorthodox enthusiasts. For the tenth anniversary of his death a colour film of the last moments of his life was shown in the Cinema Majestic. This emphasized that Padre Pio had been responsible not only for miraculous cures but also for many conversions. Entry was free.

Another sideshow which has achieved a certain amount of success in Lourdes has been organized by the followers of the Rev. Sun Myung Moon, "the Moonies." Their organization, known as the Unification Church (which is not generally regarded as a Christian Church), sells its newspaper *Nouvel Espoir* outside churches all over France, and the Domain at Lourdes is no exception. They sometimes try to sell it inside the Domain but are invariably thrown out. Moony neophytes are encouraged to give up all their own money to the cause, and then to work for up to eighteen hours a day. They aim to bring in as much as £50,000 a year each, and the resulting exhaustion has the further advantage that it is thought to be an assistance towards mind-control. The French Moony handbook, which is distributed to all members, says: "To realize our projects we need considerable financial means, and as our activities spread the Unification Church will become an even more important economic force. We have no wish to hide this fact." The Moonies have had some recruiting success in Lourdes, and have even signed up new members from among the children of the families who run the souvenir shops. From the Moony point of view there is presumably no conflict between the commercial and spiritual successes of Lourdes. And in this at least they have some historical support.

When the Holy Shroud of Turin was taken by a Christian army from the Moslem city of Edessa in what is now eastern Turkey, some of the bitterest opponents of the

move were the Christian merchants of the city who had
built up a flourishing trade in catering for pilgrims over
the nine hundred years the relic had been lodged there.
And wherever the Shroud went on its subsequent travels
around Christendom, the pilgrimage industry followed it.
In the fourteenth century, when the Shroud was exhibited
at Lirey in France, medals depicting its frontal and dorsal
images were on sale to the devout who came in great numbers to see it.* And at Santiago de Compostella the famous
scallop shells which could be picked up in such abundance
on the nearby Atlantic beaches, and which became the universal medieval emblem of the pilgrim, were actually on
sale to the pilgrims of the twelfth century from stalls set up
on the north side of the Cathedral. So long as there has
been pilgrimage there has been commerce. The mind
which arrives so eager for a sight of the place where
heaven once was, very soon starts to search for a bargain
memento of its visit. Satisfying this bathetic impulse is the
business of the low town.

The historical origins of the Lourdes souvenir trade are
still suggested by the presence of the herb vendors, who set
up their stalls in the summer just outside the gates of the
Seven Sorrows Hospital. The line of trolleys and chairs
bearing the sick pilgrims on their way to the Grotto passes
these stalls four times a day. Here are all types of vegetation proffered, against the rheumatism and the asthma, for
stomach conditions and exhausted nerves, for diabetes and
many other debilities, some of them unknown to science.
These itinerant herb-sellers with their wooden barrows and
handwritten notices for broths and infusions may seem to
have little in common with the neon-lit vendors of chaplets
and statues. But that was how the souvenir business
started. The herb-sellers are in direct line of descent from
the peasant women who were attracted to the original excitement of the apparitions and who, by the day of the
"miracle of the candle," during the seventeenth apparition,
had discovered a way of paying for their trip from the

* *The Turin Shroud*, Ian Wilson.

high pastures by selling to some of the one thousand people present the first "objects of piety."

Today's business is less hand-to-mouth. The Lourdes shopkeeper who wants to calculate his monthly purchase of stock, only has to consult the monthly returns of the town post office, which are to be found, like so much other extraordinary information, in the annual *Bilan,* or municipal balance sheet. For instance, in 1978 the monthly collection of postcards rose from 286,000 in April to 908,000 in July, 993,000 in August and back to 278,000 in October. The usefulness of these figures as an indication of tourist movements is shown by making a comparison with Tarbes, the "county town." Whereas in Tarbes (pop. 57,000) 12 million packages were collected in 1977 and 15 million were delivered, in Lourdes (pop. 18,000) 10 million were collected and only 4 million delivered. Of Lourdes' 10 million collected packages, 8 million were dealt with from April to October and 6.6 million of them were postcards.

Supported by these calculations the shopkeeper is able to order his holy medals by the thousand dozen—ten thousand dozen, or thirty thousand dozen—and his candles, Virgins and postcards can be supplied by the ton. It might be thought that such a weight of junk would be purchased with very little thought for detail, but each feature of the Virginal plastic chipling is pondered with care. A rare moment of contact between the orthodox psychological therapy of the town and the pilgrimage industry occurred a few years ago when the town's psychological centre arranged a course of therapeutic wood carving for its patients. In order to put this scheme on a sound financial basis it was suggested that the disturbed carvers should produce objects of pious interest which could then be sold to the local souvenir shops. This they did. Their carvings were of far superior quality to the usual plastic tat, and the creative possibilities were extended when a considerable supply of obsolete horseshoes came onto the market. The little carvings could then be mounted within the horseshoes. The quality of the work was assured for it was su-

pervised by Léopold and Pierre Pène, the leading suppliers
of authentic local and rustic carvings; but the *commerçants* could not be persuaded to take an interest. To represent the Virgin in the Grotto encircled by a horseshoe
was judged irreverent. The line had to be dropped.
In the bookshops of the new town the religious list is
also very evident. The bookshop in the Avenue Bernadette
Soubirous, which is one of the main routes from the hotels
to the Domain, has the following titles in its window: *The
36 Proofs of the Existence of the Devil, Nuns—Are
they Women?* and *True and False Apparitions of the
Church.* The last is an authorized work of scholarship
which disallows, among others, several of the visions listed
in the Miraculous Medal show. It advances a methodology
for discriminating between the appearances of a true mes-
senger of the divine will, as manifested in a visionary interview with the Mother of God, and the sincere but unin-
spired hallucinations of the unapproved seer. Another title,
The Pilgrims of La Salette, Why You must go there too,
makes a rather desperate plea for La Salette, the site of a
series of approved visions in 1846. But La Salette was always a pretty lost cause. Although the nimbus was recognized as an apparition of the Virgin she made no mention
of the Immaculate Conception, she was deeply critical of
the standards of the French clergy and she was strongly
against the legitimate succession of Napoleon III. Melanie
Calvet, one of the children of La Salette, paid a heavy
price for relaying this political criticism from heaven. She
was exiled to a convent *in Darlington.* But she did not stay
there for long, and the Church could never be sure for the
rest of Melanie's life where she would pop up next with
another *coda* to the Virgin's message. Furthermore, although the shrine had a high reputation for miraculous
cures, La Salette was in an extremely remote and mountainous region, and the difficulties of hauling the sick up to
it finally overwhelmed the infant enthusiasm of the devout.
It is still in business, but, by Lourdes standards, only just.
The same bookshop is also, as one would expect, well-

stocked with works, in French, on Bernadette. Most of
these are written by one man, Father René Laurentin, the
historian and chief popularizer of Lourdes, a scholar and a
theologian, as well as a journalist whose *magnum opus* has
been the seven-volume *Lourdes, documents authentiques*.
Together with the Benedictine monk Dom Bernard Billet,
and the Jesuit priest Father André Ravier, the secular Father Laurentin has compiled an enormous quantity of published material on this one life and on the story of
Lourdes. Laurentin alone has published six other works on
the subject, much of it necessitated by the even larger
mountain of inaccurate popular writing of the day. 1858
was within the age of modern communications. The apparitions were reported in the daily press as a news event at
the time they took place, and they aroused sufficient hostility and enthusiasm to ensure that any story however wild
would be spread by one camp or the other. But the result
has been that Bernadette, surely one of the simplest saints
of the historical period, has been the subject of a weight of
research which might compliment even a great doctor of
the Church such as St. Anselm or St. Teresa of Avila. At
times the amount of clerical attention devoted to Bernadette in France seems to verge on the obsessional, until
one leaves the tomes with their astonishing lists of indexed
details and steps out of the bookshop and back into the
crowded street. Here, surely, is Father Laurentin's answer.
Where else in Christendom, let alone in France, do so
many of the faithful crowd together year after year to listen to their priests?

Bernadette's own opinion of the pilgrimage industry
which grew up in her home town before her death was not
enthusiastic. She was upset to hear that her sister had
started to sell "objects of piety" and wrote to her advising
her to stop. This had no effect, and when she next learned
that her brother was going in for it she avoided the risk of
a further rebuff by merely asking him not "to sell anything
on Sunday." Before her death she told a priest that she no
longer objected to her family engaging in commerce, "pro-

vided that they do not enrich themselves."* The firm, quiet voice from distant Nevers, with its decided and quite unrealistic approach to commerce, is a good indication of how far the pilgrimage industry had moved away from the original vision, even within the saint's short lifetime.

The matter-of-fact response to Bernadette's impossible injunction is conveyed by the classic French phrase, "One has to live"—and one normally has to shrug when saying it. Even Zola, stern critic of the new town, used this argument when contemplating the shop of "Soubirous, brother of Bernadette"; and he judged that M. Soubirous was indeed not making a fortune, such was the strength of the competition. But the family business has continued and prospered; and the great number of shops in town prominently labelled Soubirous (and owned by people of the same name who are not related to the saint) includes the shop of B. J. Soubirous, great-nephew of Bernadette.

Among the leading pilgrimage sideshows is the *Maison Paternelle,* or family home of Bernadette, and "B.J.'s" premises are actually the only means of entering this. To call it the *Maison Paternelle* is rather misleading since the house was only occupied by Bernadette's family after she had been removed to the hospice, and Bernadette never slept there. Entry is free of charge, but one has to run the gauntlet of the great-nephew's crowded counters to find that the house is chiefly one rather jolly little room where a bed has been placed behind an iron grille. This *is* the bed "in which Bernadette slept"—but at the *cachot,* not here—and the grille is intended to keep back the souvenir hunters and their sharp knives. All round the grille are the little marble votive tablets, in "Recognition" and "Thanks," and devotional candles, obtainable from the shop above, burn in the fireplace. The room is completed by another bed "in which her father died"; and beside the Bernadette bed—in which she used to sleep, incidentally, with two other children—a few coins are laid out encouragingly on a chest behind another iron grille. On the walls there are some

* *Bernadette of Lourdes,* René Laurentin.

family portraits and pictures of Mgr. Laurence and Father
Peyramale, the two unwitting co-producers of this scene
and, indirectly, of the entire surrounding town. Father
Peyramale's picture is particularly appropriate since it was
he who arranged for the Soubirous family to move from
the *cachot* to this much more comfortable dwelling after
Bernadette had been installed with the nuns. Below is the
kitchen where she said goodbye to her family on the night
before she went away to Nevers for ever. And beside it is
the mill room, the habitual scene of her father's en-
deavours, the failure of which was the reason for her family's poverty and the immediate spur for her expedition in
search of firewood and bones on that important day.

In the shop above, the quality of the Virgins endorsed
by the family of the girl who saw her is no higher, and no
lower, than the goods to be found in the surrounding
shops. Indeed the only important variation in any of these
goods is the price. The closer one gets to the Domain the
more one has to pay for anything, be it a rosary or a beer.
When the price of half-a-litre of draught beer in France,
that is, on the outskirts of town, is 2.30 francs, it rises to
2.45 as one approaches the border with St. Disney's Land.
Two hundred and fifty yards down the hill it has reached
2.85, and in the cafés right beside the Domain it has
climbed to 3.60. A similar progression can be traced in the
objects of piety. At the gates of the Domain one can find a
1-franc candle for 3 francs—or a 5-kilo candle for 74.50
francs. Here a very small rosary will cost 25 francs, but
one has the consolation of doing business with the saints in
person. The shops by St. Joseph's gate are called *Alliance
Catholique, A Notre Dame de Lourdes, Au Chapelet de la
Vierge,* St. Patrick's, *Au Sacré Cœur, A la Vierge Im-
maculée,* St. Laurence O'Toole, *St. Thérèse de l'Enfant
Jésus,* the Little Flower Shop, *St. Mathias aux Nations
Catholiques* and the *Au Secours Catholique.* The last
named of these is actually an official Church welfare organization.

L'Alliance Catholique, on the other hand, which sounds
about as much like a religious association as anything

could (or possibly a movement to reimpose the Papal States), is just an enormous souvenir shop, occupying a large corner site at the end of the Avenue Bernadette Soubirous. It is decorated in the light blue of heaven and Mary, and advertises itself as "Purveyor of ecclesiastical goods to the Vatican," if not coals to Newcastle. It offers the usual German, Italian, English, Spanish and Dutch and its special tongue is Flemish. In fact it is "just another shop," according to the chaplains of the Grotto, who disclaim any connection with it on behalf of the Church. "Purveyors to the Vatican," they say, means nothing.

Lourdes is a town where even a travel agency has to call itself "the Office of Catholic Travel" or "the Pilgrim House"; this looks odd in winter when their windows are full of publicity for Safari package tours. After a while one gets used to it. If the *Au Paradis* souvenir shop, which is owned by the Hôtel St. Jean, gives hotel guests a discount card bearing a devotional picture and the motto, "I prayed for you at the blessed Grotto," one does not even think it unusual. And it can take some time to notice that the least happy Virgin design of all, "the Virgin with the eyes that follow you," is on sale at the Loyola boutique, named after the founder of the Jesuits. When the connoisseur of Lourdes gunk has registered this, it gives him such a pleasurable thrill of horror that he has to stop himself going out of his way to take another look.

The *commerçants* of the low town have recently become very defensive about their reputation. The town is a byword for acquisitiveness. *Paris-Match* prints stories about obscure connections of Bernadette who carry out confidence tricks on pilgrims by selling them bogus family relics. And the readership chuckles and shrugs its shoulders and says, "Well, those Lourdais, what can you expect?" Morale reached such a low point in 1977 that the bishop authorized a pamphlet to which he contributed his own preface entitled "The Truth about Lourdes" and referred to the fact that the town was widely "misunderstood." The pamphlet also refers to the ugliness of the original basilicas, which is due to the fact they were "built

at the turn of the century, when architecture was mere
pastiche," and the ugliness displayed in the shops which
"is such that it discourages irony." One contribution made
by Mayor Abadie opens with the frequent question, "How
can one live in Lourdes?" and later notes that, "it is
difficult to be a pilgrimage centre: if you sell services, objects, needs, you are branded as a profiteer! These are the
difficulties experienced by those who live in Lourdes." The
ex-captain of the Lourdes football team, the parish priest,
and the union of hotel keepers then speak up for the town
and refer to the difficulties of earning enough money in
four months to balance a budget, and to the "hoary" criticisms of overcrowding, overcharging and dishonoured res-
ervations.

That the need to profit from piety has proved a stum-
bling block to faith seems certain. One girl who had just
got her first job as an assistant in a rosary shop left in protest after two days. It was not the contempt in which she
held both the goods and those daft enough to buy them
which drove her out: it was because she objected to being
told to go and stand in the doorway and catch the eye of
the men who passed, "like a prostitute." Her friends were
merely surprised that she had ever agreed to work there in
the first place. To them cynicism was the natural attitude
towards the trade on which the town depended. They expressed it in such "hoary" stories as the possibility of getting Virgins at cut prices in the January sales, when all the
shops put their soiled stock on display. (In fact you can't
because the souvenir shops never hold sales.)

Little of this, however, is of importance to the pilgrims
who come to the town for a week, and whose first task is
to get settled into a hotel room. In the words of the Union
of Lourdes Hotel Keepers, "the hotel staff has learnt over
the years that its clients are not only tourists but above all
pilgrims. And the requirements of a pilgrim are quite
different from those of a tourist." Puzzling over the exact
meaning of this confident distinction and looking around
his hotel room, what will the Lourdes pilgrim find?

The hotel room in Lourdes has a certain something about it. Its one essential function, in the opinion of both management and many guests, is to provide shelter from the weather. The view is unimportant, the vital thing is to get a bed. Consequently, the hotels have been crammed together, as close to the Domain as possible. In the words of one Lourdes hotelier, "the position of the hotel is vital. Everything depends on that. It is like the beach. Obviously the most successful hotels at the seaside are those nearest the beach. And the Domain is our beach. If you have a hotel or a shop down there you can pull in hundreds of thousands of francs. But my own hotel is not on the beach, and so I have difficulty in filling it in May and June, which leaves only about four months of the season. The best land available is the Pomès family land, even though the leases are very expensive. But you have no choice down there, it is all leasehold. That is why the family no longer work. It is no longer worth their time. I must say," and here one waits for a familiar refrain, "they were very well advised."

In the light of these reflections, let us return to the hotel and consider it again. Let us take the Hôtel du Cachot, an establishment first imagined by Dom Hubert van Zeller, "curiously but not inappropriately named," and "the only house I have ever been in which included the simultaneous smells of mouse and cat."* The Cachot will not be found in the official *Guide des Hôtels de Lourdes,* but we can be confident that it is not near "the beach"; we should place it somewhere near the noisome cell where Bernadette once lived, and after which it is called. When the happy pilgrim arrives in his room in the Cachot and flings open the window he will see that almost immediately outside is the wall of the neighbouring establishment, and beyond that the next and so on. Though the shutter which the newcomer so lightly throws open does strike the window of the hotel-next-door, there is some space between them. It is just enough to contain the ventilation equipment of the next hotel's kitchen. And beyond that there is a grubby little

* *First Person Singular,* Hubert van Zeller.

palm tree, which got left behind when the rest of the tiny
patio was turned into an extension for the hotel-beyond-
the-one-next-door. Turning from the window, the pilgrim
will note that his room contains two double beds and one
single one and may be surprised to see that *Chambre No.
217* is to be shared with four other persons, only one
of whom is vaguely familiar to him. In the corner of the
room, which is necessarily dark, there is a flimsy partition,
half-way to the ceiling, or sometimes just a curtain, which
conceals a basin, a mirror and a bidet. Over the bidet there
is a stern notice (in English only) describing it as a *foot-
bath* and to be used as such. Behind this partition curtain,
thunderously and in turn, each occupant of the room can
perform his or her ablutions. There will invariably be a
crucifix on the wall. There will inevitably be the chance to
hear every remark uttered by the four or five people next
door. There will at regular intervals be a comprehensive
rattling throughout the room as the device below the window turns itself on and off by day and night. Shortly after
it turns itself on we will all know what the pilgrims in the
hotel-next-door will be having for their next meal.

The Hôtel du Cachot, like all the pilgrim hotels, em-
ploys seasonal workers. Generally speaking, these workers
are quite incurious about Lourdes. They follow *le mètier*
and will go wherever it takes them. In the winter a ski
resort, in summer a pilgrimage centre or Nice or Paris. To
them, the clients are just guests, not pilgrims. One waiter,
for instance, a Frenchman from Toulouse, which is all of
108 miles away, looked hard at a prominently labelled
group of Basque pilgrims and announced that they were
speaking *Béarnais*. He had worked in Lourdes for several
years and had long ago concluded that any Frenchman
whom he could not understand was talking a local dialect.
Another French waiter who was asked the meaning of a
sign that stared him in the face every day of his working
life said that it was in "the language of the Jews" (this
was over a rosary shop). It actually said, "Alsatian spoken
here." The waiter was not translating, he was repeating a
local myth.

Many of these incurious seasonal workers are foreign, and one of the chambermaids in the Hôtel du Cachot was an Australian called Rosy. She had come to France for a holiday, run out of money in Orléans in central France and been directed to Lourdes where she "would be sure to find work." She described the work she found.

"We start at 6:45. First I clean out all the loos for half the hotel. There are eighty bedrooms, and me and one Spanish boy, the *valet de chambre*, have to look after forty of them; that is ninety-five beds. I do the basins and he works the vacuum cleaner in the corridors. That was his idea. 'In Spain, machinery is a man's work,' he said. Then we both make all the beds. At 11:30 we get half-an-hour off for a bit of stale bread and a cup of coffee. From 12 to 2 I have to wash up in the kitchen. Then I get three hours off. From 5 to 6:30 I iron towels and linen. There are only two other chambermaids, both French, and they have the other forty rooms. At 6:30 we get our tea. The food is lousy, much worse than they get in the dining-room and we have to eat chips every day. We get a green salad once a week. No peas are ever dished up for us but we get meat, which is not very good. They deduct this food from our pay and they also deduct a charge for accommodation. After tea we do the dishes again from 7 to 9. So that makes a total of ten hours a day and at 9 o'clock I normally want to go to bed as I'm to be up again at about 7. The next day, every alternate day, we don't start till 8. Then we just straighten the beds and wash the basins and go straight into the laundry. We don't do any dishes that day and we don't get any teabreak.

"For that I earn 2300 francs (£287) a month, more or less, depending on how busy we are. The tips run at about a hundred francs every three weeks. They hold back about two hundred francs a month as 'a bonus,' that is to keep you there until the end of the season. And at the end there is holiday pay of fifteen hundred francs. I reckon I can save about two thousand francs a month, that is £250. And I will have done five months by the end of the season."

Rosy was not a Catholic and she regarded the pilgrims with an observant if sometimes incredulous eye. She always enjoyed the scene when the new arrivals came down from their room just after being shown into it and confronted the management. During this scene it was an important card in the hotelier's hand that her guests, being pilgrims, and sometimes making a penitential pilgrimage, did not like to stand on their rights too loudly, however outraged they might be.

"In the Hôtel du Cachot you get total strangers sharing four to a room, even two to a bed sometimes, and if they've booked a single or a double they'll frequently complain. Well, they come to Madame and she'll say 'well, she's so sorry, there's been a delay at the airport or something, some of the previous pilgrimage are stranded for the night, *but* . . . she'll see about it in the morning.' Well, in the morning she's got another reason. 'She can't turn pilgrims out into the street' or something, and by then they've got to know each other and they're all making the best of it and they feel too embarrassed to insist. Which is just as well because there's no more room anyway. Madame has an amazing ability to size the new pilgrims up as soon as they walk through the door. She just looks at them and reckons what they'll put up with and that's when she allocates the room numbers. She's almost always right on just one glance. But when the French National comes in she's different. She doesn't try it on them. The whole town seems to be on edge that week. They want to treat the French properly.

"Most of our guests are Irish. We get French, German and Dutch as well but the regular bookings mostly come from Ireland. They're very nice but it's a pity they're so mad on religion. They get conned all the time. Madame makes a hundred per cent profit on the candles, for example. The big ones cost £200 each. So what happens is that at the end of the pilgrimage all the Irish club together with their loose change, wrap the tricolor around the candle and send it down to the Grotto on a *chariot*. Everyone gets excited about it, including Madame. It only cost her

£100. We've all tried to discourage them from doing this but it's no good. The Irish are so religious.

"They also sing a lot. They sing nationalist songs and hymns one after the other, and they always seem to have a tenor or a soprano who has to be encouraged and who then sings solo. When they have a sing-song night we are supposed to serve in the bar after 9, but we refused to do it after a time, it was too much work.

"I've found that the only way to get on with the Frenchies is to act like they do. So I wave me arms about and scream at them. Once I got shouted at for putting me hands in me lap during meals. I nearly went off me rocker. That was the Spanish boy who did that. But *he* never asks anyone to pass anything. Just leant across me plate once and dangled his sleeve in me soup. He hasn't done that again.

"Not all the hotels are like the Cachot. Next door the guests get room numbers before they arrive and they often get what they book. And the staff get much better food. And they pay an extra two hundred francs a month for every year you come back. We went on strike over the food once and got better food later, but we still have to get food from the fridge sometimes.

"I've worked as a chambermaid before, in Australia. The work was just as hard but the conditions were a lot better, and the staff were nicer of course. But, the money was not so good. We have some Irish girls here who work in the hotel rosary shop. They keep me going. They're the only people I can talk to. When they first came out they were very devout, but after about a month they became as cynical as the rest of us. They were all recruited by a woman in Limerick who puts an ad for this hotel in her local paper. She checks into their background for the hotel, but then she builds the job up a bit too much. They have to pay their own fares over here, but they work with a sweet old lady and they seem to have learnt quite good French. I share a room with them. There are three of us now in one small room and only one little basin for all our

washing. We are not allowed any friends in the hotel. They
are always thrown out if they are caught."

Rosy had developed no interest in the religion of
Lourdes at all. She thought the Grotto itself was pretty,
but the rest of the town ugly, and the sound of the *Ave
Maria,* broadcast all day and every day, drove her mad.
She said, "The priests expect everything free here, so do
the nuns." But there is a traditional animosity among the
hotel workers of Lourdes against the clergy because they
are thought to be poor tippers. She could not understand
why the guests spent all day down at the Grotto instead of
taking more of the sightseeing trips which were on offer.
She admired "Madame" for her professionalism in replac-
ing late cancellations. If, as happened in 1978, the entire
Italian National, with 7,194 pilgrims booked in, was cancelled at the last moment, Madame would be the first to
find replacements at a cut-price from over the Spanish border. That was the professionalism of *le métier* which Rosy
admired without affection. She was not anti-French, she
had a French boyfriend (who had spent two years working in the town before going to see the Grotto), it was just
that she was not "at Lourdes" she was just at her latest
job. There are four thousand men and women like her
there every season.

But it would be wrong to characterize the hotel keepers
and the *commerçants,* as Rosy did, as all of a type. Some
of them still have a genuine devotion to their shrine. One,
a butcher from Toulouse by trade, married a Lourdaise
and opened a small *pension famille* in the 1930s. His wife
had grown up on a smallholding and had tended the flocks
as a little girl. Their first two children were sons and his
wife wanted a daughter. So when she became pregnant
again she went to the Grotto and vowed to do the Stations
of the Cross on her knees if she had a girl. She did have a
girl and she kept her vow. It was a considerable penance
as the Stations of the Cross ascend very steeply for 1,300
metres over a very rocky hill. Eventually the hotel prospered and one of her sons was sent to a fashionable
Dominican boarding school near Toulouse, where he stud-

ied with the children of the wealthy Champagne families. He did not, however, become a Dominican or even a priest. He became a psychologist and he has long relinquished any idea of God. In a way, he is a true contemporary son of the Vision.

The *commerçants* include M. Barthecoy, who is a pharmacist and a counsellor of the chief lay organization of the Domain, *l'Hospitalité*. This must be almost the ideal commercial position in Lourdes. On the one hand a retailer of orthodox potions in a town which is visited by thousands and thousands of invalids a year; on the other a luminary in the medicine of faith. The *commerçants* also include the keen rival photographers, Lacaze and Viron. Viron is descended from the policeman who was instructed to watch Bernadette during the apparitions and who happened to be an early amateur of photography. He was thus perfectly placed to make the important early studies of her which are still reproduced around the world, and which led him into the trade which has supported his descendants ever since. Lacaze is of the Bouriette family, descendants of Louis Bouriette (Miracle No. 2), the quarry worker of Lourdes who, like old Soubirous, had injured his eye at work and had been blind for two years when, in March 1858, at the height of the early excitement, he bathed his eye in the spring water and saw at once.

And the hoteliers include one man, Jean Buscail, who spends most of his day through the summer months voluntarily organizing the movement of the sick pilgrims. He was born in Carcassonne but his father moved to Lourdes when he was five and took a café by the station. Each summer when he was a child he saw the sick pilgrims arriving and leaving throughout the day, and for the last twenty-two years he has spent his days overseeing the same process at the airport. During that time the number of annual visitors has grown from 1.8 million to 4.2 million, and the number of pilgrims passing in organized pilgrimages through the airport has grown from a few hundred to hundreds of thousands.

To M. Buscail the growing popularity of Lourdes is ex-

plained by the growing ease of travel. "Of the people who
come here today," he says, "more than before, perhaps as
much as twenty per cent are merely curious. Another
twenty per cent are truly devout and make a serious retreat
of their pilgrimage. The rest are sincere pilgrims but they
also set out to amuse themselves. Of the curious most
remain sceptical, but a few come back as pilgrims. A few
is enough. The reason why they return is that they sense
that there is something at Lourdes, the presence of the Virgin or something. For the people of the town this 'something' is difficult to comprehend. It presents problems for
the faith of Lourdais. Most of them are too familiar with
the shrine to be moved by it. But for visitors, there comes
a moment when even idle bystanders are moved by the
events in the Domain. And after that they can no
longer venture a straightforward negative opinion about
Lourdes."

❧ V ❧

The Pilgrims Reach
the Domain

The Bishops ran loose, I chased one all round
the Grotto to kiss his ring, but I didn't catch
him till the afternoon.
Eric Gill, on a visit to Lourdes, 1928

The Grotto today bears little resemblance to the bumpy
cavern in which Bernadette saw *Aquero*. Its floor is no
longer washed by the mill channel which the child could
not cross; that has been piped underground. Above the
channel a wide parade has been laid out, several feet
higher than the level of the Gave de Pau, and this has been
extended into the floor of the Grotto, raising it and
smoothing it and reducing its size. One advantage is that
the spring can also be channelled beneath the ground.
Walking round the modern Grotto one finds the spring
flowing out like an underground stream, sealed off beneath
a glass panel and lit up so that the bright green plants
which grow there are shown to advantage. In summer the
reduced spring runs with the visible strength of three or
four bath taps at medium-low pressure: in winter it grows
to the approximate strength of six bath taps at good pressure. This lighted glass screen, and the statue which has
been erected in the niche high up in the wall of the cave,
are the centre of the cult, the final objectives of the
journey.

The stone of the Grotto is worn black and smooth. The pilgrims form up in lines, and walk round the edge of the cave, running their hands and their chaplets along the stone. A rosary which has touched the walls of the Grotto at Lourdes acquires a talismanic value. The proceedings are more or less silent, depending on the number of Italians present. Some pilgrims bend to kiss the stone, some do so frequently. The niche above them is slightly backlit. A crack above it gives onto the sky, which immediately suggests the possibility of optical illusion rather than apparition. One of the first actions taken by the police was to check for this possibility—without success. The statue which now occupies the niche, where it has been since 1864, is carved from Carrara marble. Its base is marked with the words, "Que Soy Era Immaculada Councepciou"; the Italianate spelling recalling Dante's hesitation between Provençal (or "Occitan") and Tuscan. The statue today is rather blackened around face and neck from candle smoke. It is an insipid study in white and pastel blue, the blue having been added by the sculptor when he saw the effects of the height and the backlighting. The failure of the statue seems to have had a galvanizing effect on Bernadette. She never liked it and pointed out that the sculptor had ignored several of her instructions in attempting to reproduce what she had seen. On the day when it was inaugurated, a ceremony which she did not attend, Bernadette announced that she wished to follow her vocation as a nun with the Sisters of Charity.

But whatever the objective merits of the Virgin of the Grotto, it has acquired over the years a presence which is rarer than simple beauty. Its appearance has been reproduced and copied all over the world; it is instantly recognizable to all pilgrims, wherever they may have come from. Throughout the summer, night and day, and for much of the winter, there are people before it; gazing at it, praying, kneeling, passing beneath it. It makes a strange contrast with the hundreds of famous Madonnas which are preserved for secular adoration in the museums and museum-churches of the world, and which represent an aesthetic achievement far surpassing the Virgin of the Grotto. They were made so perfectly that they could inspire belief by their beauty, and by the brilliance with which they transmitted the artist's own faith. This image, on the other hand, has acquired lustre by reflecting the faith of those who pray before it. It is the flawed but triumphant heart of the contemporary shrine.

In front of the Grotto there are rows of benches. They have even been placed over the mark in the paving where Bernadette herself knelt for the first apparition. Here, on the bitterest winter days, a few people are seated or kneeling, and in summer great crowds are gathered in the same place. To reach the baths the sick must pass by the statue twice a day, to light candles the healthy must do the same. It is this prettified, neat, over-ordered stage, once the desolate scene of fantastic visions whose fame spread throughout the world, which has become responsible for the health or happiness of thousands of incurably sick and for the comfort of millions of their healthy companions.

Once past the statue and the spring the pilgrim leaves the Grotto beneath a string of equally blackened crutches and sticks which have been suspended across the roof. Old photographs show that their numbers have been considerably reduced, though each is said to have been abandoned by a pilgrim who found a cure. From the smaller number still in place it looks as though the authorities had wished to dismantle the whole of what Malcolm Muggeridge once described as a "rather unconvincing display," but felt that to do so would be to outrage the trusting devotion of the pilgrims.* Anatole France, on seeing the original exhibition, was moved to ask, "What! No wooden legs?" but he was not a believer.

The Domain which encloses the Grotto is a pear-shaped park of thirty acres bounded by the river on two sides and by Church property, or the largest hotels, on the third. The baths form its stalk, the Grotto and the basilicas are placed in its neck and the processional area fills its swollen body.

* Not all the crutches commemorated cures which had taken place at Lourdes.

During the pilgrimage season from April to October this Domain is the scene of a devotional routine which has hardly varied for a hundred years. Its highlights are the morning bathing of the sick, the afternoon procession of the Blessed Sacrament and the evening Torchlight procession. For those pilgrims who are *brancardiers,* or porters, the day begins some time between 5 and 7 in the morning when those who have been on night duty are relieved and the sick pilgrims in the three hospitals are prepared for the day. From 8 o'clock onwards the "greatest service" that can be rendered to the sick in Lourdes commences. They are lifted onto three-wheeled carriages or onto the four-wheeled trolleys which carry stretchers and pushed down to the Grotto and the baths. For the *brancardiers* and handmaids this can mean two or three journeys between the hospital and the baths during which it is customary for them to recite the rosary with their passenger. The printed instructions for the Catholic Association pilgrimage say of this custom, "It is much appreciated by most of the sick pilgrims and is a valuable opportunity for us to pray as well as to work for them. It does feel strange for the first time, but not for long. Take it very gently and encourage them to answer up." It certainly sounds strange to the new *brancardier* when he reads it on his printed instructions before leaving home. But by the time he is in the Domain and struggling to manage the carriage or trolley—neither of which has brakes—up and down the slopes between the hospital and the Grotto, worrying about the embarrassment of praying aloud is not likely to preoccupy him for long.

The baths are usually a scene of frenzied activity. By moving them to the far side the chaplains have ensured that all those who come to bathe have to pass before the Grotto. And the blaze of candles and the silent, devout crowds are an inspiring prelude to the sick person's chief moment of hope. As he approaches, he might hear Marian hymns sung at a mass for American pilgrims at the Grotto, mingling with a distant *Salve Regina* chanted by a group of Germans at the short Stations of the Cross, leading to a crescendo of noise just outside the baths where the amplified voice of an Italian friar leads the sick pilgrims waiting their turn to bathe. Despite the prayers, the queues outside the baths have a reassuringly medical air. Perhaps it is their patience, perhaps just the clutter of equipment. This is the hospital of last resort, where the waters are certified as having no medicinal value, and where the resident staff are all without professional qualifications.

The present baths are long, low, stone buildings set against the hillside which ends in the cliff above Massabielle. They have a covered area in front of them with railings to control the large queues. These can sometimes become quite unruly, as on the occasion of the election of Pope John Paul I, when the women in a large pilgrimage from Naples, which was about to leave Lourdes, decided to take two baths each, one for their own intentions and one for the intentions of the new Holy Father. Behind the gates, which had to be locked on that occasion, there is an entrance hall and a bench facing a row of blue and white striped shower curtains. Behind each curtain is a changing cubicle, and then the steps leading down to the stone tub. The *brancardiers*, who work here for two hours each morning and afternoon, in teams of six or eight, have parallel steps on each side of the tub so that they can if necessary lift even those on stretchers down into the water. Male bathers who can walk are provided with a blue cloth to wrap around their waist. (The women, whose more numerous baths have seven separate entrances, are given a tunic which in summer is rarely dry, due to the great number of bathers. Putting it on when it is already wet is, apparently, the worst part of the experience.) To pass from the cubicle to the bath one descends the steps which form one end of the tub. On a ledge at the far end is a small statue of the Madonna, and a card of prayers. For the healthy pilgrims it is a simple matter of reciting the prayers and then leaning back while the *brancardiers* lower you into the water. Early in the day this is clean and freezing. Later, as the pilgrims pass through it, it becomes warmer. It is changed once, at midday. In winter the assistance is provided by full-time attendants, but in summer it is the stronger *brancardiers de pelerinage* who volunteer for the work and who bathe the sick of all the pilgrimages that are in Lourdes that day. The healthy pilgrims are bundled through the procedure as quickly as possible. But it can take a considerable time to prepare the very sick for immersion. A paralysed Italian boy who could sit in a wheelchair when supported by his leather harness had to be lowered into the water on a special stretcher. When he was eventually undressed and ready he was carried by four men down into the water and immersed for ten or fifteen seconds, moaning with the shock, his bearers meanwhile praying for him loudly. One can see how, in the concentration of the moment, John Traynor's bearers would have taken his struggles for a fit rather than a cure. So many people bathed, so many hopes dashed, a cure would be the last thing that those working in the baths would expect. Indeed the continual prayers, the ordered routine, the steady pressure from those still unbathed, seem designed to distract each supplicant in turn from the absence of his particular miracle.

While the Italian boy was being dressed the queues outside waited under the direction of the chanting friar, the healthy rather inattentive during the delay, the sick praying with more fervour as they approached the door. The water in the baths that day had a light grey tint, the same colour as the stone of the tub. It was not clean, but neither was it one of the busiest days.

Beyond the baths there is a statue which may bring a measure of reassurance for the English-speaking pilgrim after the dual irritations of Latin fervour and violated hygiene. At the foot of a steep, tangled bank, attended by two damp palms, and coolly erect amid a background of firs, stands the figure of a stout woman in medieval costume. It is inscribed, "St. Margaret, Queen and Patroness of Scotland—Pray for Us—1929." This black-green bronze of a Scots giantess, equipped with kirtle, wimple and crown, gazes at a crucifix with a hint of reflective and holy abandon. She was installed two years after the first

Scottish National pilgrimage as a gift of the dioceses of Scotland, and sometimes, if there is a Scots pilgrimage in, a garland of carnations or roses will be wound into the railings that surround her towering plinth, and the awestruck wanderer through these woods may feel that the spirit of Miss Brodie lives. In truth, the evocation of Miss Brodie would be inappropriate since Margaret was of Saxon descent and raised in Hungary, even if she did restore the ancient pilgrimage to Iona. Since 1249 there has been an indulgence of forty days for visiting the site of her grave at Dunfermline.

Not all the sick are under the care of a large and experienced pilgrimage. Sitting on the lawns opposite the Grotto one day were two women from Stoke-on-Trent with a small child who lay on the grass between them. It was a sunny day and the Catholic Association had chosen to have a picnic for their sick children farther along the bank. As they passed by, they asked the two women from Stoke to join them and to bring the little boy. But they replied that there was no point. The child was nine years old, but since the age of three he had been unable to speak or see or hear or sit up. He had contracted a virus infection which had left him in this state. They said that he was happier lying in the sun, he could feel the warmth and he seemed to know his mother's touch.

Neither of the women was Catholic and they had won their tickets in a pub raffle. They had come with a small group from Manchester. Although they had no interest in religion they knew the story of Lourdes, which was that Our Lady said first build a church and then, "Let the people come here—not let Catholics come here." They talked to the child on the grass as though he were idle or asleep rather than half-senseless. They had bathed both him and themselves several times, and were amazed by the tingling effect of the bath water on the skin. They also said that there had been no need to dry the child after his bath, which they could not understand at all. Dan was difficult to dress and undress, and his mother remembered how she had undressed, bathed and dressed again before the handmaids had even got his shirt off. "They wanted the knack for it," she said. Normally Dan shivered in a warm bath, but after this cold one he did not even have goose-pimples. Her friend, who was from Newcastle, kept saying, "I think we're winning." She also said that she had told Dan that he had to walk off the plane. "And look. He can hook his leg onto the pram step already." His mother looked and said that his leg always fell that way. "I still say we're winning," said her friend.

After the gathering in the morning the various pilgrimages attend mass in one of the Domain's five churches or five outside altars. In the afternoon, from 2 o'clock on, the sick are bathed again and then, at 4:30 p.m., there is the Blessed Sacrament procession, which ends with the Blessing of the Sick. Finally, at 9 in the evening as night is falling, there is the Torchlight procession in which the pilgrimages, again with their sick, thousands and thousands of people, carry candles through the dark, forming a winding trail of light and singing the *Ave Maria,* the hymn which Zola described as "a prolonged lullaby slowly besetting one until it ends by penetrating one's entire being, transporting it into an ecstatic sleep, in delicious expectancy of a miracle." That is the daily programme of the pilgrimage.

The Blessed Sacrament procession is the most famous scene in Lourdes. Every pilgrimage in town marches behind its banners with its sick members in the van, round the long processional track and back to the esplanade in front of the basilicas. The order of ceremony has remained essentially the same since the day when Zola described Lourdes as "a new religion." He was particularly impressed by the fervour of the crowds, something his rationalist habit of mind had assumed to be a thing of the distant past. And although popular feeling is no longer stirred up to the same extent, the ceremony of the Blessing of the Sick, which is the climax of the procession, remains an emotional one. It is very unusual to see so many afflicted people together; this alone stirs the imagination. The sight is shocking at first, and then, as the newcomer

sees how matter of fact many of the sick are about their
condition, and how they are the focus of concern for the
much larger number of their healthy fellow pilgrims, the
scene becomes more compelling. There is the same air of
purpose about the procession as exists at the baths. If you
did not know where you were, you might suppose that this
was some enormous convalescent home, and that the patients being wheeled forward so briskly were on their way
to some important treatment. Then, as each pilgrimage
reaches the esplanade, with the whole procession singing
the hymns which are given out over the loudspeakers, the
marshals divide them so that the main body take up position in the centre of the square while the sick are placed at
the very front of the crowd and all around the edge of the
square under the cover of the trees.

As the monstrance containing the Host, which is carried
towards the rear of the procession, begins to approach the
esplanade, the feelings of expectancy among those waiting
begin to rise. The sick turn their faces in that direction,
many of those with them become anxious and, despite all
that is truly said about people not going to Lourdes in
search of a miracle, they cannot, at this moment, deny
their latent hopes which surge up every time they attend
this ceremony. The prayers and invocations which have
been given out in all the languages of the day's pilgrimages
throughout the procession now also rise to a peak. "Lord,
that I might *see!*" "Lord, that *I* might see," is repeated by
all present. "Lord, that I might hear!" "Lord, that I might
walk." "Lord, he whom thou lovest is sick! Lord, we hope
in You. Lord, we love You." And so on. But there is no
hysteria. The atmosphere remains calm.

Inspired by the suffering visible on all sides, the attention of the whole crowd is directed outside each individual,
to a power outside the world which could and sometimes
does intervene on behalf of those who implore its assistance. What starts as a litany of desperation—"Lord, we
hope in You"—grows into a rhythmic prayer, uniting the
weakest and strongest present, expressing all the hopes and
fears that each feels, with the meaning of each request

swinging backwards and forwards between the literal and the symbolic. As the Host is carried before the sick, its bearer pausing every few paces to raise it and bless the up-turned faces, their heads turn to follow it, craning from the first possible glimpse to the last disappearing glint of canopy.

This process of demand and anticipated intercession is addressed not to the world or its governments, not to its army of experts and officials and placemen, not even to friends or those close by, but is directed beyond the statues and trees and sky, past the river and the spring and the deaf stones of the Grotto, to memories and feelings and to the immaterial; addressed to the power of God. If it is a new religion it is a religion of the people, one that relies on visions and challenges the dominant Catholicism of the in-tellect, that subtle, temporizing, qualified faith of those who govern the Church and whose strong reason still re-tains some inextinguishable spark of the spirit. Here in-stead is the robust faith of those Christ came to save, the common humanity which all share but not all can feel without the operation of grace.

In Zola's time, and for many years after, the style of Lourdes was set by the Assumptionist Fathers who led the French National pilgrimage and roused the crowds at the Blessed Sacrament procession to a holy frenzy. The su-preme moment of this confidence trick, in the most posi-tive sense of that phrase, occurred in 1897, which was a papal jubilee year. When the French National had com-pleted the Blessed Sacrament procession a papal benedic-tion was bestowed on all present. One thousand priests chanted the *Confiteor*, then the leader of the pilgrimage, an Assumptionist, turned on the sick and *ordered* them to believe, to prove their faith and to stand up and walk. Amid a terrible silence first one and then another did this, until "forty-one poor wretches" had left their crutches and stretchers in triumph and rejoined the healthy race. The enthusiasm of the crowd on that occasion became a danger in itself.

Eleven years later a similar scene was witnessed by an

Englishman, Mgr. Robert Benson. Benson was a prominent convert whose father had been Archbishop of Canterbury and whose brother Arthur, the Master of Magdalene College, Cambridge, wrote a poem called *Land of Hope and Glory*. 1908 was the fiftieth anniversary of the apparitions and the year when the Church proclaimed a record number of twenty earlier cures as miracles. Three of them were proclaimed in August, the month of the French National, which that year totalled eighty thousand pilgrims. They included 1,200 sick, and there was a regular display, during the great processions, of 365 of the faithful who had previously been cured at the shrine. Benson certainly chose a good year to observe the untrammelled enthusiasm of the original pilgrimages. "And then on a sudden it came," he wrote, ". . . I saw a sudden swirl in the crowd of heads beneath the church steps, and then a great shaking ran through the crowd; but there for a few instants it boiled like a pot. A sudden cry had broken out, and it ran through the whole space; waxing in volume as it ran, till the heads beneath my window shook with it also; hands clapped, voices shouted: 'Un miracle! Un miracle!' . . . And then again the finger of God flashed down, and again, and again; and each time a sick and broken body sprang from its bed of pain and stood upright; and the crowd smiled and roared and sobbed. Five times I saw that swirl and rush; the last when the *Te Deum* pealed out from the church steps as Jesus in his Sacrament came home again. And there were two that I did not see. There were seven in all, that afternoon." One of them, a blind woman, Marie Bire of Luçon, was proclaimed a miracle two years later (Miracle No. 37); and in 1911 Robert Benson received the unusual honour, for an old Etonian, of being appointed private chamberlain to the Pope, the saintly Pius X.

Contrast all that with the experience of René Scher, a sixteen-year-old blind boy who recovered his sight during the Blessed Sacrament procession in 1966. As René Scher remembered it afterwards he was sitting in a wheelchair in the usual way with the other sick from his diocese. He was

a registered blind person and had been in that state since
an operation in his childhood which had gone wrong. He
was aware that the Blessed Sacrament (which was being
carried by Bishop Fox of Menevia on that day) was close
by, from the noise of the singing around him. Then he
"saw something white," which he now thinks was the
Host. Then he saw something dark, the trees above him
probably, and then for the first time he saw clearly and realized the size of the crowd around him. He had had no
idea that there were so many people there and he became
frightened and told the man next to him that he could see
and that he was afraid. Immediately the man took his cue,
and, displaying the instinctive joyous reaction of the devout pilgrim, began to shout, "Il peut voir!" "He can see!"
The brancardiers, following the usual instructions in such
cases, then hurried the boy away from the gathering and
towards the offices of the Medical Bureau, where the gates
were locked against the crowds. Those who gathered outside were told to go away and encouraged to think that
nothing very remarkable had happened, one of the most
paradoxical routines in the whole history of Lourdes. In
fact René Scher could see, and can see today, although his
cure has never been thoroughly investigated because of a
complete lack of co-operation from the Metz blind institute
where he was formerly a resident. But it seems a pity that
in the attempt to avoid the unnerving hysteria of the great
days of Lourdes cures, and perhaps in an attempt to recommend the phenomenon to rationalists, who will never
find it acceptable, the only people who should have
witnessed René Scher's wonder when he realized that his
act of faith had been followed by the gift of sight were the
usual committee of doctors, who solemnly asked him to
point out the high crosses on the three distant hills.

However cautious the authorities may have become in
the matter of miracles the popular attitude remains very
much in tune with that of René Scher's neighbour. An extraordinary number of pilgrims say that they know or have
met someone who was cured at Lourdes. One doyenne of
the Catholic Association Annual remembered the cure of a

little French Canadian boy who could not walk. This took place in 1974. "It happened in the hotel at dinner time. He was suddenly able to walk although he had been unable to do so for two years before. I remember that we tried to take photos of him for his mother, but the flash did not work." Such matter-of-fact stories are related as the high-point of a pilgrimage; and they form an area of shared acceptance. The true pilgrim never doubts that such things can and do happen every week. But when, as in most cases, nothing happens at all, the disappointment can be devastating.

One American mother who discovered that her child had leukaemia and was expected to die shortly took him to Lourdes as a last resort. She went in a rush, and without joining a pilgrimage, and when she arrived she found no one to talk to. Her first unexpected expense was for a hotel wheelchair. Her son cried all night and the people who had the next room to her complained about the noise. She remembers telling them that she had come to Lourdes because it was a place for sick people and that her son was crying because he was sick. Her son received no cure and after he had died she looked back on the experience with such bitterness that she left the Catholic Church and joined the Christian charismatic movement.

A similarly desperate journey was made by an English couple from Birmingham who arrived in Lourdes in September 1978 while the Catholic Association pilgrimage was there. Just before the final mass of the pilgrimage, which took place in the underground basilica, a young man and his wife and small daughter came into the Catholic Association office and asked for help. They said that the previous week they had heard that the man had cancer. His wife had decided that they should all drive to Lourdes as soon as possible. This they had done, bringing a tent with them, and they were now staying in the town camping site. They spoke very little French and, being non-Catholic, had no knowledge of Lourdes at all, except that it was a place for miracles. They were fortunate that they were able to find an English pilgrimage to join, or their ex-

perience might have been as embittering as that of the
American mother. But almost the first person they spoke
to was one of the Catholic Association's doctors, and it
also happened that the pilgrimage was led that year by
Bishop Cleary, the auxiliary bishop of Birmingham. In
fact, no sooner had they arrived than they found a priest
from their own city, three English doctors and one thousand pilgrims to lose themselves among. They were more
fortunate than other strangers. Throughout the mass the
husband appeared calm and reassuring, but his wife
seemed exhausted and his daughter bewildered.

Some of the reasons for which pilgrims come to Lourdes
can be seen in the different ways in which the national
groups organize themselves. To see the Derry pilgrimage
applaud their bishop as he leaves the hotel one might suppose that they came as a gesture of diocesan or even national solidarity, which to some extent they do. Derry is
one of the few parts of western Europe where holding the
Catholic faith has resulted in penalties in the last ten years.
The pilgrimage to Lourdes has nothing to do with asserting
a defiance of that fact, but Derry's pride in its faithfulness
has taken on an inescapably defiant air. It can be seen in
the great attention paid to appearances, in the smartness of
the uniforms worn by the *brancardiers* and handmaids and
the children, and in such old-fashioned details as the fact
that Irish bishops still dress in full canonicals. The use
found for symbolism is shown in such details as the Irish
respect for Lourdes water. Whereas the English pilgrims
cheerfully mix it with their duty-free whisky, pointing out
that unlike most commodities in the town it is free, the
Irish worry over what to do with any Lourdes water they
may have left over. They are more likely to bless themselves with it than to mix it with their whisky. To do otherwise, to take the cheerful commonsense view, would be to
violate the respect owed to the symbol of their journey and
their faith.

The sense of belonging to a universal church is also emphasized, paradoxically, by this devout nationalism. This is
never stronger than during the afternoon procession, when

the pilgrimages line up behind their separate banners. To a patriotic French priest it is a sight which must recall the splendours of the papal exile at Avignon. During the Catholic Association's week there were contingents from Derry, Rome, Naples, Aix-en-Provence, Tours, Bourges, Poitiers, Nevers, Chartres, Lugano, Holland, Oldenbourg, Strasbourg, Pamplona, Munich and Kerry. At the end of the line, just before the party bearing the Blessed Sacrament, there came a group of the Knights of the Holy Sepulchre, who wear white robes, and who are one of the more flamboyant of the Catholic lay societies, with their paramilitary ranks and paraclerical manner, a sort of bemedalled lay priesthood which dates back to the Middle Ages and whose ribbons and cloaks suggest a visible mark of invisible grace, the surviving equivalent of medieval indulgences. They provided an irresistible attraction to Joe, one of the most regular of the Catholic Association's clients. Joe could always be recognized from a distance by his habit of dressing in his usual English pullover, jacket, flat hat and two carrier bags. He never varied this kit whatever the weather or wherever he was. He lived for much of the year in Sheffield, where he used to take a box round the pubs marked, "Send a poor person to Lourdes." He did not mention that the person in question was himself. He paid for his ticket in irregular postal orders, and was about the only pilgrim who did not want a single room. He liked company and conversation. Once, in the Domain, seeing one of the Association doctors dressed in the robes of the Order of the Holy Sepulchre and drawn up in a prominent position surrounded by bishops, Joe knelt before him, kissed the hem of his robe and asked for his blessing. Dr. Tangney had to bless him before Joe would release his hem, and just hoped that none of the bishops would notice. Given the confusion at Lourdes between the healing roles of doctor and priest, it was an apt joke for Joe to devise.

Most pilgrimages include a tour of the town and its neighbourhood somewhere in the week, and the Catholic Association managed to take their sick pilgrims on an out-

ing to the village of Bartrès. The transportation of the sick
made a one-hour jaunt into a half-day expedition, but it
was happily undertaken by sick and helpers alike. In the
village there was one souvenir shop and two or three cafés,
but otherwise the visit to the farm where Bernadette
stayed, to the sheepfold where she worked and to the
church, took place in unspoiled surroundings. Delia, who
was mentally sub-normal, but also mentally hyper-active,
headed straight for the souvenir shop. Since she was staying in the new hospital that year, which is well away from
the town, she had been wondering where all the souvenir
shops had gone. At Bartrès she picked out one small plastic car, one tiny crucifix, one small plastic purse and one
small plastic television set showing a version of the apparitions; and then called for assistance from anyone who
could speak French to translate her bill. The sum came to
£5. Delia's purse did not contain that much money, and
so she was invited to choose between her selections; but
she decided that if she could not have the lot she did not
wany any of them, and left the shop in rather a bad mood.

Further up the sloping village street the party assembled
in the church for benediction and a penitential service on
behalf of the sick. Delia joined them to get out of the sun,
but when Mgr. Lawrence started his sermon her still ag-
grieved tones could be heard enquiring, "We're not having
another service here are we?" But we were. And losing interest in the hymns Delia went outside to sit among the
gravestones and watch the lizards under the palm tree
hunting for insects in the forest of marigolds and rockfoil.
She therefore missed her chance to kiss a relic of Bernadette, which had been bestowed on the parish to stimulate
the interest of just such parties of pilgrims, and which was
passed among the congregation encased in a small glass
phial.

The majority of the pilgrimage were taking the same
day as a "free day" and were making excursions further
afield in the Pyrenees. One of these was to the grottoes of
Bétharram, advertised on the Catholic Association itinerary as "an underground fairyland." The grottoes have

been professionally exploited but they are nonetheless one of the most extraordinary things in the Pyrenees. Five tiers of caves filled with stalagmites and stalactites; or, as they are currently described, "petrified forests, drapes, tassles, lacework" and (more originally) "Halls of Chandeliers, an Arabian minaret, a Sphinx Window, a Joan of Arc, a Pulpit, a Pool of Water Nymphs, a Cloister and a Hall of Hell." There is an underground stream which is two miles long and subterranean cliffs rising to 160 feet. The descendants of the painter Leon Ross, who arrived from St. Malo in 1898, have added a cable car, to save the steep climb to the entrance of the caves, a train which runs on rubber wheels, and a cruise by barge down the stream, as well as a loudspeaker system which has mastered seven languages, and all for £2. Meanwhile, the statue of the Virgin of Bétharram still stands in the usually deserted village church, reminding those who see it that in 1858 Bétharram was the holiest shrine in Bigorre. The implication for the future of Lourdes might trouble the devout pilgrim enjoying his rest day.

One of the last ceremonies before departure was the Pilgrimage Mass in the Pius X underground basilica, with the new rite of anointing the sick. On the Catholic Association itinerary, all British pilgrims were "urged to attend this Mass, which is for our pilgrimage only"; and the general assistance offered to the sick pilgrims throughout their pilgrimage reached its climax with this occasion. Once again there was the reminder of eternal life, which at Lourdes starts with the message to Bernadette about "no promise of happiness in this world." Bernadette was herself for much of her life an invalid who was eventually to suffer a cruelly painful death; and the modern message of Lourdes contains frequent references to the ill-health of the saint. The second and less obvious assistance which the sick receive from the services comes from the emphasis placed on sin and the forgiveness of sin. Here is a human experience of failure which unites rather than divides the sick and the healthy. And here is something which for the devout, in

the final analysis, exceeds even the importance of health.
Here also is a task which the sick can execute on behalf of
the healthy, that is to pray for them. To see the intense
happiness on the faces of the sick as they realize something of this is an extraordinary sight. Their suffering has
some meaning, even some use. They are strengthened.

The importance attached to sickness by the pilgrimage
to Lourdes is stated quite baldly, sometimes almost un-
feelingly. "We should be grateful to our sick," Mgr.
Lawrence told the Catholic Association Annual. "God has
chosen them to suffer for us." This is in sharp contrast
with the encouragement offered by the secular "caring" society, which looks on all reference to the acceptability of
other people's sickness by the healthy as trite or hypo-
critical, and which places as its first priority the provision
of money or equipment or professional companionship.
These may be adequate goals for a ministry to aim for but,
seen in the light of Lourdes, they are less than sufficient
for either comfort or reconciliation.

The Mass with Anointing of the Sick was the only occasion when the pilgrims sang "Faith of Our Fathers," the
traditional hymn of English Catholicism, now considered
rather unecumenical. The sick pilgrims were wheeled out
of the basilica singing it as lustily as any, the second verse
along with the rest.

> Our fathers, chained in prisons dark,
> Were still in heart and conscience free:
> How sweet would be their children's fate,
> If they, like them, could die for thee.
> Faith of our fathers, holy faith
> We will be true to thee till death.

That afternoon, for the last time, the pilgrimage joined the
Blessed Sacrament procession. For the last time the pilgrims formed part of the assembly of the dying, the crippled and the blind. Here for the last time was the awe-ful
sight of the multitude of those who could not rise or feel
or breathe unassisted, who were dependent on their friends

for the least thing and who were in that state for year after year, their least little movement needing painful calculation. In some cases only their eyes seemed alive. In some cases not even that. Every increase in their helplessness was a further stage in the reduction of life to the mind. All their life was mental life. This was the unexpected terror of their fate. It was from this that the journey had released them, so that they could turn refreshed to the year ahead.

The day of departure came and the air party started to leave at midday. By 6 p.m. the coaches had arrived at the hotels for the train party, and the pilgrims were driven back to the station to board the train on which they had arrived, and which had spent the past week in one of the dozens of sidings outside Lourdes station. Between 5:30 and 8:30 that evening, eight ambulance trains with about 24,000 passengers and 2,400 sick had to pass through the station. This was more than had ever done so before in a three-hour period, but at Lourdes such records tend to get broken every year, and the time passed with the minimum of confusion.

When the train eventually drew out through the hot evening air the Lourdes hymn was sung for the last time, with the same beaming faces on the platform singing it and waving, just as they had six days previously. It was the last truly communal moment of the pilgrimage. The corridors packed again, the now familiar tune with its desperate and hopeful associations, the pleasure of new friendship, the week of shared purpose; and finally the sunlight on basilica and rocks, and the Grotto almost hidden in the deep shadows of sunset, with the sputtering glare of the candles banked up before it, tended by all those other pilgrims whose return journey had not yet begun, and whose cures were still a possibility.

Comparing notes on the journey back the three pilgrimage doctors were able to congratulate themselves that at least none of those in their charge had died; although in the case of one woman with diabetes it had been a close thing. She had a short life-expectancy and was partially blind, with symptoms of neuropathy. She presented a special problem of stabilization. It had been arranged that she should enter hospital before she set out, but the doctor caring for her at the hospital left in the interim and, unknown to anyone, she embarked on her pilgrimage without being properly prepared. She had collapsed just after arriving in Lourdes and was sent straight to the town hospital on the second day, where she spent the rest of the week. But she was well enough to travel home with the air section of the pilgrimage. If one of the pilgrims had died on the journey, it would have caused complications. French regulations for dealing with the travelling foreign dead are not designed to fit in with the problems of travel directors. And it is not unknown for the pilgrimage doctor to delay certifying the death of a pilgrim *en route* until the corpse is once more within its own national jurisdiction. Transferring the body from train to boat is the tricky bit, but it has been done, common sense overruling legalism.

The problem presented by George, a young man who suffered from Wilson's disease, a form of liver and brain degeneration, had also been solved. George had a yearning for the pubs of Lourdes and on more than one occasion had escaped from the hospital at night and headed for a drink. In his condition this was not advisable, and a special watch had to be kept over him. The most unnerving experience of all was provided by David. David had thoroughly enjoyed himself at Lourdes and had made innumerable new friends, particularly among the girls. On the journey back he was strapped into his cot to prevent him from perambulating off the train during the night, and his cigarettes were taken away to prevent him from setting the bedding alight. As Dr. Dowling was finishing his night round he passed David's cot, which was on the upper tier, and David rolled over, stuck his head out and said, "Please, would you get me a ladder so I could get down?" Since David had said nothing relevant for two years, and was diagnosed as having irretrievable brain damage which rendered him incapable of coherent speech, Dr. Dowling was rather taken aback and pressed on with the reply, "Where the hell do you expect me to find a ladder at this time of night?" One of the handmaids also reported that she thought she had heard David singing towards the end of the pilgrimage. If this was a miracle nobody seemed inclined to make very much of it.

That night there was a packed meal which included *terrine de marcassin, poulet en gelée* and half a bottle of wine. And next morning, on a damp, grey Channel day, a final mass was said in the Boulogne Customs Hall, which at that hour was quite deserted, and then the pilgrims were released to the outside world.

Lourdes leads to unrealistic expectations of the world around it. Our fellow-travellers were the usual jumble, but their restless behaviour and inquisitive faces made them as recognizably different from the pilgrims as if they had been in uniform. Settled patiently into a bench on the boat, and looking around at the returning holidaymakers, it seemed as though everyone who had not been on the pilgrimage was profoundly disturbed. Some of the younger ones with their loud jokes and self-conscious posture seemed in more urgent need of treatment than many of the pilgrims who were classed as mentally ill. The invalid pilgrims, on the other hand, had spent a week in a hospital that took its patients out at night in a candlelight procession, and the impressions of the experience would continue until they were redelivered to the place where they had to spend the remainder of the year. And the rest of us had spent a week almost as far apart from our normal world as the invalids had been from theirs. We had been thoroughly jumbled together and it would take more than a boat trip to re-separate us into Scott Fitzgerald's clear-cut categories. For some of the pilgrims, who had already decided to return next year, the two worlds would never be entirely separated again.

Sitting among a group of holidaymakers were a handsome, middle-aged woman and a retarded girl who suffered from anorexia. The child made an exhausting companion. She was continually encouraged to eat, and would agree to do so, but she was infinitely resourceful, in the way of

some retarded people, at one particular thing—in her case
at disposing of her food without swallowing it. The woman
was helped by an elderly and rather distressed priest, a
man with a plummy voice and a prosperous air who would
have looked much more at home in the pavilion at Lord's.
Now and again he dropped into sleep, quite outlasted and
driven to his wits' end by his sly charge. But the woman
was patient with her, and attentive. She was not, however,
the girl's mother. Before the pilgrimage the child had been
a complete stranger to her. It was the woman's third pilgrimage to Lourdes. She was a Protestant who had first
gone there two years earlier with her son who had contracted a brain fever. "He wasn't cured," she said. "He
died a few days after we returned. The miracle was that he
didn't die at Lourdes. My husband didn't come with me
and he would never have forgiven me if that had happened." She had been each year since, alone.

Passing through customs was a formality, as one would
expect with so many invalids. But there must have been
thorough inspections in the past. There was a stern warning in the Association itinerary, "Attempts to smuggle du-
tiable articles bring discredit not only on the individual but
also on the whole pilgrimage." Then there were reunions
with waiting families, and those sick pilgrims who reported, as some always did, that they felt much better were
advised by the pilgrimage doctors to see how they felt in a
year. Here at least there was no disappointed expectation
of miracles. If anyone felt better, well and good. If anyone
wanted to be registered as a cure, that would be done in
due course, but it was incidental to the general purpose of
the journey. A slow train made its way back to Victoria
station, and the journey was complete. For those who were
sick it was possibly the end of their only pilgrimage. They
would not be encouraged to apply to come again. Each
year the organisers had to turn down many applications
from people who were seriously ill but who had been to
Lourdes before, and who therefore had to give up their
places to others who had never been. On the crowded platform I saw a fellow pilgrim pushing a nearly empty lug-

gage trolley and asked if I could share it. "Of course," she said. Then after a while she could contain it no longer. "I've just been to Lourdes," she said. "So have I," I replied. "Oh," she said, looking for the badge.

But it was already in my pocket.

❧ VI ❧

A Limited Number of Altars

Dear people. I've some relics in my bale
And pardons too, as full and fine, I hope,
As any in England, given me by the Pope.
If there be one among you that is willing
To have my absolution for a shilling
Devoutly given, come! and do not harden
Your hearts but kneel in humbleness for pardon . . .
The Pardoner's Tale, Chaucer (Trans. Nevill Coghill)

The Domain of Our Lady, which the pilgrimage had left behind for another year, is owned and run by the diocese of Tarbes and Lourdes. It is administered by the chaplains of the Grotto who are appointed by the bishop from the priests of the diocese, and who are led by the Rector of Sanctuaries. Apart from the Grotto, the Baths (or *"Piscines"*) and the five churches, the main institutions of the Domain are the Medical Bureau, two hospitals (with a third outside the enclosure), and the confraternity of "the Hospitality" of Lourdes, which organizes the voluntary helpers. There also are offices for forwarding water all over the world and for arranging for masses to be said for private intentions, a press centre, information offices, a printing press, a social welfare office, and a shop selling books, records and pictures. It is a religious centre, a medical centre, a recruiting and propaganda and money-raising centre, a centre for holidays and for social work, and a thriving business. It is, all told, a very odd place indeed.

The whole paraphernalia of the Domain, from the order of service to the appointment of the medical director to the

policy adopted on suitable clothing for pilgrims, is ulti-
mately authorized by the Bishop of Tarbes and Lourdes,
or, as he was known until Lourdes was fully established,
the Bishop of Tarbes. It is this responsibility for the shrine,
the monstrous cuckoo chick which has hatched out in the
diocese, that makes the formerly obscure bishopric of
Tarbes possibly the most important in France. The greatest
bishop of Tarbes, after Mgr. Laurence who authorized the
apparitions, was Mgr. Théas—the present bishop's immediate predecessor. Mgr. Théas was in office during and
immediately after the Second World War when the Vatican, encouraged by the success of Lourdes, was launching
Fatima as a shrine of rival status and authenticity. He rejuvenated the various institutions of the Domain and, in
1946, prodded the medical bureau and his brother bishops
of France into doing the work necessary to proclaim the
first miracles since 1913. Mgr. Théas became something of
a figure in local politics, and at one time took such an am-
bitious line that the Vatican appointed a coadjutor to assist
him in the management of the diocese and the Domain.
John XXIII, a devotee of Lourdes, withdrew this coadjutor
shortly after his election.

After the bishop, the most important figure is the Rector
of Sanctuaries, who is the head of the corps of chaplains
and the descendant of the enflamed Father Sempé. But
unlike Father Sempé, the present rector, Father Bordes, is
no longer in the order of Garaison Fathers, for the interesting reason that the Garaison order was actually expelled from Lourdes in 1903 when the French State
suppressed the preaching and teaching orders. This persecution reached its height in 1910 when Massabielle, which
had been confiscated from the Bishop of Tarbes in 1906,
was handed over to the municipality of Lourdes. The town
promptly ceded control of it back to the bishop. But ownership was not officially restored until the rule of Marshal
Pétain in 1940 (an act which, as the chaplains are quick
to point out, was later confirmed by General de Gaulle).
Ever since 1903, the responsibilities of the Garaison order
(now rechristened the Fathers of the Immaculate Con-

ception) have been taken up by the bishop's corps of chaplains. Today there are seven secular chaplains, and ten to twelve seasonal assistant priests from other countries. There are also seven Garaison fathers whose activities are confined to pastoral work, such as the hearing of confessions and giving of sermons; no mean task at Lourdes.* The Garaison order was recalled by Mgr. Théas, who at the same time ordained that all the administration should continue to be done by his chaplains. The only point of contact comes in the ceremonies, which have to be worked out between them.

The Hospitality is one of the most important institutions in the Domain. It is run on nominally democratic lines, that is to say by an appointed council which elects its own president, but there would be no question of electing a president of whom the bishop did not approve. It started—to retell the romantic story—when an old lady who was too weak to get to the Grotto from the station was assisted by the Comte Roussy de Sale, who, with two friends, wheeled her to Massabielle. Subsequently, a regular confraternity of hospitallers, based on the Knights Hospitallers of St. John, was founded and the first president took office in 1885. The business of the Hospitality is to concern itself with the comfort and needs of the sick pilgrims, but it has developed over the years a complex structure of grades and honours. The last president of the Hospitality once said: "There are two sorts of *brancardiers*. The *brancardiers* of the pilgrimage and the *brancardiers* of Lourdes. And it is the second category which interests us." This is an unofficial distinction. But it refers to those *brancardiers* who place themselves at the disposal of the Hospitality for the length of their stay in Lourdes, for year after year; thereby acquiring many months of service and eventual promotion to the rank of medal-holder. They are assigned to work at places like the railway station, the baths, the airport, or directing the processions, leaving the daily care

* Visiting priests may only hear confessions within the boundary of the Domain. If they wish to hear confessions elsewhere in Lourdes, they must obtain a special faculty from the Rector.

of their fellow pilgrims to the *brancardiers* of that particular pilgrimage. Neither job is easier, but working for the Hospitality is like joining a club. The other is a more private way of caring for the sick.

Over the years the Hospitality has acquired about three thousand *voitures,* or bath chairs, about a hundred and fifty stretcher trolleys, and several thousand wheelchairs, frequently donated by pilgrims. It has also acquired a certain amount of property in and around the town. There is the *Abri St. Michel,* where the *brancardiers* can eat, and where, it is generally agreed, the food is not at all bad. Zola caught the original atmosphere in this passage:

> . . . The feature of the place which more particularly struck you, as you crossed the threshold, was the childish gaiety which reigned there; for packed together at the tables, were a hundred and fifty hospitallers of all ages, eating with splendid appetites, laughing, applauding, and singing with their mouths full. A wondrous fraternity united these men, who had flocked to Lourdes from every province in France, and who belonged to all classes and represented every degree of fortune. Many of them knew nothing of one another, save that they met here and elbowed one another during three days every year, living together like brothers, and then going off and remaining in absolute ignorance of each other during the rest of the twelve months. Nothing could be more charming however, than to meet again at the next pilgrimage, united in the same charitable work, and to spend a few days of hard labour and boyish delight in common once more; for it all became, as it were, an "outing" of a number of big fellows, let loose under a lovely sky, and well pleased to be able to enjoy themselves and laugh together.

But to join in this fellowship it is necessary to apply and to be enrolled. A pilgrim could come to Lourdes for fifty years and help with the sick, and, as far as the Hospitality was concerned, he would have to work his way up through their ranks from the bottom if he had not put himself at the disposal of the Hospitality rather than his own pilgrimage director.

The Hospitality has also acquired various houses where the *brancardiers* doing a *stage,* the basic six-day stint, can put up. And last year they also acquired the *Villa de la Forêt,* a house in one of the prettiest outskirts of the town, where hospitallers can stay with their wives and children, who would formerly have seen nothing of them during their *stage.* It is a concession to the times, an acknowledgement that the "big fellows" find it more difficult nowadays to get out under a lovely sky, but tend to have family responsibilities which have to be shared on a more level basis.

Among other responsibilities the Hospitality is responsible for the *piscines.* The spring which was uncovered by Bernadette is now stated to have been there, below ground in the Grotto all the time, and the saint's function was simply to uncover it. The course of the spring has even been traced to beneath the hill of Le Béout, the summit of which is well known to visitors as it is served by a funicular. The official attitude to this water today is more ambivalent than ever. On the one hand it is clearly stated that the water is not magical, nor even mineralized. In fact it has fewer minerals than the normal water supply in the town. It is just "good mountain water, pure and drinkable. Moreover," continues the *Official Guide,* "there is no obvious link between the water and the cures in Lourdes; many of them take place during the Blessed Sacrament procession." The *Official Guide* recalls that in the nineteenth century the essential message of "prayer, penance, poverty" was replaced by the slogan, "Lourdes water cures," but that this deviation has now been corrected.

The ritual of the bath, for both sick and well, remains as popular as ever, despite official prevarication. On 14 August 1978, on the third day of the French National pilgrimage, 1,800 men and 4,750 women were bathed at the *piscines.* This means that on average 316 men and 678 women passed through each tub, the water having been drawn twice during the course of the day. The doors were opened at 7 a.m. on that occasion, allowing for an exceptional six hours of bathing; even so each of the 13 tubs handled an average of 85 pilgrims an hour, or one every 45 seconds, an astonishing rate when one considers that this included thousands of sick pilgrims, many of whom would have taken very much longer. At such busy times there are 6 to 8 *brancardiers* by each bath. To assist the speeding penitents through their prayers, prayer cards are available in nineteen languages (as well as French and Latin), including Arabic, Mandarin Chinese, Korean, Croatian, Japanese, Slovenian, Tamil, Thai and Ukrainian. Braille prayer cards are also provided in the five principal languages of Lourdes.

The water is filled to knee depth, and is only drawn more than twice a day if it has been visibly fouled. That it is invisibly fouled is indisputable. There is a devout rumour, what Dr. Jean Louis Armand-Laroche terms *"un bruit dans le vent,"* that microbes die in Lourdes water. Dr. Armand-Laroche, who is on the International Medical Commission of Lourdes, considers this theory to be "all wrong." In fact it was once rather more than a rumour. The *Guide to the Grotto* which was circulated as recently as the 1960s, stated that "microbial analyses have found that the water contains a mass of noxious germs. However, it is a medical fact that this naturally polluted water remains, in fact, exceptionally sterilized, powerfully abiotic, that is to say it destroys the malignity of the most dangerous germs. It is completely innocuous." The tests on which this arresting claim was based were carried out in 1934 and 1935, when laboratories in France and Belgium analysed Lourdes bath water and found it to be polluted with colon bacillus, staphylococcus, streptococcus, pyocyaneus and other microbes. Guinea pigs inoculated with these microbes after culture were, however, unaffected. So the bacilli were reported to be inert. At the same time guinea pigs inoculated with water taken from the river Seine in Paris which was polluted by the same microbes died. But this experiment is no longer regarded as of any importance by the Medical Bureau, which states that there is nothing abnormal about the polluted water of the Lourdes baths.

Dr. Armand-Laroche says that he could never recommend bathing from the point of view of a professional hygienist, and that he finds it an effort to bathe when he goes to Lourdes. But, "I do it," he says, "as a believer. I do it in humility, in the spirit of penance and as a spiritual exercise." The total surrender of caution is more common among the women pilgrims than it is among the men. Whereas in the men's bath new arrivals frequently have to be encouraged to enter the water at all, and then sometimes have to be further encouraged to immerse themselves above the knees, in the women's baths the handmaids are instructed not to allow the bathers to immerse themselves completely. It is a case not of pushing the bathers down but of pulling them up, and the women are told that they are not allowed to lower their heads into the water.

The spring water now passes through a complicated system of pipes. It rarely runs at more than 42,000 litres a day, and in summer, when the demand for baths is at its height, it may drop as low as 21 litres a minute or 30,000 litres a day. Two storage tanks have been installed, one of 300 cubic metres and a newer one of 2,000 cubic metres, but the same source also has to supply the tens of thousands of pilgrims who come to the taps to wash and to fill their bottles. The practice of allowing so many pilgrims to bathe in the same water has long caused people to wonder that there has been no outbreak of cholera or typhoid at Lourdes, particularly during the hot and busy August seasons. But no record of infection from the baths is kept at Lourdes.

There are, however, occasional stories in the press throwing doubt on this record. In 1964 a party of English schoolgirls were admitted to an isolation hospital in Surrey suffering from typhoid, but they had visited the Costa Brava as well as Lourdes, and there was no proof that they had been infected in the baths. And the Chief Medical

Officer at the Ministry of Health said, in the same year, that there was no evidence of any British case of typhoid having been contracted in Lourdes. The whole question of the wisdom of bathing in spa water is an old one, and was even raised by Samuel Pepys, who, on a visit to Bath in 1668, tried to get into the baths early to avoid the crowd. He wrote: ". . . Much company came very fine ladies and the manner pretty enough only methinks it cannot be clean to go so many bodies together in to the same water." Despite his misgivings he stayed happily immersed for two hours.

At Lourdes the sick are invariably bathed at the beginning of each session to reduce the time they have to wait, and though it may be a considerable act of penance for the healthy to follow them into the water the overwhelming majority of bathers are usually healthy. The *brancardiers* who assist in the men's bath are brisk and most insistent that each bather immerse his body up to the neck. They will not allow you just to paddle in, say a few prayers, and paddle out again. It is demanding work but some of the experienced *brancardiers* have found it so rewarding that they have made it their main occupation. André Mourot has worked as a *brancardier* in the baths since 1956 and is one of those who have retired to Lourdes, in his case from the Jura, in order to work for the Hospitality throughout the year. He has plunged two cures to his own knowledge. The first was that of his son who suffered from persistent verrucas in the hand which did not respond to treatment and which cleared up at once on being bathed. Verrucas are notorious for clearing up suddenly and would be most unlikely, even if they were sufficiently serious, to be considered for an official cure, but the circumstances of the case convinced M. Mourot of the miraculous nature of the event. The second case was that of a pilgrim from Toulons who had a withered arm that healed after bathing. M. Mourot learnt of the cure when the man returned in the following year. In all his years at the baths he can recall no trouble except for the occasional *Paris-Match* photographer who attempted to breach decorum and rever-

ence, and minor incidents with men who had decided at
the last minute that they did not wish to bathe after all.

The reasons people find for not bathing are sometimes
quite ingenious. When I bathed on a February afternoon
the water was cold but clear, and the cubicle—the only
one in use—was heated, contrary to all expectations. Nevertheless, a burly middle-aged man who had come in with
a friend declined to take his coat off, let alone bathe. He
sat on the bench shivering with horror at the prospect and
in response to all entreaties merely moaned and clutched
his overcoat round himself more tightly. Common reasons
for a last-minute refusal from men include: "I want to go
to Confession first"; "my heart will stop"; and "I'm only
in here because the wife sent me." If there is time the *pis-
ciniers* or *plongeurs* will tease or chivvy them into changing their minds, but many leave having observed the whole
process carefully—presumably with a convincing enough
account of their imagined experiences to satisfy any subsequent questions.

The *plongeur* who bathes is called "the duck" in professional slang, and he has the choice of bathing first, when
the spring water is fresh and freezing, or last, when it is
warm but soupy. Certainly the shock of the cold water in
February is sharp enough to drive any other thoughts out
of one's head, but if one follows the prescribed practice
and does not dry oneself (no towels are provided) one
leaves with a delightful tingling sensation and a feeling of
well-being and virtue. I was curious about the bathing
habits of the senior staff of the Domain, and, since the
winter would seem to be the ideal time for them to bathe, I
asked one of the Grotto fathers about this. "Whether or
not the chaplains bathe is up to them," he said. "It is not
obligatory to do so, it is not an order. Our Lady left an invitation only." It seems then that the chaplains do not
make a weekly habit of bathing. One of them mentioned
that he had already bathed once that year (that is by
February), on behalf of an American lady who could not
get to Lourdes, and who had requested him to bathe on
her behalf.

Dr. Armand-Laroche, who comes from a family which has been on regular pilgrimage to Lourdes for fifty years and whose father was also a doctor and also on the council of the Medical Bureau, does bathe regularly, as an act of mortification. Dr. Théodore Mangiapan, on the other hand, who is the director of the Medical Bureau and is present in Lourdes for most of the year, when asked if he had ever bathed said emphatically, "Never."

The habit of Lourdes bathing, the most characteristic practice of the cult, has become more idiosyncratic as time has passed. When it was started there was nothing to distinguish it from the usual practice followed in European spas. But there was one hidden difference; Lourdes had a very limited supply of water. This meant that as the number of pilgrims started to increase, Lourdes' standards began to resemble those of seventeenth- and eighteenth-century Bath rather than nineteenth- and twentieth-century fashionable thermalism. That was not a problem, in the absence of outbreaks of infection, since the bathing was an act of faith in itself. In the official literature the act of undressing is compared to Christ's being stripped during his passion, and the act of descending into the water is compared to being covered with the prayers of one's fellow pilgrims. But in an age when a massive industry is devoted to persuading people that they are dirty and malodorous and in need of new drains and new bathroom machinery, and an ever cleaner skin, more and more pilgrims find that in bathing at Lourdes they are making a conscious decision to do something which would, in the outside world, be considered foolhardy or repellent. This has caused no loss of enthusiasm among the pilgrims, indeed it seems to increase the penitential nature of the bath; but it does mean that, for the authorities, the penalties of an outbreak of infection would be much greater than before. And, at the back of many of the decisions which are made in favour of change at Lourdes there is this same preoccupation with appearances. The official fear about the continued practice of bathing is not only that the growing demand will exhaust the daily water supply, but also that the penalties

(if there was an outbreak of infection, the baths would
have to be closed and there would be a public enquiry)
would be too high.

As a result, the Council of the Hospitality has been considering ways in which they might persuade more of the
pilgrims to wash at the taps rather than bathe. In their own
defence the council can point out that *Aquero* never said
anything about bathing. The bathing just came naturally to
the people of Bigorre; all the vision said was "drink the
water and wash in it." They also say that many people are
put off washing altogether by the long queues at the baths
and the absence of basins at the taps. In future it may be
that bathing will be presented as something which only the
sick require; and the healthy, who form the majority of
pilgrims, will confine themselves to using the taps for
washing and for filling their bottles. This separation of sick
and healthy, it is added, would reduce the risk of infection,
reduce the pollution in the baths, ease the work of the *pis-
ciniers* and reduce the inconvenience suffered by the sick.
It would also make it possible for each of them to spend
more time at the ritual of bathing. In an age of increasing
hygiene and decreasing independence of thought, the new
scheme will probably be implemented. But it is a far cry
from the days of the old Comte de Beauchamp who was
president of the Hospitality from 1922 to 1957, far longer
than anyone else, and who used to make a habit of going
down to the baths at the end of each day's session and
drinking a glass of bath water, declaring that he had
"drunk a whole hospitalful of microbes" and never come
to any harm at all. That *was* an act of faith.

The only direct connection between the Church and the
spring is in the bureau for sending Lourdes water through
the post. The only charge the Church makes for the water
of Lourdes is for the flask and for packing, handling and
postage. There is an office near the Domain which will arrange for this, and which distributes a detailed price list.
For instance, to post a quarter litre flask anywhere in the
world costs £1.90; anything larger than that has to be

sent by train or ship. The largest flask, 10 litres, costs £23 to send to the U.S.A. It cannot be sent on any terms at all to Ireland, Zambia, Cyprus or Uganda. The leaflet explaining this procedure states that "Rev. Father Bursar" of the Grotto Society will receive applications in response to the Virgin Mary's *dicta*, "Go and drink at the fountain and wash there." The leaflet continues: "The Grotto Society is willing to send this miraculous water in plastic flasks to sick people and to people from distant lands. This water is for drinking and for applying to affected parts of the body. It is not a magic remedy to do with witchcraft. Great faith and insuperable confidence in the Immaculate Virgin is a prerequisite. The Grotto water is sent to every corner of the world. *It is always free.*" And according to a spokesman for the chaplains the amounts charged do not always cover the expenses involved.

The carriage of water must be a considerable item in the postal figures, helping to swell the totals for the summer months, just as the postcards do, but it is impossible to be too precise about this because the Church retains a certain independence in its arrangements, sending the flasks on Tuesdays and Fridays "from Easter to All Saints," and on Thursdays only for the rest of the year. A calendar which opens with a moveable feast and closes on another unnumbered day of celebration is liable to baffle even the French statistics service.

Under French law no one can sell Lourdes water if it is given to them free, and the Grotto fathers do what they can to prevent this happening. It is a matter on which the chaplains speak with some feeling. They are well aware that they could have made millions by selling the water if they had "chosen to behave like Evian or Vittel." Indeed the mayor of Lourdes at the time of the apparitions immediately seized on this idea. But he was overruled and the Church has consistently stated that to sell the water would be shameful.

But one local firm, Barrère, seems to have found a way round the regulations. Barrère sell "Pastilles de Lourdes," little white sweeties bearing a vague outline of the Virgin on one side, composed of sugar and natural perfume, and "guaranteed to be made with water from the miraculous source." It is rather difficult to prove that "more" is charged for these sweeties than for similar confections based on standard H_2O. But it cannot be considered entirely satisfactory from the chaplains' point of view, that a local enterprise is selling a product on the basis that it contains the miraculous water which is known to be associated with cures. Barrère do not of course advertise that cures have resulted from sucking sweeties. If the manufacturers were to suggest that, they would no longer be able to rely on the classic Gallic defence, "one has to live." That is how the chaplains live; the cures are their business, just as the sweeties are the business of Barrère. But the connection is implicit all the same. The water of the source remains the symbol of the waters of baptism and of the Jordan, to use the Church's imagery, even if it has been carted away in Barrère's sizeable plastic barrels, rather than in a pilgrim's little flask.

And Barrère has a rival—Malespine. Malespine, whose sweeties tend to be half the price of Barrère's, presents them as even more authentically "of the source." "Beware of Imitations," says Malespine, and his packet actually uses the words of *Aquero*, "Go, drink at the fountain," and refers to the cures which flow from it. Then Malespine draws attention to the need, since not everyone can come to the water of Lourdes, for the water to go to everyone, instead. And fortunately science, which comes from God, need not be exclusively employed in temporal works and in curing bodily ills; it can also be turned towards the infirmities of the soul. It can, more precisely, be used to transform drops of the precious water into the Malespine sweeties, which is done in a special factory Malespine has built near the station, in response to a large public demand and putting aside all odious calculations of speculation and profit.

Even if the chaplains did wish to put a stop to Malespine's long-established enterprise they might have a job to succeed. His leaflet also records that during the thirtieth anniversary celebrations of 1888, the original Monsieur Malespine had the pious inspiration of offering a box of his holy sweeties to His Holiness Pope Leo XIII—naturally not just any old box, but "a magnificent gold casket filled with" these delicacies. Leo XIII seems to have had a sweet tooth because he sent a papal benediction through Cardinal Rampolla, the Latin text of which is included in every crackling little packet. The negotiations for this papal endorsement must have been carried out in the previous year, which was a good time to write to Leo XIII since it was the fiftieth anniversary of his priesthood and he was showered with gifts, each of which had to be acknowledged. A close study of the text suggests that the Malespine company, in claiming that the Pope had blessed them *and their work*, are stretching the facts a little. But Cardinal Rampolla's seal makes a handsome trademark, and certainly assists the faithful sweety suckers in distinguishing between the genuine Malespine and the products of "certain unscrupulous persons who sell *bonbons* which have been manufactured in Lyons, Marseilles or Toulouse, as Lourdes *bonbons.*"

But if they can do nothing about the vendors of sweeties or soap ("Go drink . . . go wash"), because they can only control the use to which the water is put if more is charged for it, the chaplains can at least stoke up their indignation and come down very heavily on anyone selling medallions at a higher price because they have been blessed at Lourdes or dipped in its water. "An increase in spiritual value cannot be made commercially more profitable," said one of the chaplains. And he was talking about simony, one of the classic medieval frauds, immortalized by the presence of the Pardoner, or seller of indulgences, among Chaucer's pilgrims. "Modern simony," continued the chaplain, "is particularly prevalent in America, and we have been warned about it by some of the American consumer groups." Shortly after he spoke an interesting example cropped up in Philadelphia.

In December 1978 a Philadelphia company, American Consumer Inc., one of the largest mail order firms in the

United States, agreed to refund more than 5,500 customers who had each spent $15.95 on something called "the Cross of Lourdes." These crosses were advertised as having been "dipped in the waters at the Shrine of Our Lady of Lourdes and blessed in Rome by Pope Paul VI." This claim had been made in such papers as *Grit* and the *National Enquirer*. Somehow this advertisement came to the attention of the Justice Department, and American Consumer Inc. faced a one-thousand-count mail-fraud indictment and a possible fine of $1m. As part of an arrangement in mitigation, or a plea bargain, the company agreed to repay $103,000 to 5,500 customers who had purchased crosses in good faith. All but 240 of the customers, who had already changed address, were repaid.

It might be thought rather odd that the American Justice Department should be concerned with simony, and with the erroneous idea that grace can be acquired by the passage of money from hand to hand. It even raises the possibility that there are Jansenists at work in Washington, concerned at this late date to deny all suggestion that grace can be "acquired" at all. But in fact Assistant U.S. Attorney Michael Cohen's objections were quite distinct from those of the Grotto chaplains. The prosecution case was based on the claim that the crosses had never been taken to Lourdes but had been sprayed in the United States with bottled Lourdes water. Nor had they ever been blessed by the Pope. In other words the chaplains were concerned that a papal blessing had been given and then sold. Mr. Cohen was objecting that the blessing had never been given. Mr. Cohen considered that because the crosses had only been sprayed with Lourdes water and had never been to Lourdes that was another misrepresentation, whereas the chaplains, as consignors of Lourdes water to all parts of the world, would have seen no difference between spraying the crosses in Philadelphia and immersing them in Lourdes. God and Mammon, though united in disapproval, continued to demand quite different values from their bewildered subjects.

Another sensitive point of contact between the Domain

and commerce occurs with the sale of candles. Candles play an important part in the ceremonies at Lourdes. The nightly Torchlight procession consists of thousands of people each carrying a candle with a special hood which they have purchased in the town. The hood is printed with the words of the *Ave* processional theme tune and the *Credo* in Latin. As to those candles, there is no problem. They are sold by shopkeepers and used at will by their customers. It is the other candles about which questions are always asked.

Within the Domain directly on the way to the Grotto, there are enormous racks containing candles at many sizes and prices. The sale of these candles is one of the four commercial enterprises conducted by the chaplains within the grounds of the Domain—the other three are a bookshop, a printing press and an office for receiving offerings. The candles, which are in blue and white, the Marian colours, are then carried past the Grotto to the great wrought-iron candle racks which have been set up in the open air. Things turn out in such a way that what with the breeze, the jostling, and the continual need for new candles to be set up, very few of the candles purchased are actually burnt for even half their length. Once the candles are extinguished they are taken away by the permanent staff who are employed solely to attend to candles, and stored in nearby huts. Pilgrims who see this happening are inclined to ask what will happen to their candle next, and, in the words of the *Official Guide*, the "suspicious" people even wonder if it is going to be sold again. The townspeople, or some of them, are quite convinced that the chaplains arrange for these candles to be melted down and reworked into another candle. The chaplains say that in truth the candles are stored and then relit and burnt during the winter. "When silence falls once again in Massabielle, from November to March, more than a ton of candles will burn each day. Whoever comes to Lourdes during this period is struck by the sight of this great light blazing in the night, bearing witness to the prayer of millions of men and women," says the *Guide*.

Though it is, of course, a conventional point of ritual that a candle lit in prayer should burn right down, nobody is likely to make much fuss if it does not do so. But there are those in the town who adopt a cynical view. The son of one hotelkeeper said that in his father's hotel the *chariot* which is supposed to be heading for the Grotto loaded with enormous votive candles turns instead in the opposite direction towards the premises of the candle makers. That, if it happens, is not the act of the Church. And the cynicism of the townspeople may be no more than an unwillingness to believe that the chaplains could act better than they do themselves. Investigation in February showed that both claims could be partly right.

In winter the huts are indeed full to the roof with unfinished candles, and these are indeed wheeled out, relit and burnt by the ton in the blustery air until they dissolve. Most Lourdes candles are probably burnt far more thoroughly than most votive candles lit in enclosed churches the world over. But the candles are placed close together and they burn very fast, as they must if they are to stay alight in that damp, windy place. The result is that a great quantity of molten, liquid wax collects in the drip trays beneath. This is run off into smaller drip trays, in which there is no discernible trace of a wick, and the attendants are then faced with the alternative of throwing away a lot of molten wax or re-using it. An unmarked van carries the molten wax away and one can only hope that if it is eventually recycled, the price of the candles produced will reflect that economy.

Delving into the great candle question, it is possible to go too deep. The candle has a value and is bought for a purpose. It is sold on the understanding that it will be thoroughly burnt. Lighting it is a ritual and while it burns it is a symbol of prayer. That is all that matters to the pilgrim who buys and lights a candle, and to accomplish that is entirely within his power. Beyond that it is a matter of doubt how many pilgrims are at all concerned about what eventually happens to the candles. They come to Lourdes trustingly. They are accustomed to using various symbolic de-

vices as an assistance to prayer. They do not regard prayer
as a mechanism like an electric light bulb. That is why the
dishonest *commerçants* find it so easy to cheat them. And
that is why they are not concerned about the ultimate fate
of their candles. They are accustomed to trusting. However fly they may be at home, in Lourdes they consider
that the accomplishment of the intention outweighs the ac-
complished fact.

The crowds in the Domain include certain visitors
whose presence is as great a tribute to the popularity of the
shrine as is that of the regular pilgrims. These are the
criminals. Departmental statistics show that Lourdes has a
very high rate of crime. In 1976 in the Department of the
High Pyrenees the total number of criminal offences was,
at twenty-three per thousand of the population, lower than
the national average of thirty-six; but Lourdes had fifty-
four cases per thousand people, against the national average for small towns of twenty-five, and exactly twice as
many as Tarbes, the departmental capital, which has three
times the population. Nineteen per cent of all delinquency
and medium-serious crimes that occur in the High
Pyrenees occur in Lourdes, and thirty per cent of the most
serious offences. Furthermore, since the overwhelming majority of Lourdes crimes occur in the summer, it means
that the high season rate is higher than London's, possibly
as high as West Berlin's, which, at 105, is the highest in
Europe.

In view of this, it is hard to understand the chaplains'
insistence that "although there is crime in the Domain it is
very small in view of the numbers. The police always say
so." There have been rapes and attacks in the Domain, to
the point that it was once rumoured that they were the
reason for the main gates being closed at night. Others said
that it was the famous bomb which blew a hole in the roof
of the underground basilica in 1977. Responsibility for the
bomb was never established. Some officials blamed it on
the Tridentine Catholics, who were on pilgrimage at the
time—without any evidence. A more likely group might

have been the Spanish Basque separatists. Lourdes and the surrounding regions shelter numerous Basque refugees, many of them atheists who have carried out numerous outrages in the area, usually against Spanish government property. The buses bringing Spanish pilgrims to the shrine have sometimes been burnt.

But in any case the unexplained bomb was hardly typical of crime in the Domain. The common offences are purse snatching, pickpocketing, hotel-room rifling (not shoplifting, since very little in the piety shops has a value outside the town), and impersonating a priest, usually in order to obtain money. Less usually, there is trouble with members of foreign sects such as the Moonies, who were once thrown out for scribbling obscenities in front of the statue of the Crowned Virgin. The favourite place for pickpockets is by the water taps on a busy day when there is considerable jostling. Sometimes genuine priests behave in an inappropriate manner, and are discreetly removed. Sometimes genuine pilgrims, seeing the opportunity, turn to theft. Sometimes naturists choose to sunbathe on the grassy roof of the underground basilica, which is still supposedly set aside, like all the grass in the Domain, for the bishop's cattle. Until recently people would approach the box of petitions set into the wall of the Grotto and just help themselves, confident that they would find money in some of the envelopes. (The box has now been moved farther out of reach.) Even overdevout pilgrims who try to chip away some of the Grotto stone are committing an offence, in direct line of descent from the early cultists who destroyed the rose bush associated with the visions within weeks. The rose bush pruners were not perhaps criminals; but the fourteenth apparition was postponed from morning to afternoon, and some thought it was because the Grotto had been defiled during the night. As the devout say today, "the Lady said 'let the people come,' not just the good people." The chaplains rely on a large force of plain-clothes policemen and policewomen to be present in the Domain during the summer.

The most frequently maligned of all the writers who have
come to Lourdes and criticized it is also one of the greatest
to have devoted his time to the subject. The popular Catholic attitude to Émile Zola was set in rigid lines as soon as
he had published his novel, *Lourdes*. He was described as
a fraud and a liar who had falsified the facts, and as an
atheist fanatic. This remains the official attitude today. As
recently as 1956 a popular book stated that:

> One of the worst frauds against Lourdes was perpe-
> trated by Zola, who, by his own confession, in his
> novel *Lourdes* deliberately altered the facts in ac-
> counts of three cures and made their stories come out
> to suit himself—i.e. in death, not health as actually
> occurred. "My characters are my own," Zola grandly
> wrote to Dr. Boissarie. "I shall do whatever I like
> with them." But they were *not* his characters. They
> were living persons whose stories he had purloined
> and abused; only using enough of the truth to leave
> no doubt as to *who* they were, but changing the ends
> of the stories so as to make the conclusion entirely
> false. When his ruse became known he secretly visited
> the cured persons and offered them comfortable sums
> of money to leave Paris and live in a foreign country.

Ruth Cranston in *The Mystery of Lourdes* gave no evidence for her last allegation, but it sounds most unlike the
high-minded crusader of the Dreyfus affair.

The hero of Zola's book is a priest who has lost his faith
and who witnesses the "miraculous" cure of a dying girl
who, he is convinced, was suffering from an hysterical illness. The book has been described as "hardly a novel,"
and like most of Zola's novels it was also intended as a di-
dactic work. But enough time has now passed for the devout to give Zola's book the credit it deserves. It paints a
very lively picture of the town as it was in 1890 and 1891.
It shows great sympathy for the religious feeling. It lev-
elled some criticisms against the early system of medical
inspection which were subsequently acknowledged by the

Lourdes authorities when they altered that system. And in an interview in 1894 Zola acknowledged that there had been many genuine cures at Lourdes, although he attributed these to undiscovered natural causes. The most interesting and most deadly argument that Zola puts forward is that the phenomenon of Lourdes was "the story of the foundation of all religions." He believed that at Lourdes he had perceived "almost a new religion."

That there was an element of truth in this cannot be denied. There was for a start the authority given to the private visions of an uneducated young girl, somebody who—viewed from the peak of the male, educated, elderly, clerical hierarchy that governs the Church—was of negligible importance in theological argument. There was also the terrific impetus which Lourdes gave to Marianism in the nineteenth-century Church—to such a degree that a rival movement was started to encourage pilgrimages to shrines directly associated with Christ, starting with Avignon.*

The distance travelled in these controversies by "Lourdes" can be measured from a stone, which is set into the statue of St. Peter at the entrance to the crypt of the Upper Basilica. This statue, which reproduces the famous statue of Peter in Rome, was donated by the French National pilgrimage of 1878. By kissing the right foot of the statue pilgrims may gain the same indulgences as would be theirs if they had journeyed to Rome and kissed the famous worn-out right foot of the statue there. The difference is that the Rome right foot became worn by reason of its convenient kissability, and popular devotion and the passing of time. The Lourdes right foot has become worn by cosmetic art.

Cut into the pedestal of this statue there is a prayer which ends with a declaration of belief in the dogma of the Infallibility of the Pope. That dogma, which may have done more to separate the Catholic Church from the rest

---

* This developed into the series of international eucharistic congresses presided over by a papal legate. It was a great success, but its counter-Marian uses were rather limited; the Eucharistic Congress was itself staged at Lourdes in 1899 and 1914, and will be there again in 1981.

of Christianity than any other promulgation of the nineteenth century, was an inspiration for the early, middle
and quite recent Lourdes. It is not so any longer.
Consider the words of a Grotto father in 1979 who was asked first
about the possibility of Anglican pilgrimages to Lourdes.
"Yes," he said, "we like them to come. It would be rather
difficult for them to hold divine service in a central position perhaps, but that is not a problem because they are always quite a small group, and so they fit naturally into one
of the smaller sanctuaries. They are most welcome to worship in their own liturgy discreetly." Then the Grotto father was asked about pilgrimages of the Tridentine Catholics, that is those who follow the authorized and ancient
liturgy that was universal until the Second Vatican Council
which opened in 1958. The chaplain's face darkened. "The
Tridentinists," he said, "need reminding that the Domain
is private property, and belongs to the diocese. We allow
them to enter but we succeed in isolating them. Last time
they came they wanted to say mass in the Grotto. This was
not possible, but they seized the altar anyway in an act of
disobedience. There were three hundred of them, and at
that time there were forty thousand regular pilgrims in
Lourdes."

As a matter of fact this description does not do justice
to the alarm which was caused when the Tridentine pilgrims turned up. As soon as the bishop heard that they
were coming he took the novel step of publishing new
regulations covering behaviour in the Domain. Demonstrations, parades, public prayers, singing and music, the
very business of the shrine since it had first opened, were
henceforth banned, presumably allowing the rector to call
for police assistance if any such devotions took place without his approval. This move recalled the original ner-
vousness of the ecclesiastical authorities in 1858 when they
approved the police barricades around the Grotto, and it
was about as successful. The Tridentinists paraded into the
Domain anyway, their reverence only diminished by the
Rector of Sanctuaries in person, who equipped himself
with a loudspeaker and "forbad" any pilgrims present

from joining the Tridentine procession "even out of curiosity."

"Lourdes," bellowed the rector, "is a place of fraternity, peace and prayer which wants to remain in close communion with the Holy Father and with the bishops united with him. The threats which the Tridentinists have proffered publicly on the occasion of this gathering are stamped with aggression and violence." But the three or four hundred traditionalists filed down to the Grotto anyway, singing the Lourdes hymn. And finding that so far from seizing it they could not even approach the altar, as it was barricaded, they crossed the bridge and said mass in the meadow opposite. "Our intention was not to occupy the sanctuaries," said their leader afterwards, "but to pray." However, the rector, in the true spirit of the old Garaison fathers, filed an official complaint with the police against the Tridentine Abbé for "failure to respect the private Domain of the Grotto." The spirit of Father Peyramale must have felt very much at home.

For Lourdes, this was an extraordinary scene.* Lourdes, the traditional stronghold of Marianism and the ultramontane movement and a bastion of the temporal power of an infallible papacy, was here rejecting that segment of Catholic opinion which could most easily be represented, since it was traditionalist, as the natural heirs to the ultramontane movement. As late as the 1950s the Vatican, in attempting to heal the post-war divisions and uncertainties of the Church, had chosen to emphasize Lourdes (and Fatima, as a second Lourdes), Marianism and papal infallibility, drawing on the strength of its most traditional positions. But following the Second Vatican Council the changes which overtook the Church were to become more visible at Lourdes than anywhere else. To some extent this may have been because it came naturally to Lourdes to act as a liturgical innovator. Strengthened by the traditionalist

* The battle continued in 1979, when a group of youthful traditionalists imprisoned the Rector in his own Basilica. This incident evoked a letter of protest to the President of France from the hotel managers of Lourdes.

approval of Pius XII, Lourdes was in the perfect position
to ride on the new wave undammed by John XXIII, even
though this was running in exactly the opposite direction.

There was another and a particularly French incentive
to do this. The French priesthood, and the French Church
generally, is weak. Faced with an internal crisis, the
French hierarchy has placed its trust in liturgical innovation. It has repeated the original tactic, only this time the
bishops have looked for their model to the supposed future
of religion rather than to its known past.

The newest sanctuary in the Domain, the underground
basilica, which was completed in 1958 in time for the centenary celebrations, has proved to be admirably suited to
this new purpose. The Pius X Basilica is one of the largest
underground structures in the world, and with its naked
concrete ribbing and wide approach ramps it resembles
nothing so much as a gigantic underground car park. It
has been designed to make it possible to hold the usual
ceremonies in bad weather, with the eventual possibility of
extending the Lourdes season throughout the bitter Pyrenean winter. (The *commerçants* gave ten per cent of their
takings in the record centenary year towards its cost.) But
with the new freedom of liturgical practice it has become
an ideal forum for the "concelebrated mass," at which several hundred priests can gather around its vast central
altar. Sometimes the ministers grouped together in such
numbers and in uniform vestments make it impossible for
the congregation to see past them to the ceremony they are
performing. The concelebrated mass has obvious advan-
tages in Lourdes, where so many priests come from all
over the world, and where there is a limited number of
altars, but, to anyone aware of the crisis of numbers in the
French priesthood, and craning his neck for a view of the
ceremony beyond, it sometimes seems as though every
priest in France is standing on the altar steps of Pius X in
a reassuring display of strength. And the concelebrated
mass, so impressive in theory, is not always so impressive
in sight. The beautiful vestments, dignified when unique,
are less dignified when they are worn by a hundred simul-

taneous celebrants—ninety-nine of them superfluously shadowing the actions of the single, central priest who was formerly supposed to be sufficient to perform the sacrifice; the increase in priestly numbers inescapably suggests a loss in individual priestly power.

Asked about the great number of liturgical changes at Lourdes one of the chaplains replied, "Everything changes. Not substantially, just in its form." The heart of this defence is of course that the form is unimportant, it is the substance which is essential. But that invites the retort, "Then why change the inessential, since it was for many the means of approaching the substance. What evidence is there that more damage will not be caused by changing it than not?" The chaplain continued, "The younger chaplains and *brancardiers* feel differently to the old ones." No doubt he is right; and, no doubt, a little variety in the work of the chaplaincy would be very welcome, but does the new generation of pilgrims feel differently? Since the most numerous group of individuals among Lourdes pilgrims are French women aged over sixty it is hard to imagine that much pressure was placed on the authorities for "liturgical innovation containing increased amounts of spontaneity and informality" from that direction. On the contrary, the modern liturgy of Lourdes suggests that all the pressure for change came not from the laity, whose support for it is always used as its justification, but from the clergy themselves. The reform of the liturgy was the response of priests, rational men charged with the task of defending an irrational belief in an age of increasingly insistent rationalism, who suffered from a growing sense of isolation.

The strengths and weaknesses of the new approach are well illustrated by the changes which have overtaken the rite which was formerly known as the Last Sacrament, or extreme unction. The rule was that this could only be administered to the dying. It was reserved for them as a special comfort and support, to reassure them that everything that man could possibly do had been done to assist their salvation. It was a final honour to be anointed with the sa-

cred oils which were otherwise reserved for the consecration of priests or monarchs. All this has now been replaced at Lourdes by "the anointing of the sick," a
ceremony which does not require the anointees to be
dying, and the intention of which is "to take the fear out
of extreme unction." It seems that under the old arrangement many of those who received the Last Sacrament, that
is to say those who were dying, were put in fear of their
lives. Now they can be slipped in among the routinely invalid.

In its desire for the appearance of compassion the new
arrangement ignores the fact that extreme unction, by preparing a person for the impending fact of his own death,
was itself "designed to take the fear out of" that event. By
acknowledging the imminence of death it concentrated the
dying man's mind on the question of his immortal future.
The fact of death was accepted rather than obscured. And
if it did arouse fear, that might, to some extent, be a good
thing for the members of a Church which taught that the
state of one's soul and the life after death were of more
importance than the state of one's body and the life upon
earth. By conceding the possibility that the Last Sacrament
might be more frightening than comforting, the reformed
Church was responding to the temporal priorities of the
world at the very moment in the life of a soul when, by
the Church's own teaching, it should have been doing the
exact opposite; and at the very moment when, by general
secular agreement, its spiritual ministrations were of su-
preme value. It was also, incidentally, diluting the symbolic power of its sacraments.

The visitor to Lourdes who was looking for evidence of
a reaction among the pilgrims against this democratic enthusiasm of the reforming liturgists would soon find it.
Lourdes is a natural forum for the idea of the Universal
Church, and the obvious language for a universal church is
a universal language. That, until the reforms took hold, the
Church always had. Once a day the *Credo*, the only part
of the central daily liturgy still to be said in Latin, concludes the Torchlight procession, uniting all present more

completely than any number of multilingual invocations. Everyone, French, Italian, German, English and Irish, Vietnamese, African, Polish, suddenly feels the strength of the Universal Church. And the frequent annoyance among those foreign pilgrims who have missed the daily mass in their own language and cannot find a Latin mass in its place, reinforces this impression of loss.

The degree of innovation which Lourdes has undergone can also be seen in the smaller sanctuaries, such as the chapel of St. Joseph. Here it is not unusual for the priests to outnumber their congregation. It makes a melancholy contrast with the embattled times when the members of a congregation would travel for days to a secret meeting with one fugitive priest, all present facing the possibility of martyrdom, to see the benches of St. Joseph's today, crammed with celebrants while a scattering of lay worshippers look on from the rear of the church. At the moment of communion the priests who are assembled in the front pews crack their consecrated Hosts, scattering the crumbs all over the floor (a mishap which would formerly have resulted in a ritual—now dubbed "scrupulous" —triple scrubbing). Then a congregation of mainly plain-clothes nuns walk up for their communion. They receive the Host on the altar steps, and proceed to the altar where they lift the chalice to their own lips. This provides the unusual sight, for a Catholic mass, of a group of fashionably dressed women standing around the altar making the ritual gestures of a priest. There is something almost perverse about the delight with which some of the religious and clergy present in Lourdes take the opportunity not just to abandon the mysterious symbolism of the old liturgy, but to parody it. Outside the chapel after the service a Dominican friar in traditional habit but carrying a leather handbag chats to a Sister of Charity of the Order of Nevers dressed in a fur hat, fur-trimmed coat and leather boots.

At another mass in St. Joseph's, celebrated during the Catholic Association Annual Pilgrimage, it was proposed to bless the sick children. This idea developed into a "party-mass" with audience participation. After the conventional reverence of the consecration, there was a period of charismatic inspiration, when anyone moved by the spirit could shout whatever came into his head; and then there was a confirmation ceremony for one of the children who was dying. The presiding priest said that for confirmation one needed a bishop but unfortunately there was no bishop present. However, if all the children clapped loud enough a bishop might appear. This the bishop, who had been waiting in the sacristy, duly did. Balloons and paper streamers were then thrown around and the concelebrating priests joined hands and skipped up the side aisles singing "Lord of the Dance." Flowers were distributed among the worshippers. Everyone looked very happy, particularly the priests.

❦ VII ❦

The End of the Season

> All visions, revelations and impressions of
> heaven, however much the spiritual man may
> esteem them, are not equal in worth to the
> least act of humility: for this brings forth the
> fruits of charity, which never esteems nor
> thinks well of self, but only of others.
>
> St. John of the Cross

Many of the pilgrimages that cross France on their way to
Lourdes select a route that passes through Nevers. This enables the pilgrims to see the final miracle associated with
the life of Bernadette, her uncorrupted body, which is exposed in the chapel of the Convent of St. Gildard.

After her retirement from the public stage in Lourdes,
Bernadette went to live up the hill at the Convent of the
Sisters of Nevers. At that time this was the only convent in
the town. Then, as her fame spread, there began a period
of fairly intense competition between many of the con-
vents of south-west France to see which of them could attract Bernadette's permanent interest. Over the next six
years, during which time Mgr. Laurence sanctioned the
cult at the Grotto and the Sisters of Nevers provided her
with a strictly disciplined education, Bernadette gradually
acquired the certainty that she had a religious vocation. In
April 1864 the statue of Our Lady of Lourdes, which still
stands in the Grotto today, was inaugurated. Bernadette
had been critical of the statue and did not attend this ceremony but remained in the convent where she received

communion at that morning's mass. After mass she told
the superior of the house that she wished to enter the
Order of Nevers. Previously she had been attracted to the
Carmelites, a contemplative order whose life would have
been too hard for anyone in her state of health. She had
also considered the Bernardines, the Sisters of the Cross
and the Sisters of St. Vincent de Paul. But the first would
not have her, again because of her health, and because of
her public following, and when she visited the second and
tried on their massive headdress she said, "I want nothing
to do with this tunnel."

There seems at that time to have been a curious
skittishness in the solemn matter of a nun's vocation, about
the differing costumes of the rival orders. Thus when Bernadette was accepted into the Order of Nevers, but before
she had joined it, the sisters gathered together and took
two group photographs, one with Bernadette in civilian
clothes, and the other with her "trying on" the habit.
There is an element of fashion here. Again when she
visited the Sisters of Saint Vincent de Paul she returned
saying, "I had quite a bad time of it today . . . those nuns
tried their habit on me, but I didn't feel at all attracted."
(The conventional response to this discomfort was to say
that it was the sign of a vocation.)

Similarly when Bernadette was welcomed to the convent of St. Gildard in Nevers she had to describe to the
assembled community all the headdresses that had been
tried on her by the rival orders. (And when she spent
some of her early days in tears she was again told that this
was the sign of a solid vocation.) But fashion or not, the
telling point for Bernadette was that the Sisters of Nevers
had had the sense not to solicit her interest. And she once
said, "I am going to Nevers because they did not lure me
there."

Nevers today is a town of 47,000 people. It has a cathedral, a ducal palace, a museum of local earthenware and
the river Loire. Its tourist board proposes the town as a
historic and religious capital, which it is—like all the old

towns of the Loire. It is a pleasant place with some well-preserved walls and battlements, but the province of Burgundy has many towns which are more historic, and the river Loire passes through several which are more beautiful.

Nevers Cathedral is not one of the showpieces of medieval architecture. In winter it is as bleak a building as one could find. The town was severely bombarded by the allies in 1944 and the cathedral now has no stained glass. Outside, the blackened and spiky gargoyles form its chief curiosity. Inside, on the Feast of Our Lady of Lourdes, there was water dripping from the roof, and only two old believers praying in the afternoon gloom. Their breath rose in clouds, which was curious because mine had not done so outside in the full chill of February at 4 p.m. Two large rubber plants had been placed behind the high altar to celebrate the Feast, but their tropical associations did not warm the stark and blasted surroundings.

In a side-chapel there were candles burning in front of the statue of St. Anthony of Padua, the saint who finds things which have been lost, and the image of St. Teresa of Avila was also attended by candles and flowers. But one had to peer high up into the back of another unlit chapel to see the undecorated statue of Our Lady of Lourdes. There is supposed to have been some rivalry between Lourdes and Nevers over the question of memorials, but if so it must have died years ago, at least as far as Nevers is concerned. The town was far more interested in the "return" of a middle-aged pop singer, Johnny Hallyday, on 26 February, eve of the Feast of St. Gabriel of Our Lady of Sorrows. Posters for this earthly resurrection everywhere outnumbered those for the Abbé Laurentin's illustrated lecture, "The Face of Bernadette," promoting his latest work on the subject—which is a two-volume collection of the many pictures of the saint.

The finest old church in Nevers is, in any case, not the cathedral but the terrific Romanesque fortress of St. Stephen's, an eleventh-century bastion which seems to have absorbed such of the town's religious life as survives. Here a whole wall is studded with *"reconnaissances infinies"* tablets to Mary, to St. Anthony (again) and to St. Jude, the patron of lost causes rather than lost objects. It seems to be a town which has mislaid a lot.

The ducal palace is advertised as "the first of the châteaux of the Loire" but in fact even the distant view of this from the river has been lost. As one makes one's way through the barren municipal flower beds in front of the palace and reaches the terrace overlooking the Loire, it is to discover that a beneficent municipality has placed a nine-storey, flat-roofed, drip-marked, concrete lump between the bank and the slope. This improvement is marked in large letters, Maison de la Culture de Nevers—Animations—Spectacles—Cafeteria—Bourse du Travail—Maison des Sports—Motel; a hideous complex of sustaining projects that manages to drain the famous light from the broad waters and all the life from the brown stones of the magnificent road bridge which not even the allied bombs could mark. As one descends the slope to the Fun palace/Labour exchange/Motel one passes the memorial to Achille Millien 1838–1927, a forgotten celebrity, who gazes back in panama hat and copper bas-relief from the far bank to the distant town: "Land of Nevers, my cradle," says the inscription. "I never left You," from which one concludes that he did. If Achille is looking back still he will see all that he was yearning for so deliciously, the old town clustered above the water, the imposing distanced height of the cathedral, the just-so angles of the bridge, obscured by the grey glob of the House of Culture. One resident questioned on the subject replied explosively, "Don't even mention it to me. The municipality has, I calculate, placed the entire town in debt for the remainder of all our lives. And we already had a sports stadium." He had to retire into the Café du Pont de la Grippe to restore himself.

In the street named rue de Casse-Cou, which pitches from the town to the river at an alarming rate, there was another poster, this time advertising a High Mass billing the Archbishop of Sens, on 18 February, the centenary Feast day of the saint's death. In the list of Local Feasts in the *St. Andrew's Daily Missal* (issued on the highest authority 1958, semi-obsolete 1963), the entry for 18 February states:

> St. Mary Bernard Soubirous [Bernadette] after hearing the Blessed Virgin say "I am the Immaculate Conception" [which confirmed the dogma officially proclaimed by Pius IX in 1854] left everything to purchase the kingdom of heaven and entered the convent of the Sisters of Charity at Nevers in 1866. Here she was given the name of Sister Mary Bernard, and died on 16 April 1879, after a hidden life of prayer and penance. She was canonized by Pope Pius XI on 8 December 1933; in 1936 her feast was allowed to be celebrated in some places a week after the feast of Our Lady of Lourdes.

What the *Missal* does not mention is the degree of suffering which Bernadette experienced before she died. The last three years of her life were spent in a state of unremitting illness, until she finally succumbed to a number of conditions and in particular to tuberculosis of the lungs. In view of the state of her body when she was alive—tuberculosis with ankylosis of the knee, which was hideously swollen and painful, a back that was almost completely peeled of skin from bed sores, as well as advanced decay of the lungs—the subsequent state of her corpse is all the more unusual. For three days after her death her remains were displayed for public veneration. The body was photographed, suitably arranged with a rosary and a double coronet of roses. During this time (according to Zola), "the body underwent no change, but was interred on the third day, still supple, warm, with red lips and a very white skin, rejuvenated as it were, and smelling sweet." Zola's description almost suggests that she was buried alive, but he was merely reporting the popular beliefs of 1894, at which time the cause of Bernadette's canonization had not yet been opened. That the possibility was, nonetheless, in the minds of the nuns from the moment of her death is

shown by the lying-in-state. Every religious order is naturally greedy for saints, who boost morale and influence
recruitment. But in the case of Bernadette there was
influential opposition from Mother Vauzou, her former
novice mistress, who was never entirely convinced of the
genuineness of the vision, and whose own spirituality was
founded on a devotion to Christ and to the Sacred Heart.

When the three days were up, Bernadette's body was
placed in a double coffin of lead and oak which was sealed
in the presence of witnesses. Six weeks later, after obtaining a special permission, the coffin was placed in a new
vault beneath an outlying chapel in the gardens of the convent. In 1909 an episcopal commission enquiring into the
possibility of her canonization, and wishing to discover
whether the body had been spared the customary putrefaction, retrieved the coffin and opened it.* Among those
present were two doctors. They later reported on their unusual task as follows:

> The coffin was opened in the presence of the Bishop
> of Nevers, the mayor of the town, his principal dep-
> uty, several canons and ourselves. We noticed no
> smell. The body was clothed in the habit of Berna-
> dette's order. The habit was damp. Only the face,
> hands and forearms were uncovered.
>
> The head was tilted to the left. The face was matt
> white. The skin clung to the muscles and the muscles
> adhered to the bones. The sockets of the eyes were
> covered by the eyelids. The brows were flat on the
> skin and stuck to the arches above the eyes. The
> lashes of the right eyelid were stuck to the skin. The
> nose was dilated and shrunken. The mouth was open
> slightly, and it could be seen that the teeth were still
> in place. The hands, which were crossed on her
> breast, were perfectly preserved, as were the nails.
> The hands still held a rusting rosary. The veins on the
> forearms stood out.

* The absence of putrefaction in a corpse is traditionally regarded
by the Church as a sign of sanctity.

Like the hands, the feet were wizened and the toe-
nails were still intact (one of them was torn off
when the corpse was washed). When the habits had
been removed and the veil lifted from the head, the
whole of the shrivelled body could be seen, rigid and
taut in every limb.

It was found that the hair, which had been cut
short, was stuck to the head and still attached to the
skull—that the ears were in a state of perfect preservation—that the left-hand side of the body was
slightly higher than the right from the hip up.

The stomach had caved in and was taut like the
rest of the body. It sounded like cardboard when
struck.

So rigid was the body that it could be rolled over
and back for washing.

The lower parts of the body had turned slightly
black. This seems to have been the result of the car-
bon of which quite large quantities were found in the
coffin.

In witness of which we have duly drawn up this
present statement in which all is truthfully recorded.

Nevers, 22 September, 1909

Dr. Ch. David, A. Jourdan.

After the examination was complete, the nuns washed the
body and placed it in a different coffin lined with zinc. In
the few hours of the examination it had all started to turn
black. The coffin was then re-lowered into the vault.

Approximately the same procedure was carried out
twice more, once in 1919 and once in 1925; an extraordinary triple investigation in which the meticulous formu-
lae of the civilian French administration stand in odd contrast to the ancient preoccupations of the Church. So, in
1919, at the second exhumation, the police commissioner
made out his routine form which was normally intended
for posthumous murder inquiries. But in this case the
name of the deceased is not "Jean Dupont" or "Chantal

Souris," but "the Venerable Sister Marie Bernard, née Bernadette Soubirous."

By the time of the final examination in 1925 the repeated exposures had caused the process of normal putrefaction to start. And so when various relics, two ribs, part of the liver and diaphragm and the two kneecaps, had been removed, the forty-six-year-old corpse, as after any surgical procedure, was swathed in bandages and the somewhat macabre undertaking drew to a close. Imprints of the face and hands were then moulded in wax and taken to Paris so that a leading firm could make a mask based on the moulds and on contemporary photographs. This was done because "it was feared that . . . the blackish tinge to the face and the sunken eyes and nose would make an unpleasant impression on the public." While the mask and a suitable shrine were being made the body lay exposed for a period of three months in a locked chapel, and the nuns of that day were able to observe it through a window. Finally, when the Paris firm had delivered the mask and the Lyons firm had delivered the shrine, the nuns opened the chapel and dressed the body in another new habit. Then the masks were put in place, the nuns posed for one last group photograph around the body, and the remains of Bernadette were laid in the shrine. It is this arrangement which is now on view in the chapel of the convent.

The Sisters of Charity, an order which once extended to 200 houses, now face the crisis familiar to so many religious orders—lack of vocations. The solution favoured by these nuns has been drastic if not original. They have abandoned the veil and closed many of their foundations, and the mother house, once a place of strict seclusion, has become a conference centre and an installation which can be hired for retreats. It is a handsome early nineteenth-century building which has been extensively altered. The long communal dormitory has been broken up into a line of twin-bedded compartments with modern furniture for the conferees. Room after splendid room designed for prayer, study or work, now stands highly polished and empty of purpose. Each has been labelled with its former use, "library" or "sewing-room," and the remarkable thing is that this transformation of a living house into a museum has taken place while the community is still in residence. The little dispensary where Bernadette did her last work as infirmarian is now marked *"Mutuelle"*; the nuns subscribe to an insurance scheme.

The only nuns who do retain the habit and the veil confine themselves to the upper floors where the stream of restless or curious pilgrims do not intrude. There they can continue to lead the regulated life for which the whole community once claimed to have a vocation. Their work is still prayer, and their business-minded, kindly, efficient sisters below refer to the nuns on the upper floors as "our lightning conductors." There is certainly plenty of work for the free-ranging nuns to do. For pilgrims, the attraction of the convent grows with the increasing popularity of Lourdes. In 1979, 150 special trains bearing about one hundred thousand pilgrims were booked to stop at Nevers *en route* to Lourdes from Germany alone. It might be thought that for women who had been brought up within the routines of the old rule, organizing such an invasion would be too hard a task. But the life under the rule was not all that restrictive either. Sister Marie Noel, one of the few English members of the order, who was kind enough to show me round, had spent much of her life as a nun teaching at a foundation in Tunisia. Before that she had worked as a missionary sister in Japan, where she was interned during the war. She was in Nagasaki when the atom bomb went off, and she faced the prospect of a hundred thousand German pilgrims with equanimity. In the year that she joined the order and submitted herself to a supposedly sheltered future, there were thirty-six novices.

But the object of the pilgrimage to Nevers was not to hear of Sister Marie Noel's dangerous adventures but to see the body of the saint. The story of Bernadette's miraculous preservation is known by every regular pilgrim to Lourdes, and the feeling of expectancy as the devout enter the chapel of the convent is high. The body is the first

thing you see. It lies in a golden casket with glass sides
which is the shape, and about twice the size, of a coffin.
The body rests as on a death bed with the hands crossed
on the breast in an attitude of prayer; it is dressed in the
traditional habit of the order, with the head raised by an
embroidered silk pillow and turned slightly towards the
rail at which the public kneel. The mask bears a close resemblance to some of the photographs of the living face,
although the Parisian master was unable to resist the temp-
tation to improve imperceptibly on God and nature by reducing the hook in the nose and by giving the eyebrows
a slightly plucked appearance. It is nonetheless, without
quibbling, an impressive sight. Even Edith Saunders, the
English rationalist, and one of the most hostile writers ever
to publish a book on Lourdes, admitted to being moved by
the reliquary at St. Gildard. "The heart of any feeling
woman would be broken if she stood before the reliquary
at Nevers and saw within it her own child," she wrote.
"The saint looks so weary and so sad, although she sleeps
so peacefully."

The chapel itself is partly in the neo-Gothic style with
sharp stone vaulting and narrow windows. The casket,
made in 1925, includes such details as Roman burial urns
and gilded wreaths, themselves reminiscent of the imperial
glory of Napoleon I. There is a splendour and solidity to
the casket which would not be out of place *Aux Invalides*,
or at the tomb of a national hero such as Joan of Arc (if
she had one). The shrine includes stylistic references to
ancient Rome, medieval Europe, the late eighteenth century, the mid-nineteenth century and, in the virulent colours of the stained glass, to the taste of the 1950s. There
is nothing visibly evocative of the 1920s when the scene
was actually designed. And the religious habit, which provided the only genuine link between the saint's life and
today has, of course, recently been laid aside by most of
Bernadette's successors.

In leaving the convent of St. Gildard the pilgrims pass a
bookshop where they find a blow-by-blow account of the
three autopsies carried out on the body of Bernadette, and

the significance of its preservation. It is startling to read in the midst of these harrowing details the following passage:

> The fact that Bernadette's body was perfectly preserved (in 1909) is not necessarily miraculous. It is well-known that corpses decompose less in certain kinds of soil and gradually mummify. It should be noted, however, that in the case of Bernadette this mummified state is quite astounding. Her illnesses and the state of her body when she died, the humidity in the vault in the chapel (the habit was damp, the rosary rusty and the crucifix had turned green) would all seem to be conducive to disintegration of the flesh. We should be glad, therefore, that Bernadette benefitted from a fairly rare biological phenomenon. But this is not a "miracle" in the strictest sense of the word.

"The strictest sense of the word"; stony phrase—what can it mean? What can any of this whole, incredible business mean if the incorruptibility of the body is not to be regarded as a miraculous sign of personal sanctity? What was the purpose of the three autopsies, why is the corpse displayed, why indeed is the booklet published, what on earth are the pilgrims trooping in to see, if it is only to be regarded as a natural freak which might happen to any of us? The Church's consistent preoccupation with the weakness of the flesh, the mortality of the body, the transient unimportance of all worldly things, and its delight in the occasional echoes of the glorious resurrection of Christ, are all included in its ancient concern for the relative state of putrefaction in the corpse of a supposedly saintly person. It may be more awkward to insist on miracles when spontaneous mummification can sometimes occur naturally, but if a distinction is not to be made in the case of such Christian exemplars then the process of investigation and display had better be abandoned. Or, once again, the equivocal note of a modernized faith will have raised more questions than it answers.

Somewhere among the crowd attending the centenary mass held in St. Gildard on the Feast day of Our Lady of Lourdes there was one silent sympathizer with this point of view. For among the authorized leaflets which were available in the porch an unseen hand had secretly inserted an unauthorized communication. "Extract from the message of the Very Holy Virgin, the Queen of Heaven, given at San Damiano in Italy on 9 November, 1969," it read. "Tape recorded and then translated from the Italian." The message had been delivered to a pious clairvoyant, the Mamma Rosa, who said that the Queen of Heaven had appeared on a pear tree, *draped in red,* in a light which covered the whole world and that she was accompanied by the angels and martyrs. The message of the Queen of Heaven was lengthy and devoted to stern criticism of the post-Vatican II usage with regard to the Holy Eucharist. Priests, bishops and Pope Paul VI were criticized in turn for authorizing the taking of the host in communion by hand rather than on the tongue. "The Eternal Father grows weary . . . He is weary, the Eternal Father, I repeat, is weary." There then followed a promise of punishment if the old usage was not restored.

The chances of Mamma Rosa's vision being accepted are absolutely nil, since it is almost a cardinal principle in such matters that no vision which indulges in "negative criticisms," let alone criticisms of the hierarchy, can be regarded as authentic. Indeed the messages of Mamma Rosa have become something of a joke in Catholic circles. But somewhere in that obedient and well-drilled congregation there beat a rebellious and evangelizing heart, which still placed trust in an apparition.

Not all the international pilgrimages to Lourdes go by air or train. The Hosanna House Trust, for example, books the entire journey through by coach when the flights are finished. In October, just before the end of the season, a party of twenty-eight pilgrims from a small parish near St. Albans boarded an unconverted coach which was scheduled to make the trip in thirty hours. Seven of the pilgrims

were classed as sick. There was to be no diversion to
Nevers this time; just a straight dash to Lourdes.

The road journey, which is the cheapest method, is also
the penitential route. There was a thick fog in the Channel
that night. The coach was delayed on the road to South-
ampton by fog, and when it did arrive, just in time, it was
to find that the boat it was booked onto was cancelled because of a seamen's strike. But fortunately there was room
on another boat. Although the pilgrim coach arrived last
and without advance warning it was driven on first, and
the sick with their helpers were settled into reclining seats
before any other passengers had boarded. Such a small pilgrimage can be organized much less formally. There were
no *brancardiers,* though two of the adult sick were paralysed and the youngest pilgrim of all, a girl of four, was
dying. The group included one priest, one nun and four
nurses, and the other pilgrims helped out as they were
needed. In the morning, in Le Havre at seven o'clock, the
fog was even thicker. But eventually, after leaving the port
and driving in the pre-dawn past the smouldering indus-
trial furnaces on the banks of the Seine, and after climbing
up to the level of the toll bridge, the fog parted and the
pilgrimage found itself in thin clear sunlight and in the late
autumn of Normandy.

The villages on the penitential route have unusually interesting names. There is Captieux, which might be translated as "fond of taking exception," and Liverot and
Lieudevin and Les Nègres and even Roquefort. By the
roadside there were the black and white timbered barns
which always seem to spring up from apple country, with
a cider press below the loft and the yellow apples stacked
up against the trees in sacks, or rolling off the apple carts
and bouncing onto the road in front of the coach. In the
watery light a girl in jeans was hand-milking the big cows
that stood in a patient circle around her churns. She had
chosen the corner of the field nearest to the village
creamery.

Later it grew hotter. The corn stalks stood for mile upon
mile in the fields, brown, stripped and dead. A crumbling

white dry stone wall led to a crumbling stone gateway
leading to a crumbling château. Nothing barred the passer-
by except a crumbling signboard reading "private." We
drove for eight hours without a stop, which seemed an age.
Then in the early afternoon the coach reached a motorway
petrol station, where a lunch of soup and dry cake came
from a machine. This was a long way from the creameries
of Normandy.

As the day wore on the pilgrims dozed, and their coats
fell onto them unnoticed from the racks above. Outside
Angoulême the road passed *le Centre Psychothérapique*
with its spread of football pitches and its distant faceless
patients, playing for a cure. At Aire sur l'Adour there was
a "Pub Twickenham," first sign that we were in the south
and rugby country. There was also an advertisement for
les Grottes de Bétharram, the tourist diversion which had
once been a shrine. It was to be many miles farther before
the coach passed the first reference to Lourdes, and the
first statues of the virgin, blue and white and two feet high,
massed by the side of the road.

Eventually, after night had fallen, and after a long period of increasing pain for the sick, the coach arrived at
Bartrès. The pilgrims were staying in this village above
the town, at the Hosanna House hostel. The full moon lit
up the mist above the woods and the hills beyond. And occasionally, between the trees and the wide barns, one could
see a distant cross illuminated on a hilltop beyond the
town.

Lourdes in October, at the end of the season, seems to
recede into its past. There are still enough people to make
a press which requires supervision, but not enough to dis-
turb devotion. The misty drizzle which is characteristic of
the month is barely enough to make the candles sputter.
Watching the diminished crowds in the processions one
can see the essential simplicity of the arrangements. The
Torchlight procession is managed by no more than a few
lighted signs and a paved circuit. It works just as well for
two thousand people as it does for fifty thousand. In the

Grotto after the procession there is silence, but then, as
one walks back towards the river bank, about twenty yards
away, one hears people praying. By the embankment wall
there are two groups of seventy or so, one Italian, one
Irish, close together and saying the rosary, the same prayer
in different languages and at different speeds. But the arrangement of space, cliffs, water and air is such that they
cannot be heard by the people kneeling in the silence of
the Grotto. In October the chestnuts and planes which are
planted so thickly to guard the sick from the summer heat,
shed their leaves. These are swept into heaps and burnt,
and the green-grey smoke rises straight up through the
stillness of the thin twigs outside the empty windows of the
hospital.

As the crowds depart the spring grows in strength, and
the water starts to run down the slab of rock behind the
suspended crutches in the Grotto. But the Grotto is never
completely abandoned. Even if the pilgrims flag, there are
still the resident devotees. Two nuns from a nearby convent spend more than an hour there every day. They talk
to no one outside their order. They wear old-fashioned
workmanlike habits, full-length and of coarse grey material, beneath thick navy-blue overcoats. An old priest, a
pilgrim, with a livid poteen-patched face, arrives with a
carrier bag full of postcards from his Irish parishioners.
He kisses the ground in front of the Grotto, dumps his
postcards into the iron basket and then sits down near the
nuns to write some more of his own. Explaining the procedure about the letters left for Our Lady, one of the chaplains said that they were left for four days "for Our Lady
to read" and then the Sisters of Nevers opened them, removed any money and burnt them. He described them as
"a kind of superstition of humble people." Since people
would leave messages and money in the Grotto it had been
decided to tidy the whole business up. A blackbird rustled
in the ivy above the priest's head as he wrote, and spar-
rows crept through the moss near his feet. It was hard to
see why the written supplication of the letter was more su-

perstitious than the prayer spoken aloud, or even the silent
prayer of those considered cleverer than this priest.

The pilgrimage from St. Albans spent its time no
differently from any other. When the pilgrims were not occupied with their devotions there was enough left of the
town's busy summer life to interest them. One evening
they met two women who had flown in from Dublin and
who belonged to a society called "All Night Vigils of Dun
Laoghaire." Their party had arrived late on Saturday and
had gone straight to the crypt of the Upper Basilica where
they had spent the night in prayer, ending with early
morning mass. Then they had gone back to their hotel
where they were allowed the use of a room for the rest of
the day. They spent Sunday resting or going to the baths,
or taking part in the two great processions. They were to
fly home at about 2 a.m. and would be back at work on
Monday morning. They were treating the pilgrimage as a
fast, and neither of them would drink anything more than
coffee.

The younger one, a chubby blonde of eighteen, said that
neither she nor her friend were particularly religious. The
older one, who was about seventy, said that she had come
"because Our Lady wanted me." She might come again
next year and she might not; it depended on Our Lady.
The younger one said that she had come to thank Our
Lady for an improvement in health since last year, "when
I was not particularly well." "Is that all you prayed for, in
thanks?" asked the older one, who had red hair. "Didn't
you ask for a bonus?" "Well, I never turn down a bonus,"
said the younger one. "Oh, it's not the done thing, you
know, to ask for a bonus when you come in thanksgiving,"
said the older one, delighted to have caught her out.

In the Domain the crowds remained sufficiently large to
require one visiting spiritual director to guide his flock in
single file with the help of a walking stick held over his
shoulder, to the top of which he had attached a flashing
red torch. Outside the underground basilica a thin Italian
priest, who looked like a bank manager with his horn-
rimmed spectacles and briefcase, was hearing the confes-

sion of a handsome middle-aged woman, as both continued
to walk down the ramp. To give her absolution he had to
transfer the briefcase from his right hand to his left. One
afternoon there was a flurry of interest because a Jumbo
jet full of Japanese Roman Catholics had landed at the airport without warning. But they did not stretch the town's
resources. They only stayed three hours.

At the time the St. Albans pilgrimage was in Lourdes a
small group of English Poles were staying in the *Chalet
Across*, quite close to the Domain. It was the evening of
the election of John Paul II and the pilgrims were having
supper in the kitchen with a radio crackling away in the
corner, but it could hardly be heard because of the noise
of the conversation. Suddenly a nun in strict habit who
was standing beside the radio called for silence. She had
just caught a faint French voice amid the crackling saying
that a Pope had been elected. But the pilgrims did not hear
her and continued to talk. The nun, Sister Zenona, continued to listen by the radio, she looked strained as though
she knew what was about to happen. Then suddenly she
cried out and flung up her arms like a football fan. The
voluminous sleeves of her habit fell back and her white
arms, fists tightly clenched, stuck up in the air. "It is
Wojtyla," she cried. "Wojtyla is the Pope." Then she burst
into tears and ran out of the room.

Everyone else was stunned into silence. Nobody but
Sister Zenona had heard the radio, and she was gone. Then
the announcement was repeated more clearly, and the
room, apparently full of Englishmen but actually full of
Poles, realized that there was a Polish Pope for the first
time in history. A woman doctor started to jump up and
down with excitement. The pilgrims stopped eating. One of
the old men began to sob. For the older Poles everything
had to be translated by their children and grandchildren
who spoke French as well as English and Polish. Then, apparently spontaneously, all who could, rose and sang "God
protect Poland," the hymn which is also the Polish an-
them, and (if you include the original words asking for
Poland to be free again) is also an act of defiance against

the present régime. Many were in tears as they sang. Only when the hymn was finished would they accept the applause and congratulations of the other pilgrims in the chalet.

Sister Zenona came back, her face streaked and puffy, and apologized for crying. She went out onto the balcony to hear the bells ringing through the night from the spires beyond the river. She had been Cardinal Wojtyla's secretary in Cracow until "he sent me to England to learn English for him. When I heard his name just now I had such mixed feelings. I wanted the honour for him and for Poland, but I also wanted him to come back to Cracow, because we need him so much there." Then the leader of the pilgrimage, a young priest, came in from a long walk. He had heard the bells and was wondering what had happened. When he was told he clapped his hands and burst out laughing.

When they heard that at the election of the last Pope, two months earlier, the Italian pilgrims had led the Torchlight procession, some of the pilgrims started to make a banner. They got a large white sheet and some sellotape and covered half of the sheet with red paper napkins stuck together. They had not intended to go out that night, but four of the sick said they were well enough, and so this small group with its wheelchairs and home-made banner hurried down to the esplanade and arrived at the head of the waiting procession just as it was about to set off. The *brancardiers* there would have sent them back, having long since allocated the position of honour to a large Italian group from Lombardy, but when the Italians learned that these were the Poles they made way for them. And an Italian priest came up and thanked them, in French, for giving the Church a Pope. So that night the procession was led by twelve Polish pilgrims, the rest having been conscripted to the choir microphones. And by next morning Sister Zenona had received a summons from the Vatican, via Cracow and England, to attend the papal coronation, and the rest of the pilgrims had clubbed together and then raffled two extra bus tickets, and that afternoon she and the two raffle winners were on the bus for the Italian border.

Before the election of John Paul II, a French observer of the Poles, speaking perhaps slightly enviously, had searched for a word to describe the quality of the Polish faith and had chosen not "traditionalist," or "besieged" or "uncompromising," but "cerebral." It is a union of spirit and intellect which marks the Poles at Lourdes. Compared to the faithful of other nations they are distinguished by a fierce certainty which makes light of the doubts which trouble those raised in less tested communities. The Polish faith is strengthened by the opposition it faces from a left-wing tyranny. Such an ideology challenges the essence of Christianity; that is it challenges Christianity's other-worldliness and its claims for the immortality of the individual soul. The result is an increase in the spiritual strength of Polish Catholicism.

At Lourdes this makes a vivid contrast with the prevailing character of the Western Church. That character contains the ideal of "the revolutionary Church," which was formed in opposition to the right-wing tyrannies of South America and the Third World. Right-wing tyrannies do not feel any need to attack the religious life until the Christian churches intervene to protect their members from political persecution or social injustice. The ensuing battleground is always temporal. And the result, for Christianity, is that it becomes politicized with its religious identity weakened. Left-wing tyrannies encourage a more spiritual Christianity, right-wing tyrannies a more political one. And the purified enthusiasm of the Poles enables them to make light of the disagreements about points of theology which have sprung up at Lourdes over the years.

The nineteenth and twentieth centuries have been, for the Catholic Church, the Marian age, and Lourdes has been at the centre of that enthusiasm. It has accounted for the success of the shrine but it has also caused a steady criticism. Even today one English priest recalls his relief after his first visit to Lourdes that "the Marian side was not overplayed as much as I had feared." Both inside and outside the church, the Marianists have been accused of "mariolatry," of substituting worship of Mary for worship of God and, in the words of the *Official Guide*, of "a superfluous devotion to the Virgin, relying on trinkets, rosaries and medals; a perversion of authentic religion, bordering on superstition." In their defence the authorities quote François Mauriac: "I cannot walk a few steps in Lourdes without asking myself what I believe and what I don't." In other words there is room at Lourdes for many shades of Catholic opinion. Increasingly in recent years the tendency has been to get round these differences of opinion by concentrating on the role of Bernadette.

One of the first difficulties about the story of Lourdes is in supposing that, if God were to direct his Church through visions, he should select the indistinct perceptions of a child. It was an obstacle which Mother Vauzou, Bernadette's novice mistress, could never overcome. It seemed to many absurd to suppose that an omnipotent deity would ever use such an inefficient form of direction. But in reply the Church advances good arguments about Bernadette. It meets the fundamental objection of absurdity head-on, by glorifying the child's simplicity and poverty. And it points out that a simple child, raised in a settled faith, is capable of the most unambiguous and sincere account of such a vision. What is new is not that such children should experience visions, but the degree of attention which their experiences attract. Any revealed religion, as it grows older and its founding revelations recede into mythology, needs renewal; and the most authoritative form of such renewal is a new revelation. But once the new "revelation" itself, in this case the doctrine of the Immaculate Conception, has passed into the body of familiar faith the shrine is left with the problem of renewing its own impetus. The Church at Lourdes has decided to solve this, for the time being, by directing the attention of the pilgrims towards Bernadette. She was young, she was poor, she was sick, she was "working-class," and she had visions; altogether a very fortunate combination for a hero of both the revolutionary

church and the charismatic church, two of its most recent
postures.

The most convenient point for this annual "orientation"
is the conference of pilgrimage directors, which takes place
in the depths of the off-season, in February, and which co-
incides with the feast days of the Lourdes stories—11 February being the day of Our Lady of Lourdes, 18 February
that of St. Bernadette.

The annual conference of pilgrimage directors is a mixture of horse-trading, public relations and pilgrimage, and
to give the whole event some tone, and in order to assert
the Church's controlling position, there is a pastoral day
for the assembled directors during which the bishop gives
an address. The directors form two groups—there are the
spiritual directors and the travel directors. The latter are
travel agents, the former are their clients, usually priests.
An address to both groups therefore has to start from quite
a broad base. In 1979, designated as the year of Bernadette, the bishop said that "a good number of pilgrims
among the young, but also among the adults, and especially among those who come from countries other than
France, are almost completely ignorant of everything
about Bernadette." This, said the bishop, was partly due to
such films as The Song of Bernadette (which was mainly
memorable for the performance of Gladys Cooper as
Mother Vauzou), and to the lack of more authoritative accounts. But now, thanks to Fathers Laurentin, Billet and
Ravier, particularly the first, it may be possible to hear
"the irreplaceable note which she represents in the sym-
phony of the Communion of the Saints." And he quoted
Abbé Laurentin's view that Bernadette characterized "the
holiness of the poor." The poor find in her someone who
resembles them. And the young find in her a "sister" who
was as powerless as they are in the face of the leaders of
the moment, yet able to face life with "an imperturbable
and tranquil audacity."

This week of the pilgrimage directors' conference is the
best time to see Lourdes as a business. Even the hoteliers

are prepared to interrupt their holidays and open up, to confirm pre-arrangements for the coming season and occasionally to enter into new ones. It is during this week that one can see how difficult it would be for a newcomer to break into the Lourdes trade. Many of the pilgrimages have been coming for twenty or thirty years. They may be booking two or three thousand beds, four or five years in advance, and some of the "travel directors" will be bringing more than one such pilgrimage each season. There is of course always some marginal change to be negotiated, a dozen beds here or there which can be switched from one of the hotels, which only takes the overflow of any particular pilgrimage. But the main bookings stay the same for as long as both parties are in business. In a way they have to. There is an increasing demand for beds at Lourdes every season, and it would be difficult indeed for any travel director to find four or five hundred beds at only eighteen months' notice for any given week.

The other stabilizing factor is that the spiritual directors have to compete with each other for the facilities of the Domain. A new pilgrimage arriving in Lourdes, even if it secured accommodation, would find itself at the end of the queue for priority at the various ceremonies and altars. There is terrific competition, for instance, to say mass at the Grotto. But there are only a few hours each day when the Grotto can be set aside for mass, since this interrupts the crowds of people who have come thousands of miles to walk around it and pray there. In such competitive circumstances the oldest established pilgrimages whose directors have the longest friendship with the chaplains are bound to have first choice. "Spiritual directors" do not give up that sort of advantage easily. They know that if they change their dates they are likely to cause problems and start competing with different groups. They also know that their own regular pilgrims have come to rely on roughly the same dates, and so they are the last to allow the travel directors any leeway, even if a new and cheaper booking opportunity should turn up.

The winners in all this are of course the hoteliers and

chaplains of Lourdes. The former because it means that they can evade the normal market pressures to hold prices and improve facilities that much more easily. And the latter because it increases the area of their own influence and control. But it is not an advantage anyone has been able to engineer deliberately. It would dissolve at once if the demand for pilgrimages to Lourdes were ever to slacken.

The pilgrims are unanimous in complaining about the prices of Lourdes. In 1930 boat and train fares and a week in a good hotel might cost an English pilgrim £5. In 1931 there was widespread complaint, not surprisingly, because this had risen to £7. 10s. 0d. In the mid-fifties the price had risen to £18 for a sick pilgrim and about £27 for a healthy one, prices that remained fairly stable for ten years. But by 1978 it was £78 and £118 respectively, and in 1979 it was £90 and £137. The air fare in one year rose from £140 to £169.

Although the travel directors are well aware of the pilgrims' views on Lourdes prices they take the view that they are if anything lower than prices in the rest of France. Their preoccupations include such matters as why British Caledonian charge the same price for a flight from Gatwick to Lourdes as to Barcelona. The official answer is that they have to charge the extra amount because of the extra time spent unloading the sick. So is it worth arranging for sick pilgrims to be carried off more quickly, or are British Caledonian saying that they don't really want the business? The travel directors have also to spend more time building bridges with the Lourdes hoteliers, as English travel agencies have been noted in the past for the number of bad debts. Even agencies which have been approved by the Church and recommended by parish priests have gone into liquidation overnight, leaving both pilgrims and hoteliers out of pocket. Another hitch occurred in 1971 when a plane chartered to fly Lourdes pilgrims was intercepted before reaching Ireland and found to be loaded with a consignment of Czech arms purchased by the I.R.A. In that case the pilgrimage seems to have been used as a cover for gun-running. This was made pos-

sible by the expansion of Tarbes airport, and the increase
of charter flights between Ireland and the Continent.

When a pilgrimage starts to go wrong the travel agents
notice the falling numbers; but they also notice that all the
priests are staying in the Hôtel Imperial, that none of the
pilgrims can find out what's going on and that they start to
tag onto other pilgrimages which happen to be in town at
the same time. The travel directors notice these things because it means that there will be an opening for new customers in the near future. There are few other opportunities for entirely new pilgrimage business, although Spes
Travel have found one which is connected with the unrecognized shrine of Garabandal. There was a spectacular
series of visions at this northern Spanish village between
1961 and 1965. Part of the message of Garabandal was
that there will be a miracle on a Thursday evening, of
which there will be eight days' warning. The Lady of
Garabandal has a considerable following, and Spes run
regular pilgrimages to the village. But "in response to popular demand" they have also opened a "miracle list," that
is a list of people who pay a deposit and who wait for the
prior warning of the miracle when they will be contacted
by Spes and flown out for the event. Updating this list
(the coming miracle was first announced on 13 November 1965) is a regular chore for the Spes staff.

Sometimes at the conference more immediate problems
arise. One spiritual director who was responsible for bringing a hundred "children in care" from Salford, aged from
twelve to eighteen, was very scathing about the military
side of Lourdes; the medals, the flags, the emphasis on national badges and the "over-disciplined" ceremonies. It
turned out that his objections had started when he realized
that he could hardly give his children a banner, since he
did not want to advertise which school they came from.
Nor could he put them in hotels since they would certainly
have had the taps off before unpacking. He was finally advised to put them in the town camp site, which he did.
During their week at the shrine his charges, oblivious of
the quality of the goods, spent some time lifting a rich

array of virgins, bottles, rosaries, medals and other objects
of piety. One of them even returned the water bottle which
he had just stolen because it leaked, and obtained a replacement. When their spiritual director realized what had
been going on he was faced with a problem. So he called
them all together and said that since they had been steal-
ing, and since it was now impossible to return the goods,
there being no reason at all why any particular piece of
tinsel should have come from any particular shop, the only
thing to do was to hold a sale of the proceeds on the camp
site and send a handicapped child to Lourdes on the proceeds. Everyone greeted this solution with enthusiasm, and
the priest was quite pleased with his ingenuity—until one
of the boys, worried about the prospects for the unknown
handicapped child, came up to him and asked if he "was
sure they had obtained enough?"

Following this story a terrific argument broke out between this priest and one of the travel directors about the
morality of making a profit from pilgrimages, the travel director pointing out that the priest himself, like all the other
spiritual directors present, had had his fare paid for him.
The argument only stopped when it was interrupted by the
appropriate climax to the week of the pilgrimage directors'
conference, which was the reconsecration of one of the
hotels.

The hotel had changed hands for £250,000 and its new
owner was one of the leading travel agents, or "pilgrimage
directors," in Dublin. The happy event was marked by a
little ceremony. All the English and Irish pilgrimage directors were invited to a champagne reception and one of Ireland's leading spiritual directors put down his glass,
donned alb and stole and marched through the crowded
bar with brush and bucket of holy water sprinkling the assembled company and the fixtures and fittings. He then
marched out of the bar on an extended sprinkling expedition of the upper and lower floors (he was quite young
and refused the lift), which left rather an awkward silence
in his wake. But nobody broke it, until the white-robed
figure had returned, still sprinkling, to make a warm

speech of "thank-you and welcome" to J.W., the hotel's
new owner, who had, he said, "always been a gentleman.
And I should know because I'm one of his oldest customers." M. and Mme. Abadie, the newly enriched sellers
and bearers of an old Lourdes name, watched from behind
the bar, their granite features faintly illuminated by an expression of decorous rapacity.

This occasion inspired one of the English spiritual directors to suggest that it would be sensible if the English dioceses combined to purchase one or two hotels which could
be used to enable more English pilgrims to be brought to
Lourdes at less cost. Everybody agreed on the good sense
of the proposal, and nobody mentioned that it had first
been mooted years before, and always come to nothing for
the same reason of inter-diocesan rivalry.

Returning at the end of the week by the way they had
come, the St. Albans pilgrimage stopped at Lisieux to visit
the next best thing after Bernadette, which was the shrine
of St. Teresa. While they made their visit, George, their
poker-faced driver, expressed a personal view. "It doesn't
interest me in the least—quite frankly," he said. "Everyone to his own taste, and Lourdes isn't mine." He had had
plenty of opportunity to find out as he had been driving
pilgrims backwards and forwards between London and
Lourdes all summer. He considered the present group very
quiet. The most difficult pilgrims he had ever taken were
from an approved school for girls in southern England.
Half-way across France one of the pupils, aged about fourteen, had revealed that she knew what to expect at Lourdes
because she had once been to Fatima. When she was
younger and living in Dublin she had run away from home
and stowed away on a boat which ended up in Lisbon.
There she had taken to prostitution and eventually, by
chance, found herself in Fatima, from where she was sent
to the nuns who ran the approved school. "It was the first
time she had gone into her adventures in detail," said
George, "and it certainly made the drive pass quickly."

In Lisieux, in the chapel of the Carmelite convent, the

pilgrims inspected the various relics of this other saint. There is a *chasse* with a nun's figure lying inside, but, contrary to the case of Bernadette, there has been no miraculous preservation. The body decked out in nun's habit is frankly described as a waxwork, and the saint's bones are concealed in the trunk beneath it. The best relic is undoubtedly Teresa's hair, which was cut off when she took her solemn vows and which, rather than being sold to ransom an African slave (as was Bernadette's), was carefully kept by the convent. The hair makes a superb ringleted, golden display in its glass case, dressed as though for a wedding; it is so long that it looks as though she was scalped. Teresa had four sisters, all nuns. If each had hair like that, their father must have been a sad man.

Outside in Lisieux, the town was just starting its evening diversions, and before reboarding their bus the pilgrims found somewhere to drink coffee. The café they chose was just beside a bookshop which contained in its windows a silent reminder of the world they were returning to. This was a thickly illustrated series entitled *The Encyclopaedia of Sex*. Volume One was recommended for children aged seven to nine.

❧ VIII ❧

The Ultimate Goal

"One *can't* believe impossible things . . .
[said Alice]"
"I dare say you haven't had much practice,"
said the Queen. "When I was your age I always did it for half-an-hour a day. Why sometimes I've believed as many as six impossible
things before breakfast."
Alice Through the Looking-Glass, Lewis Carroll

At the very end of the Blessed Sacrament procession there
walks a rather motley group who, despite their respectful
air, seem a little out of place. As the procession reaches
the esplanade, and the Blessed Sacrament is carried between the lines of sick pilgrims, the members of this group
lose interest in the ceremonial and turn instead to watch
the faces of those who are lined up in their chairs and
stretchers under the trees. The observers are the members
of the Medical Bureau, that is to say any doctor of whatever belief who happens to be in Lourdes that day, and
who wishes to take an interest. They are accompanied by
Dr. Théodore Mangiapan, the director of the Medical Bureau, like the head of a hospital department on his ward
round.

The position of the doctors at the end of the procession
gives them an opportunity to observe the demeanour of the
sick as the Blessed Sacrament is carried past. And it is
symbolic, scientific medicine, for the purpose of these proceedings and in the case of these patients, giving way to
religious faith. If the processing doctors are also members

of the International Medical Association of Lourdes, as most pilgrimage doctors are, they will wear a small enamel badge marked with the word "Credo."

The doors of the Medical Bureau at Lourdes are the ultimate goal of every sick pilgrim. If you receive a cure at Lourdes you have the opportunity, some would say the moral obligation, to go to the Medical Bureau and report the event. By doing so you start a process of investigation which can take many years. Nobody knows how many people have experienced cures at Lourdes. But records of one sort or another have been kept since the twelfth apparition, and the archives of the Medical Bureau go back to 1878. More than five thousand cures have been recorded, of which only sixty-four were eventually proclaimed "miracles." The activities of the Medical Bureau are the first step in achieving this bold reduction.

For Marie Kerslake, from Norton St. Philip in Somerset, who experienced her cure in July 1978, arriving at the Medical Bureau was a rather intimidating experience. She had been increasingly disabled by chronic arthritis for sixteen years; her condition was deteriorating; she was in constant pain and her finger joints, knees and back were all so badly affected that she was virtually crippled. In July 1978 she joined the Order of Malta Volunteers pilgrimage. After mass in the church at Gavarnie, during one of the pilgrimage excursions, she found herself able to leave her chair and her sticks and collar and walk for some distance up a steep hill. She felt no ill-effects at all. Ever since then her mobility has enormously improved, she has never needed her equipment again and she is now able to run, weave tapestry and lead a fully active life. But she remembers her first entry into the Medical Bureau as a worrying moment.

The Bureau's initial investigation deals with about two reported cures a week, although the number can fluctuate considerably. As in the normal course of events, Mrs. Kerslake saw Dr. Mangiapan, who made a preliminary investigation, mainly to see whether she gave a sensible account of her story. In Mrs. Kerslake's case her account and his examination were sufficiently interesting for him to discuss her case with the pilgrimage doctor, and to open a dossier. She was then asked to return in 1979, and to bring her medical records and a report from her own doctor at home. The real work of the Bureau begins with this second visit, when any doctor in Lourdes can attend the examination. Any medical records which the patient has are produced at this meeting. Dr. Mangiapan's main task is to supervise the proceedings and ensure that a record is made of everyone's opinion. When the examination is complete its findings make the second entry in the dossier of that particular case, and the patient is asked to return again for a third time, a year later, together with any additional records that seem relevant. At this stage the initiative moves to the doctor of the pilgrimage and to the pilgrim's own doctor. The Bureau cannot normally proceed with the investigation if the pilgrim's own doctor refuses to cooperate.

The director of the Medical Bureau is in a curious position for a medical man. All his patients come to him because they are feeling better; the better they feel the more concerned he becomes about their condition. If they start to feel worse he must start to lose interest in them. Dr. Mangiapan qualified in 1953 and was formerly in practice in Marseilles, where he specialized in paediatric medicine. He was appointed to the Bureau in 1972. He says he was drawn to Lourdes partly from spiritual conviction and partly by the opportunity to do something so different after twenty years of practice in Marseilles. When I asked if he had a personal belief in the miracles he said "Yes, but it fluctuates." He believes in them "as a son of the Church believes in a proposition of the Church."

As director of the Medical Bureau, Dr. Mangiapan is an employee of the bishop and chaplains; he is paid from the budget of the Domain. But in medical matters he is given such independence as he needs. He is the only person entitled to speak officially about the medical aspects of Lourdes, with the exception of the members of the International Medical Committee of Lourdes, who only pronounce about those few cures on which they, as a second investigative body, have reached a decision. The International Committee sits for only one day a year; the director's is a full-time appointment, and so his position is the more influential. He supervises the early process of investigation. He has to pursue any recalcitrant doctors, and, when all the documents are ready and the incidental members of the Medical Bureau have completed their examinations of the patient, it is he who has to take the final decision whether or not to send the case forward to the International Medical Committee. Even then his task is not finished because at the Committee's meeting it is he who introduces the cases and presents his dossier. The importance of the Medical Bureau's role is shown by the fact that between 1947, when the Bureau's methods were reformed, and 1978, about twelve hundred dossiers were opened, an average of roughly forty a year. But of these twelve hundred only fifty-six were forwarded by the Bureau to the second tribunal, that is the National or (since 1954) International Committee. The second Committee had the opportunity to investigate forty-four of these fifty-six cases, of which it accepted twenty-five as "medically inexplicable." Of that twenty-five the Church has proclaimed only seventeen to be miraculous. So, a cure passed by the director of the Bureau has about a one-in-three chance of being proclaimed. But a cure reported to the director has only a one in twenty-two chance of even being passed on, and only a one-in-seventy chance of being proclaimed.

In the popular mind, "Lourdes" means "miracles." But miracles are a problem. Dr. Mangiapan tells a story about a newcomer to Lourdes who went to the Medical Bureau and asked, "Please, can you tell me at what time the miracle will occur?" In the Church of the Real Presence there has never been any trouble in persuading the faithful to believe in miracles; they see them everywhere. In New Mexico, in 1977, Maria Rubio was frying tortillas for her husband's dinner when she noticed that the crispy burn marks on the dough resembled the face of Jesus crowned with thorns. "A miracle," she cried, and within twelve months eight thousand people from the surrounding Mexican-American community had come to her house to venerate the sacred batter, now mounted behind glass. These pilgrims have donated enough money to build a small room to house the miracle, which is always surrounded by candles and flowers. This is the sort of thing which embarrasses bishops, and the Archbishop of Santa Fe has tried to discourage the holy pancake cult, so far to no effect.

It is only a small step from here to out-and-out superstition, divorced from religion, such as the English jeweller's catalogue which advertises the Pyramid Ring, "the most powerful ring known to man, containing the miraculous and mysterious power of the pyramid whose biomagnetic energy enriches the aura effect enabling you to attempt to discover forces emanating from people around you, and which contains a handy secret compartment which can be used to energize seeds." The same catalogue contains "Lord's prayer pendants," "Cornish pisky necklaces" and "crucifix key rings." To the jeweller it is all the same market. Religion can be confused with superstition or diluted by rationalism, and the second is an encouragement for the first. "What else can you expect? . . . Religion will out, and when it is suppressed it breaks its way through in strange and sometimes poisonous forms."* If religion will not express the sense of the mysterious and will not make use of the human need for symbolism, then superstition is sure to revive. If the Vatican today is correctly reported to be disturbed by the new readiness of people to accept miraculous claims, it surely need not look far to find the reason.

The medical investigations of Lourdes are a determined attempt to restrict the number of miracles. The old method of testing a cure followed a formula laid down by Pope Benedict XIV. It was compiled in 1734, and asked seven questions intended to distinguish between natural or medically induced recoveries and acts of God, but over the years certain changes have been made in the questions

* *The Lawless Roads,* Graham Greene.

posed. The first point to be made at Lourdes is that the
question of an inexplicable cure and the question of a miracle are separate. The Bureau and the International Committee are solely concerned with the question of an inexplicable cure, as to which the following requirements have to
be satisfied.

Was the cure:
Sudden, unexpected and without convalescence?
Complete?
Lasting (a minimum of three or four years)?
Was the disease:
Serious (through the degree of invalidity or risk to
life)?
Organic and not functional (based on a definite dis-
ease)?
Objectively proved (proved by tests, X-rays or biop-
sies)?
Finally, was the treatment given, if any, responsible
for the cure, wholly or in part?

The actual list of questions which the International Committee asks is more detailed and technical than this, and is
itself in process of revision. But the exact conclusion to
which the Committee works is that: "the cure established,
considering how it was produced and maintained, constituted a phenomenon contrary to the observations and expectations of medical knowledge and was scientifically inexplicable." It can be seen that between the cripple who
gets up and walks, and the cripple who gets up and walks
and is proclaimed to have benefited from a miracle, there
is a very long distance.

Of course the popular phenomenon of a "Lourdes miracle" has very little to do with this careful process of investigation. "The miracle mother of Lourdes"* turned out to
be a reference to a woman from Worthing who had been
told eleven years earlier that she could never have chil-

* Newspaper headline, 1978.

dren. While on holiday in the South of France she and her husband realized that they were close to Lourdes and made a detour to pray. Three months later she was found to be pregnant. She duly gave birth to twin boys and said that though she was not very religious this was certainly a miracle to her. (The boys, oddly, were then christened "Darren" and "Stuart.") An event like that, whatever its meaning to the person involved, would never be considered an official cure, let alone a miracle.

As far as the authorities at Lourdes are concerned, such reports are significant only for the continuing public interest they reveal in the possibility of miracles. The chronicle of their own investigatory activities is one long list of prevarications. As an example of a cure which was judged "incomplete," for instance, there was the case of a woman who was completely paralysed. She was then cured in the baths, but one hand remained inert. It is quite common for miraculees to bear some reminder of their previous state, but it must not, as in this case, be so marked as to compromise the completeness of the cure.

Sometimes the cure is complete but does not last. This happened to one English pilgrim, a woman of about forty who came to Lourdes with Parkinson's disease on the Catholic Association pilgrimage. She was a believer and was cured, but her husband, an agnostic, remained unimpressed. After a year she came back for her first examination and seemed to be well but one of the doctors noticed a very slight tremor in one hand. Her disease had returned and she is now very ill again. But she does not feel bitter about her relapse. She says that she and her husband still "had a wonderful year."

Sometimes a cure owes more to human excitement than to anything else. So, on a day when Princess Grace of Monaco was making a highly publicized visit with the Monaco pilgrimage one of the sick Monegasques was reported cured from three different parts of the Domain in the same morning. *Life* magazine immediately described the event as "a miracle," but the Monaco pilgrimage doctors said that the girl in question had been suffering from an unhealed wound to the leg after a motorcycle accident in which her fiancé had been killed. They were delighted that she felt better and that the wound had finally healed, and they expressed the view that if she soon found a new boyfriend they would hear no more of her accident.

For the pilgrim who wants to know about the genuine cures the best place to apply is the picture gallery outside Dr. Mangiapan's office. Here the walls are lined with the portraits of famous old cases dating back to the nineteenth century. The overwhelming impression is of an army of bold, stout women, glowing with health. What did these confident and healthy matrons do? Nothing. Something happened to them.

The two cases supposedly distorted by Zola are both proudly displayed. Marie Lemarchand, whom the novelist called "Elise Rouquet," appears as a handsome middle-aged person surrounded by two sons, two daughters, two twin daughters and a husband with a splendidly waxed handlebar moustache. She was cured instantaneously in the baths on 21 August 1892, of lupus (T.B.) of the face, and of something vividly and chillingly called "dog's muzzle." Zola describes it as follows: "It was a case of lupus which had preyed upon the unhappy woman's nose and mouth. Ulceration had increased, and was hourly increasing—in short, all the hideous peculiarities of this terrible disease were in full process of development, almost obliterating the traces of what once were pleasing womanly lineaments." One looks again at the picture of the husband and family of Mme. Authier, as she became in real life (Miracle No. 17), and sees the full reward of her cure. Zola put the event in its place by making his young doctor suggest that the lupus was a skin disease of nervous origin due to faulty nutrition. Time has not helped Zola in this; the T.B. bacillus is not connected with the nerves or with the subconscious mind. Justin Bouhort, who was cured in July 1858 of a condition then diagnosed as consumption, at the age of 2 (Miracle No. 5), the last miracle for a Lourdais, is also pictured—as a man of about sixty. It is pleasant for the pilgrim to realize that he is looking at a photograph of one of the saint's contemporaries.

For English pilgrims there is of course a picture of John Traynor, who is considered one of the greatest of Lourdes cures, and a picture of Sarah MacLoy of Birmingham. The caption says that she was cured of cancer of the cervix on 8 August 1962, and that this was registered as a cure by the Medical Bureau in 1965. (It was not accepted for investigation by the International Committee because eight months after the registration of her cure she became ill again of a possibly associated condition.) The only other British cure to have reached the same level recently, that of Margaret Gresham, whom the Medical Bureau certified in 1963 to be certainly and inexplicably cured, was not passed on to the International Committee on the grounds that she had had a functional condition which could not be related to an organic disease. Her picture is not displayed in the exhibition.

A recurring reason for the elimination of a possibly miraculous cure is "absence of co-operation from the patient's own doctors." Professional hostility to Lourdes was once so fierce that it could bring a brilliant man's career to an end. But today total hostility is the exception rather than the rule. The most it usually amounts to, in the opinion of Dr. Armand-Laroche, is an aggressive "Cartesianism" in sceptical doctors, who immediately demand proof not of the inexplicability of a cure but of the existence of a miracle. However the hostility remains strong enough to persuade many doctors who have the "misfortune" to treat a patient who is subsequently cured at Lourdes to withhold all co-operation, lest they become guilty by association. According to Dr. Mangiapan, "We have two sorts of critics, those who criticize old dossiers on technical grounds, and those who are *parti-pris*. Of the second class, no dossier will convince them." And for the first group there is no answer either; old dossiers cannot be updated, any more than old treatments can be modified.

The medical hostility towards Lourdes probably reached its peak with the attack on Alexis Carrel in 1902. Carrel,

202 THE ULTIMATE GOAL

who was eventually awarded the Nobel Prize for his work
on blood-vessels, was then a young doctor attached to the
Faculty of Medicine at Lyons University. Mainly out of
curiosity, he accompanied a Lourdes pilgrimage. On the
train he noticed one case in particular, that of a young
woman called Marie Bailly who presented all the symptoms of tuberculous peritonitis. She was in such a bad condition that Dr. Carrel considered it rather scandalous that
the pilgrimage had agreed to take her. She had a family
history of T.B. She was spitting blood. Fluid had been
drawn off her lungs. She had a pulse of 150 and her face
was already turning blue. She presented the familiar symptoms of a case in the last stages of the disease, and Carrel,
among others, considered that she was dying. Her sudden
and complete cure after the bath and during the Blessed
Sacrament procession took place before his eyes and Carrel made a report on the matter, which he accepted as a
miracle. Zola, who had also accepted the stories of extraordinary events, invited scientific doctors to investigate
Lourdes. Carrel in a sense took up this invitation. He went
to Lourdes as a scientist and described what he had seen.
Then he stated certain conclusions. He said that all that
mattered was scientific investigation of the facts. Every period saw the birth of new facts which seemed extraordinary and dangerous to the learned mind. It was the duty
of the investigator to break the fetters of organized
scientific systems when new facts required him to do so.
Scientists must never jeopardize proven facts, but must
remember how much remained unknown. *They should not
deny what they had not themselves seen,* any more than
Catholics should look on research as sacrilegious. Science
was a method. It had neither country nor religion.

Accordingly, Carrel, having reported what he had seen,
concluded that these were highly significant events which
"prove the reality of certain links, as yet unknown, between psychological and organic processes. They prove the
objective value of the spiritual activity which has been almost totally ignored by doctors, teachers and sociologists.
They open up a new world for us." Few doctors would

now disagree with this opinion. But the reaction of his colleagues at the university was so hostile that Carrel had to
leave. He went to New York, joined the Rockefeller Institute and carried out the research which was to win him the
Nobel Prize nine years later. As he said in *Journey to
Lourdes,* his account of the case of Marie Bailly: "There
is no denying that it is distressingly unpleasant to be per-
sonally involved in a miracle."

Current scepticism about Lourdes cures was sum-
marized in *The Dictionary of Common Fallacies* (1978),
the fallacy in this case being that "there are miraculous
cures at Lourdes." The basis of the criticism is firstly the
same as Zola's; that the cures are caused by "the excitement of the journey, the prayers and the hymns . . . the
ever-increasing emotion generated by the atmosphere of
the shrine . . . the healing breath produced by the unknown force which emanates from crowds during violent
demonstrations of faith." In another writer that might be
considered a fair description of the preparation for any intense religious experience, and therefore a proper preparation for receiving "the sign from God" which, according
to the Church, is what "a miracle" is. Furthermore, there
is nothing "scientific" about Zola's explanation. Neither
"prayers," nor "hymns," nor "the healing breath," nor the
"unknown force of faithful crowds" form part of the
scientific doctor's vocabulary. They are merely secular
ways of describing a religious occasion.

The second criticism mentioned in *The Dictionary of
Common Fallacies* concerns the standards of the Medical
Bureau, as evaluated in a book entitled *Eleven Lourdes
Miracles* by D. J. West. Dr. West's book, published in
1957, was funded by a grant from the Parapsychology
Foundation of New York, and Dr. West was at that time
the research officer to the Society for Psychical Research.*
The experience of Marie Kerslake when she returned to
Lourdes in July 1979 for her second examination shows

* He has since become Professor of Clinical Criminology at Cambridge University.

something of the investigatory procedures which for various reasons Dr. West found defective.

On the second day of her pilgrimage, Marie Kerslake faced her first full examination at the Medical Bureau. As an English pilgrim she might have expected a smaller panel than a French or Italian proto-miraculee, but there were fourteen doctors, almost all English-speaking, waiting for her. They had her complete medical history, her X-rays from the Royal National Hospital for Rheumatic Diseases, Bath, and reports from her own doctor, Dr. J. D. Corcoran, and from the specialist who had treated her at Bath, Dr. Cosh. The examination took three hours. At 5:30 that evening she returned for another examination, this time by twenty-five doctors, which lasted until 7:45. The examinations were very thorough, quite painful and sometimes quite hostile. The atmosphere was not at all like that of a normal medical consultation, where a sympathetic doctor is trying to heal a patient. These doctors were detached, sceptical and, in the words of one of them, inspired by the spirit of the devil's advocate. An attack of meningitis, suffered eighteen years before, aroused a certain interest. Her eyes and co-ordination were tested; she was weighed and measured.

The report from Dr. Corcoran, made after her cure, simply said that she had had a

> longstanding and widespread osteo-arthrosis which over a period of five years gave her much pain and stiffness, restriction of movement of the back and shoulders, and constant pain and limitation of movement of her swollen fingers. This was treated by a variety of oral medication and on several occasions by steroid injections into her joints. In the past year [that is since her original visit to Lourdes] this has been markedly improved and she has had no treatment for this condition.

The year before first going to Lourdes Mrs. Kerslake suffered a heart attack which was demonstrated by an electro-cardiograph. The report continues:

For two months subsequently she had a lot of central chest pain and was admitted to hospital for investigation. [After her visit to Lourdes] a further ECG showed T wave inversion in lead III, but there were no other abnormalities. Minor changes in leads V5 & 6 and V2 and AVL having returned to normal. In the past year Mrs. Kerslake has had no pains relating to her heart condition.

In April 1979 she had a minor episode of right-sided sciatica which responded quickly to a simple analgesic. Otherwise she has remained very well and free of all symptoms.

This bare report exemplifies the understated nature of many medical records. In conversation with the author Dr. Corcoran said that although the specialist, Dr. Cosh, diagnosed osteo-arthrosis, *he* had always assumed that it was a case of rheumatoid arthritis, and that if it was indeed osteo-arthrosis it was a very severe case in his experience. A few years ago, he said, she was "a very sad picture," and he would have expected her condition in the normal course of events to have left her completely incapacitated by 1979. A doctor who had worked in the Guy's Hospital Heart Unit and who saw her after her heart attack had been pessimistic about her future on that account as well. Dr. Corcoran regarded Mrs. Kerslake as an emotional person and "a worrier" who had had a lot to worry about. She had a history of illness. At various times since 1956 she had been treated for a slipped disc, operated on for a duodenal ulcer, treated for viral meningitis with a possibility of polio, and treated for pneumonia. She had borne seven children and had lost two others in infancy. Twice in his experience there had been a possibility that she was suffering from "anxiety states," once when a niece had died in an accident, once when her daughter had been attacked; but otherwise most of her illnesses had been pathological. He therefore excluded the possibility of hysterical illness and, in the case of the heart attack, a functional illness was excluded by the ECG. Before going to Lourdes she had been in a partially crippled condition and was sometimes unable to get around the house. She had also been unable to walk up the short hill outside her home in Norton St. Philip. Now she was an extremely active woman and could run up the same hill. She was more remarkably improved than anyone in his experience.

If Marie Kerslake's case is considered sufficiently interesting she will be asked to attend again in 1981 (she has already agreed to attend in 1980) and possibly for further years after that. And, provided that the Medical Bureau eventually obtains enough information about her previous condition, and satisfies itself that her cure was genuine, lasting and complete, her case will be passed to the International Committee.

Despite this apparently painstaking procedure, Dr. West was not impressed with the cases which he examined for his book, which comprised the eleven most recent miracles at that time. "Close examination . . ." he wrote, "yields scant indication of any absolutely inexplicable recovery. The great majority of the cures concern potentially recoverable conditions and are remarkable only for the speed and manner in which they are said to have taken place." No layman can evaluate Dr. West's criticisms, so in order to find out if they could themselves be criticized I asked Prof. David Morrell to read *Eleven Lourdes Miracles* and comment on it. David Morrell is professor of general practice at St. Thomas's Hospital, London, and a member of the Lourdes Medical Association. Prof. Morrell, in his turn, was not impressed by Dr. West's paper. His criticisms might be extracted as follows.

Eleven Lourdes Miracles was written in 1957 and describes events which occurred mainly in the 1930s and 1940s. The case histories recorded at the Lourdes Medical Bureau were supplied by doctors practising at that time in European countries. They were the case histories of ordinary people who experienced extraordinary cures. The fact that certain investigations or X-rays appropriate in the late 1950s had not been

carried out is not surprising as medicine in the thirties
and forties was much more dependent on clinical
findings. Had it been known that the individuals concerned were to become the subject of remarkable
cures, doubtless their cases would have been carefully
documented, but they were not individuals being entered into a clinical trial. They were very ordinary
people receiving very ordinary medical care. The fact
that records were sometimes missing and reports were
sometimes at variance with each other almost supports their validity. In 1978 at a London teaching
hospital 25 per cent of records were not available at
out-patients sessions because they had been lost in the
system.

Further points which Prof. Morrell makes in answer to Dr.
West's criticisms are that:

1. The previous medical records which appear from
the dossiers to be the only source of information are
nearly always supplemented by the observation of the
pilgrimage doctors. In my own experience over the
years, having travelled with sick pilgrims on long and
often difficult journeys, the written medical reports do
not reflect the true seriousness of the patient's condition on arrival in Lourdes.
2. The clinical diagnosis of neurological complaints is
often of far more value than laboratory tests even
today.
3. The physicians and surgeons of the 1930s and
1940s were very familiar with the clinical signs of tuberculosis.
4. The suggestion that some patients will have a spontaneous remission while at Lourdes is very convenient. It is up to the scientist putting it forward to
support the likelihood of such a coincidence from his
knowledge of spontaneous remissions in tuberculous
peritonitis and malignant disease.

Prof. Morrell's conclusion is an attempt to answer the modern scepticism about Lourdes cures.

Dr. West's whole emphasis in this critical review is concerned with obtaining laboratory or X-ray support for diagnoses, many of which were made when medicine was much more based on clinical descriptions and when laboratory and X-ray diagnosis was very poorly developed and very expensive for patients who often were by no means rich. In some cases, he objects because the doctors certifying a particular illness do not give a detailed account of how they reached the diagnosis. This is not surprising to me. If I am asked to certify that one of my patients is suffering from a particular disorder and to provide a summary of the case, I assume that my academic standing will be sufficient for the recipient of the certificate to accept my judgement. In many cases, more details may well be available if one goes back to the original records but ten or twenty years later this may be very difficult, particularly in a country where war existed for six of these years [1939–45].

As regards his interpretation of the evidence he presents, he appears to start out with the hypothesis that the illness is "functional" [of uncertain origin] unless proved otherwise [i.e. "organic," due to detectable changes in an organ], and then tries to rebut such evidence as proves it otherwise. . . . His suggestion that some of the illnesses are "hysterical" or "functional" really stretches the reader's credibility. These illnesses have continued for many years with multiple operations, eyewitness accounts of haemoptysis [spitting blood], wasting, and fistulae [passages communicating with a deep-seated abscess]. In particular, he appears to ignore evidence of the pathetic state in which these patients arrive in Lourdes. . . . This evidence seems to me very important. If I see a semi-comatose patient with fistulae and swinging temperature, or a paralysed patient with contraction, flex or spasms and gross neurological signs, suddenly cured, I find this difficult to explain irrespective of the diagnosis. The startling thing to me about these cases is that desperately-ill patients got suddenly better and stayed better. This is hardly typical of hysterical or functional illness, which would be expected to relapse when the attention and emotional uplift of Lourdes is suddenly removed and the patient goes home. I have seen many of those "miracles" at Lourdes where the patients come back the next year and for a few days feel and perform better.

If indeed all the miracles declared were cures of hysterical people who in their hysteria could vomit blood, discharge pus through their vaginas and abdominal walls, be incontinent of urine, paralysed and blind, then it is really rather remarkable. If psychiatrists could achieve the same results, their value to society would be greatly enhanced because it is doubtful if there are any illnesses so resistant to traditional therapy as "hysterical" or "functional" disorders.

Dr. Daniel O'Connell, who is the head of the Department of Radiotherapy at Charing Cross Hospital, and who has been a member of the Lourdes International Committee since 1956, points out that whatever one decides about the evidence for or against a particular cure, the fact remains that "the therapeutic index of Lourdes is practically zero." Nonetheless he has himself devoted years of his professional life to supporting the investigative work of the Lourdes International Committee, and he and his English and Irish colleagues considered the Committee's work sufficiently important for them to stage a walk-out from the annual meeting in 1972 because certain improvements which they had asked for repeatedly had not taken place. (It was at this period that the report on the cure of Vittorio Micheli, Miracle No. 63, was being prepared.)

The International Committee meets once a year and usually in Paris, for the convenience of its foreign members. The Bishop of Tarbes and Lourdes is present at its meetings, but it has its own president, drawn from among its majority of French doctors. At the moment the president is Prof. Henri Barrière. Other members come from nine other countries: Ireland, England, Scotland, Belgium, Italy, Germany, Spain, Holland and Luxembourg. The meeting starts with mass, and its deliberations are "placed under the sign of the Holy Ghost," a provision which "for metaphysical reasons," in the words of Dr. Armand-Laroche, would exclude the participation of any non-Christian members. In fact all the members of the Committee are Catholic. The procedure, in so far as the cures are concerned, is for Dr. Mangiapan to introduce the dossier, and the Committee then appoints one or more of its number, preferably a specialist in the disease in question, to be *rapporteur*. He would normally see the cured person and talk to his doctors. He would also review all the papers in the case. About three months before the next meeting his report is circulated to the Committee members, so that it can be debated on an informed basis. The Committee frequently delays for some years after a report is presented to see if there are any further developments in the patient's condition. The Committee pronounced on the case of Serge Perrin (Miracle No. 64) four years after it had been put forward by the Medical Bureau; and delayed a similar time in the previous case of Vittorio Micheli. The final decision is taken on the basis of a simple majority.

It is clear that by the time a case is approved by the International Committee it has been considered at numerous levels. It has impressed the patient's own doctor and the pilgrimage doctor. It has also been approved by the Director of the Medical Bureau over three or four years and it has been considered by several dozen doctors, selected at random from among those who go to Lourdes from all over the world. It has further been carefully reinvestigated by a committee of senior doctors drawn from all the main European countries which send pilgrimages to Lourdes. In other words, there is a convincing medical argument for an inexplicable event. But that does not mean that it is a miracle. All the International Committee can do is pass its decision and its report to the bishop of the diocese in which the pilgrim lived at the time of the cure. All further action, if any, must be at his initiative.

Here is the last obstacle, and no slight one, in the path of those who have been cured at Lourdes and who believe that they have experienced a miracle.

The canonical commission is an antiquated inquisition which is preoccupied with theological criteria, and which is quite capable of introducing an entirely new element into the centralized considerations of the International Committee. For instance, the commission appointed by Bishop Théas in the case of Théa Angele (Miracle No. 53) consisted of a president (the senior diocesan canon), two assessors (who were also diocesan canons), one *rapporteur* (who presented the medical evidence and the story of the cure), one devil's advocate or "promoter of the faith" (who was the principal of the diocesan seminary and who argued against it), and one medical expert, a doctor from Tarbes. It is hardly surprising that such a singular body, pursuing its canonical investigation in various French or Italian dioceses, should occasionally appear to be a law unto itself.

It is not uncommon for a bishop to make absolutely no response to the report of the International Committee, not even an acknowledgement. This happened with the Archbishop of Liverpool in the case of John Traynor. And there have been other cases too. Since the war the Lourdes medical authorities have heard nothing of four cases in which the dioceses of Nantes, Lille (twice) and Milan have either failed to reply to all queries or refused to give any reasons for taking no action.

And when the Church does speak it is sometimes less illuminating than when it remains silent. Its own demands for a miracle are that it be "medically inexplicable," that is to say a cure of a definite illness that had been objectively demonstrated, with a poor prognosis with or without treatment; a cure of a serious and incurable illness; and a cure that happened without convalescence and was perfect and lasting. But in fixing such guidelines the various diocesan commissions have sometimes contradicted one another. So, until 1948, the medical dossier usually said that the cure was inexplicable "in the light of current medical knowledge." Then the Bishop of Nantes refused a ruling on the grounds that that phrase was "unfortunate and clumsy," and that it made all judgement of the cure invalid and pointless. So that formula was dropped and replaced by "a cure that was outside the laws of nature." This continued until 1960 when the International Committee pointed out the difficulty of defining "the laws of nature." So a third formula, "medically inexplicable," was adopted and is used today. But although this was the one used in the case of Vittorio Micheli, the Archbishop of Trento in that case in 1976 volunteered the opinion, unprompted by the medical bodies of Lourdes, that the cure could not be explained "in the present state of science."

That the canonical authority should ignore the medical reports is bad enough, but there is another form of negative decision which the International Committee must find even more frustrating. In the Bulletin of the International Medical Association of Lourdes for May 1971, Doctor Olivieri, then medical director, referring to the case of Vittorio Micheli which had just been registered by the International Committee, lamented the "unfortunate series of five cures recognized as medically inexplicable by the International Committee but postponed or rejected by the ecclesiastic authority." He was referring to the cures of one French man, one French woman, one Belgian woman and two Italian women dating back to 1952, all of which had been approved by the medical authorities in 1962 and 1964. And in each case the bishop's reason for taking no further action was a medical one. For although the canonical commission is primarily concerned with theological matters it has to understand the medical report, and this means that it usually appoints its own medical adviser. So here the whole medical question can be reopened, but this time it can be effectively decided by a single doctor. That is what happened in these five cases.

The Archbishop of Antwerp ruled that he was "not in a position to pronounce in favour of the miracle" relating to the cure of Simone Rams, of cancer of the thyroid, because of the different interpretation of the case history by his medical expert. The Bishop of Dijon reached the same conclusion in the cure of Berthe Bouley of multiple sclerosis. The Bishop of Blois made the same ruling in the cure of Edmond Gaultier, of the after-effects of meningoencephalitis of unknown origin, because of "an insoluble lack of medical proof." The Archbishop of Salerno produced the same reason for refusing to proclaim the miraculous nature of the cure of Anna Santaniello, from mitral stenosis (heart disease). And the Archbishop of Sassari did not even nominate a canonical commission to consider the cure of Marchesa Mura, of axillary adenopathy (glandular disease) due to the rooted objections of her own specialist who lived in the diocese, and who questioned both the cure and the diagnosis made in Lourdes, and even his own patient's "mental balance."

At the end of the exhausting process of investigation which supports each proclaimed Lourdes cure one can still be left with a doubt about whether it was worth it. It is, after all, a very strange business. The hostile critics of Lourdes say that the doctors are all believers, and that when it comes down to it they have merely to rubber-stamp an unusual event and say that something "inexplicable" has happened, and that that is not really *so* much to say; and that all the records and debates and tests merely serve to eliminate some of the objective doubts about the accuracy of an essentially subjective assertion.

Certainly the whole purpose of the Bureau and the Committee is to say that medicine has nothing to say, and knows nothing of what happened. For many doctors, that in itself would serve to condemn the good sense of the proceedings. How can so many learned men sit there and solemnly compete to reassure one another about their combined ignorance? Is it a demonstration of the absurd, or a valuable exercise in professional humility?

And what, in the final evaluation, does the process of proof add to the miracle? Originally the Lourdes Medical Bureau set out to disprove accusations of fraud, gullibility and superstition. Then it battled with the suggestion that all the cures were of hysterical illness. Both those battles are long since won. So what is the present purpose of establishing a certainty about a miracle, a sign from God? Naturally, the work of the Bureau will continue. But it is impossible, after all, to prove that the most routine cure is *not* miraculous. The Bureau uses all the resources of modern science to raise doubts about the certain operation of modern science. But one wonders how many of the cures in any modern hospital could withstand equivalent investigation to the point of complete certainty about diagnosis and effective treatment. If one were to take the records of other terminally ill patients and write on the last page "Cured at Lourdes," how many of those records would not show up precisely the same possibilities for error as the critics of Lourdes claim can be found in the records of the miraculated?

And suppose one has no doubts? Suppose one sees the hand of God everywhere, as any believing Christian must? If you are such a person then you are one of those whom the shrine is for. Do you yearn for nice distinctions to be made between "fact" and "mystery"? Do you strive to reduce mystery to a minimum, and so reduce the incidence of its healing? What is the purpose of certainty about mystery? All that is written about the cures of Lourdes cannot take away the choice which exists from the very beginning of the argument. The critics of Lourdes say that, "Because something is said to have happened which does not fit with natural explanations then clearly it did not happen." The protagonists say, "Because something happened which does not fit with natural explanations there must be a supernatural explanation." In logic both are bad arguments which depend on opposing acts of faith.

And for those without either faith, does it matter? They

are left in the end with nothing to be certain of except the undisputed reality of the cure.

The epileptic boy, aged six, carried into the baths by the mother of Dr. Armand-Laroche, forty years ago. All his life, once a fortnight, this child had had a major fit. Before she bathed him Mme. Armand-Laroche told him to pray to the Virgin for his cure. "No," he replied, "I will pray for the cure of all sickness." He has never had a fit since. The experience of René Scher as he sat among the sick pilgrims for the Blessed Sacrament procession and realized he could see, and looked round at the vast crowd and was afraid. The feelings of Marie Bigot (Miracle No. 59), who was cured in successive years (1953 and 1954), first of paralysis and then of total deafness, both times during the Blessed Sacrament procession. She remained however totally blind (all as the result of a stroke) until, on the train home in 1954, lying awake in the night, listening to the sounds that had returned to her, she thought that she imagined the lights of a terrible storm, and was told that she had just *seen* the lights of a passing station. Her eyesight too was perfectly restored.

Serge Perrin (Miracle No. 64), sitting in his chair at the Anointing of the Sick, crippled, almost blind, suffering increasingly violent fits, deteriorating steadily for two years, in a dying condition, and saying suddenly to his wife in his super-precise accountant's diction: "I do not know what has happened to me, but I have the impression that I will not need my sticks much longer, and that I could walk." He was correct to the last decimal point. He could walk, and that afternoon his sight was so good that with one eye he could read the signs across the esplanade.

Or Evasio Ganora (Miracle No. 54), a farm labourer from Casale, who was found to be a certain case of Hodgkin's incurable disease. He responded to no treatment, he grew weaker and weaker, he was thought to have only a short time to live until, on being immersed in the water of Lourdes, he felt a great warmth run through his body, he got up, walked back to the hospital and at once began to work as a stretcher bearer. Years later he was crushed beneath a tractor and was invited, as he lay there, to pray to the Holy Virgin to save his life. He declined, on the grounds that he had had his turn.

And the husband of Alice Couteault, himself a non-believer, waiting on the platform at Poitiers for his wasted, twisted, incoherent and incapable wife to be carried off the train, dying, as she had been for three years, slowly and before his eyes. And waiting while the pilgrim train drew in, and waiting while it stood there, and wondering why no one got off it from one end of the platform to the other— until a door opened in the distance and one small figure climbed down and began to run towards him down the long empty platform; Madame Couteault, instantly and perfectly cured of multiple sclerosis during the Blessed Sacrament procession. By the time Miracle No. 58 reached Monsieur Couteault, *he* was unconscious on the platform, and it was he who had to be carried home.

"In that instant," said Gabrielle Clauzel (Miracle No. 46), referring to the moment at mass on 15 August 1943, her birthday, when her paralysis, pain, racing heartbeat and inability to eat, all just left her, "In that instant, I was well."

⚜ Appendixes ⚜

APPENDIX I
SOME STATISTICS OF THE PILGRIMAGE

1. The proportion of pilgrims by nationality in 1978
The total number of visitors to the town in 1978 was 4,259,000.
Since the average number of visitors to other towns of the same
size is 1 million, the "excess" drawn by the pilgrimage is estimated to have been 3,259,000; of which:

37%	came from	France
20%	"	Italy
13%	"	Belgium
7%	"	Germany
6%	"	Spain
5.5%	"	United Kingdom
4%	"	Ireland
7.5%	"	Others

The leading national groups included under the heading
"others" are, in descending order: Holland, Switzerland, Austria, U.S.A., Portugal, Yugoslavia, Canada, Luxembourg, Hungary, Poland, Malta, Czechoslovakia, Monaco, Greece, the
Ukraine, India, the Philippines, Vietnam, Egypt, Indonesia,
Japan, Korea, Lebanon, Ceylon, China, Guadeloupe, Brazil,
Mexico, Venezuela, Martinique, Argentina, Costa Rica, Colom-
bia, Chile, Australia, Tahiti, New Zealand, Mauritius, Niger,
South Africa, Réunion, Gabon and the Ivory Coast. Pilgrims

from sixty other countries also came, alone or in groups of less than thirty. The proportion of foreign pilgrims has been growing steadily since the first foreign groups arrived in 1873.

Source: Press Bureau, Lourdes.

2. The proportion of pilgrims by sex in 1977

The average percentage of all pilgrims is 67% female and 33% male.

Holland sends the lowest proportion of male pilgrims, 27%; Germany, Belgium and Spain send the highest at 38%.

Source: Press Bureau, Lourdes.

APPENDIX II

A LIST OF MARIAN APPARITIONS OF THE TWENTIETH CENTURY UNRECOGNIZED BY THE CATHOLIC CHURCH

In the book *Vraies et Fausses Apparitions dans l'Eglise,* Dom Bernard Billet lists 232 Marian visions reported to have taken place around the world between 2 March 1928 and 2 June 1975. The following tables are based on those compiled by him, divided by year and by country.

232 Unrecognized apparitions of the Virgin Mary (1928–1975)

I. By year

Year		Year		Year	
1928	1	1944	2	1960	3
1929	0	1945	2	1961	4
1930	1	1946	4	1962	1
1931	3	1947	18	1963	2
1932	2	1948	21	1964	1
1933	15	1949	13	1965	2
1934	3	1950	13	1966	7
1935	1	1951	8	1967	5
1936	2	1952	5	1968	7
1937	5	1953	9	1969	5
1938	7	1954	18	1970	5
1939	3	1955	3	1971	2
1940	3	1956	3	1972	4
1941	0	1957	3	1973	1
1942	1	1958	6	1974	0
1943	2	1959	5	1975	1

II. By country

Italy	83	Greece	2
France	30	Hungary	2
Germany	20	Lithuania	2
Belgium	17	Luxembourg	2
Spain	12	Mexico	2
U.S.A.	9	Philippines	2
Canada	6	Portugal	2
Switzerland	5	Rumania	2
Brazil	4	Algeria	1
Holland	4	China	1
Ireland	4	Egypt	1
Poland	4	Lebanon	1
Colombia	3	Palestine	1
Czechoslovakia	3	Peru	1
U.K.	2	Ukraine	1
Austria	2	Yugoslavia	1

The two British apparitions were:

1947 Stockport (The Lady was wearing a crown of roses)
1954 Newcastle (5 November)

The four Irish apparitions were:

1939–46 Kerrytown (A long series of visions to Teresa Ward and "O'Donnell")
1939 Dublin
1942–47 Cornamona, Galway (A long series of visions to Marie Morin)
1950 Belmullet, Co. Mayo (To a young girl of 12)

Many of the twentieth-century apparitions have their incongruous aspects. Those of Barbara Ruess took place at Marienfried Pfaffenhoffen in Germany between 1940 and 1946, regardless of surrounding events. The single Egyptian vision took place in April 1968 during a moderately active period of Egyptian-Israeli hostilities and was seen by a congregation of 100,000 Copts. It is recognized by the Coptic Church. Perhaps the most unexpected venue for a Marian vision was for that experienced by a French visionary in October 1954, in St. Tropez. The swollen total of visions for 1954 may be connected with the fact that it was the international Marian Year.

APPENDIX III
THE LIST OF PROCLAIMED MIRACLES

It is hard to find any pattern in the miracles of Lourdes. In an analysis carried out by Fr. Leopold Sabourin SJ, Professor of

Exegesis and Biblical Theology at the Pontifical Biblical Institute, Rome, it was said that most of these cures were of pulmonary tuberculosis, tuberculous fistulae, tuberculous peritonitis
and various kinds of eye disease.

Of the 64 people cured 52 were women and 54 were French.
There have also been 4 Italians, 3 Belgians, 1 Austrian, 1 German and 1 Swiss. The oldest miraculated pilgrim was 64, the
youngest 2.

Arranged by date of cure, and disregarding the original 7
cases which launched the fame of the shrine, the cures have
taken place over periods of twenty-five years as follows:

        1862–86:   4
        1887–1911: 29
        1912–36:   2
        1937–61:   20
        1962–79:   2

This shows a pattern of alternation. But since an essential element in any proclamation is the diocesan commission, and
since the members of such a body are human, the variation is
as likely to be in the opinion of the commissioners as in the
original events.

That there is a fashion in the proclamation of miracles is
confirmed when one examines them by date of proclamation
rather than by date of cure. Setting aside, once again, the original 7 cases we see that in the twenty-five years after the first
proclamation (1862–86) 4 cures took place that were later to
be proclaimed, but no proclamations were made at all. In the
next period (1887–1911) when 29 cures took place, 28 proclamations were made, all of them between 1907 and 1911. A further 5 miracles were proclaimed before World War I. And in
the period 1912–36, when only 2 cures took place that were
subsequently to be proclaimed, no post-war proclamations were
made.

The modern sequence did not recommence until 1946.
Clearly, in the decision whether or not to appoint a diocesan
commission to examine the findings of the Lourdes Medical Bureau, unseen and probably "political" factors are at work. The
modern sequence, of 24 proclamations in 34 years, commenced
at about the same time as the reorganization of the Medical
Bureau and the decision to encourage the simultaneous development of the Marian shrine of Fatima.

It is one thing to receive a sign of the work of God, it is
quite another thing to "proclaim" it. The French Church's final
decision to acknowledge the reputation of Lourdes as a place of
miraculous healing and to publicize it was taken at the time of
the fiftieth anniversary celebrations. The first proclamation was

made by the Bishop of Evreux on 11 February 1907, the feast
day of Our Lady of Lourdes, and the case chosen (Miracle No.
20) was that of a priest of the diocese who had been cured
fifteen years earlier. The 21 proclamations which followed in
the months leading up to the end of the anniversary season
form one-third of even today's entire list. Six of these 22 cases
were nuns and 18 of them were women. One of the proclamations (Miracle No. 8) covered events which had occurred
thirty-three years earlier. Two of the proclamations made by
the Archbishop of Paris (Nos. 16 and 17) concerned the cures
which had been slighted by Zola. The list included the first two
non-French miracles (Nos. 8 and 9). This was quite clearly a
concerted attempt by the ecclesiastical authorities to place
Lourdes on a different level of fame.

A similar though more muted concern with timing is to be
seen at the time of the centenary celebrations. So, in 1957, the
diocese of Nice decided to proclaim a cure (No. 41) which had
taken place thirty-two years earlier, although in the intervening
period the same diocese had been able to decide a case (No.
48) within two years. And in the centenary year itself (a great
year for Lourdes, when the number of pilgrims quadrupled and
the underground basilica was opened), the disappointment of the
celebrations passing without *any* miracles was avoided by the
announcement of No. 42, a relatively unspectacular cure of
tuberculous fistulae of twenty-eight years' standing.

Of more random interest is the fact that whereas Miracle
No. 8 represents the longest period of time between cure and
proclamation, thirty-three years, the shortest period passed in
Miracle No. 40, proclaimed after less than 12 months. Of the
52 women miraculously cured, 10 have been nuns and 32
others have been unmarried. Of the 12 men, 3 have been in
holy orders. The modern cures are more evenly balanced than
the old ones. There have been 5 male cures in the last 11 miracles, and 7 non-French miraculees out of the last 14 cases.

As to the cures which have *not* been declared miraculous, there
are many conflicting estimates. One early enthusiast (Georges
Bertrin) estimated that there had been 3,962 inexplicable cures
between 1858 and 1917. The Medical Bureau's records, a more
exact source, record thousands of reported cures; of which 89
were accepted as inexplicable between 1925 and 1946.

From 1947 (and the reorganization of the Medical Bureau)
to April 1977, 1,065 dossiers were opened on alleged cures; 56
of these were accepted as inexplicable by the Medical Bureau;
44 of them were forwarded to the second medical committee,
now the International Medical Committee; 25 of these were accepted and passed on to the diocesan authorities; and 17 of
these were eventually proclaimed miraculous.

Cures of Lourdes recognized as Miraculous by the Church

List no.	Name and Domicile	Nature of illness	Age at cure	Diocese and year of recognition
1	Mrs. CATHERINE LATAPIE-CHOUAT of Loubajac	Paralysis of cubital type due to traumatic elongation of the brachial plexus for 18 months.	39 yrs. on 1-3-1858	
2	Mr. LOUIS BOURIETTE of Lourdes	20-year-old injury to the right eye with blindness for 2 years.	54 yrs. in March 1858	
3	Mrs. BLAISETTE CAZENAVE (nee Soupene) of Lourdes	Chemosis or chronic ophthalmitis with ectropion for 3 years.	About 50 yrs. in March 1858	
4	Mr. HENRI BUSQUET of Nay	Adenitis of the root of the neck (undoubtedly tuberculous) with fistulae for 15 months.	About 15 yrs. on 29-4-1858	Mandate of Monseigneur Laurence on 18-1-1862
5	Mr. JUSTIN BOUHORT of Lourdes	Chronic post-infective hypothrepsia with retarded motor development. Diagnosis at the time; "consumption."	2 yrs. on 6-7-1858	
6	Mrs. MADELEINE RIZAN of Nay	Left hemiplegia for 24 years.	About 58 yrs. on 17-10-1858	
7	Miss MARIE MOREAU of Tartas	Very marked impairment of vision with inflammatory lesions especially of the right eye, progressive for 10 months.	About 17 yrs. on 9-11-1858	
8	Mr. PIERRE DE RUDDER of Jabbeke (Belgium)	Ununited fracture of the left leg.	52 yrs. on 7-4-1875	Bruges (Belg.) 1908

No.	Name	Condition	Age / Date	Place
9	Miss Joachime Dehant of Geves (Belgium)	Leg ulcer with extensive gangrene.	29 yrs. on 13-9-1878	Namur (Belg.) 1908
10	Miss Elisa Seisson of Rognognas	Hypertrophy of the heart and oedema of the lower limbs.	27 yrs. on 29-8-1882	Aix-en-Provence 1912
11	Sister Eugenia (Marie Mabille) of Bernay	Abscess of the true pelvis with vesical and colic fistulae. Bilateral phlebitis.	28 yrs. on 21-8-1883	Evreux 1908
12	Sister Julienne (Aline Bruyere) of La Roque	Cavitating pulmonary tuberculosis.	25 yrs. on 1-9-1889	Tulle 1912
13	Sister Josephine-Marie (Anne Jourdain) of Goincourt	Pulmonary tuberculosis.	36 yrs. on 21-8-1890	Beauvais 1908
14	Miss Amélie Chagnon of Poitiers	Tuberculous osteo-arthritis of the knee and second metatarsal of the foot.	17 yrs. on 21-8-1891	Tournai (Belg.) 1910
15	Miss Clémentine Trouve (Sr. Agnès-Marie) of Rouille	Osteo periostitis of the right foot with fistulae.	14 yrs. on 21-8-1891	Paris 1908
16	Miss Marie Lebranchu (Mrs. Wuiplier) of Paris	Pulmonary tuberculosis (Koch's bacillae present in sputum).	35 yrs. on 20-8-1892	Paris 1908
17	Miss Marie Lemarchand (Mrs. Authier) of Caen	Pulmonary tuberculosis with ulcers of face and leg.	18 yrs. on 21-8-1892	Paris 1908
18	Miss Elise Lesage of Bucquoy	Tuberculous osteo-arthritis of knee.	18 yrs. on 21-8-1892	Arras 1908
19	Sister Marie de la Presentation of Lille	Chronic tuberculous gastro-enteritis.	44 yrs. on 29-8-1892	Cambrai 1908
20	Father Cirette of Beaumontel	Antero-lateral spinal sclerosis.	46 yrs. on 31-8-1893	Evreux 1907

List no.	Name and Domicile	Nature of illness	Age at cure	Diocese and year of recognition
21	Miss Aurélie Huprelle of St.-Martin-le-Noeud	Apical pulmonary tuberculosis.	26 yrs. on 21-8-1895	Beauvais 1908
22	Miss Esther Brachmann of Paris	Tuberculous peritonitis.	15 yrs. on 21-8-1896	Paris 1908
23	Miss Jeanne Tulasne of Tours	Lumbar Pott's disease, with neuropathic club foot.	20 yrs. on 8-9-1897	Tours 1907
24	Miss Clémentine Malot of Gaudechart	Pulmonary tuberculosis with haemoptysis.	25 yrs. on 21-8-1898	Beauvais 1908
25	Mrs. Rose François (nee Labreuvoies) of Paris	Fistular lymphangitis of the right arm with enormous oedema.	36 yrs. on 20-8-1899	Paris 1908
26	Reverend Father Salvator of Dinard	Tuberculous peritonitis.	38 yrs. on 25-6-1900	Rennes 1908
27	Sister Maximilien of Marseille	Hydatid cyst of the liver, phlebitis of the left lower limb.	43 yrs. on 20-5-1901	Marseille 1908
28	Miss Marie Savoye of Cateau-Cambresis	Rheumatic disease of the mitral valve with failure.	24 yrs. on 20-9-1901	Cambrai 1908
29	Mrs. Johanna Bezenac (nee Dubos) of St.-Laurent-des-Batons	Pyrexia of unknown origin, impetigo of the eyelids and forehead.	28 yrs. on 8-8-1904	Perigueux 1908
30	Sister Saint-Hilaire of Peyreleau	Abdominal tumour.	39 yrs. on 20-8-1904	Rodez 1908
31	Sister Sainte-Beatrix (Rosalie Vildier) of Evreux	Laryngo-bronchitis, probably tuberculous.	42 yrs. on 31-8-1904	Evreux 1908

32	Miss MARIE-THÉRÈSE NOBLET of Avenay	Dorso-lumbar spondylitis.	15 yrs. on 31-8-1905	Reims 1908
33	Miss CÉCILE DOUVILLE DE FRANSSU of Tournai (Belgium)	Tuberculous peritonitis.	19 yrs. on 21-9-1905	Versailles 1909
34	Miss ANTONIA MOULIN of Vienne	Osteitic fistulae of the right femur with arthritis of the knee.	30 yrs. on 10-8-1907	Grenoble 1910
35	Miss MARIE BOREL of Mende	Four pyelo-colic fistulae of the lumbar region.	27 yrs. on 21/22-8-1907	Mende 1911
36	Miss VIRGINIE HAUDEBOURG of Lons-le-Saulnier	Tuberculous cystitis, nephritis.	22 yrs. on 17-5-1908	Saint-Claude 1912
37	Mrs. MARIE BIRE (nee Lucas) of Ste.-Gemme-la-Plaine	Blindness of cerebral origin, bilateral optic atrophy.	41 yrs. on 5-8-1908	Luçon 1910
38	Miss AIMÉE ALLOPE of Vern	Numerous tuberculous abscesses with 4 fistulae of the anterior abdominal parietis.	37 yrs. on 28-5-1909	Angers 1910
39	Miss JULIETTE ORION of St.-Hilaire-de-Voust	Pulmonary and laryngeal tuberculosis, suppurating left mastoiditis.	24 yrs. on 22-7-1910	Luçon 1913
40	Mrs. MARIE FABRE of Montredon	Muco-membranous enteritis, uterine prolapse.	32 yrs. on 26-9-1911	Cahors 1912
41	Miss HENRIETTE BRESSOLLES of Nice	Pott's disease, paraplegia.	About 30 yrs. old on 3-7-1924	Nice 1957
42	Miss LYDIA BROSSE of St.-Raphael	Multiple tuberculous fistulae with wide undermining.	41 yrs. on 11-10-1930	Coutances 1958

List no.	Name and Domicile	Nature of illness	Age at cure	Diocese and year of recognition
43	Sister MARIE-MARGUERITE (Françoise Capitaine) of Rennes	Abscess of the left kidney with phlyctenular oedema and "cardiac crises."	64 yrs. on 22-1-1937	Rennes 1946
44	Miss LOUISE JAMAIN (Mrs. Maître) of Paris	Pulmonary, intestinal and peritoneal tuberculosis.	22 yrs. on 1-4-1937	Paris 1951
45	Mr. FRANCIS PASCAL of Beaucaire	Blindness, paralysis of the lower limbs.	3 yrs. 10 mths. on 28-8-1938	Aix-en-Provence 1949
46	Miss GABRIELLE CLAUZEL of Oran	Rheumatic spondylitis.	49 yrs. on 15-8-1943	Oran 1948
47	Miss YVONNE FOURNIER of Limoges	Extending and progressive post-traumatic syndrome (Leriche's syndrome).	22 yrs. on 19-8-1945	Paris 1959
48	Mrs. ROSE MARTIN (nee Perona) of Nice	Cancer of the uterine cervix (epithelioma of the cylindrical glands).	45 yrs. on 3-7-1947	Nice 1949
49	Mrs. JEANNE GESTAS (nee Pelin) of Begles	Dyspeptic troubles with obstructive episodes.	50 yrs. on 22-8-1947	Bordeaux 1952
50	Miss MARIE-THÉRÈSE CANIN of Marseille	Dorso-lumbar Pott's disease and tuberculous peritonitis with fistulae.	37 yrs. on 9-10-1947	Marseille 1952
51	Miss MADDALENA CARINI of San Remo (Italy)	Peritoneal, pleuro-pulmonary and bony tuberculosis with coronary disease.	31 yrs. on 15-8-1948	Milano (Italy) 1960
52	Miss JEANNE FRETEL of Rennes	Tuberculous peritonitis.	34 yrs. on 8-10-1948	Rennes 1950
53	Miss THEA ANGELE (Sr. Marie-Mercedes) of Tettnag (Germany)	Multiple sclerosis for six years.	29 yrs. on 20-5-1950	Tarbes-Lourdes 1961

	Name	Disease	Age and date	Place and year
54	Mr. EVASIO GANORA of Casale (Italy)	Hodgkin's disease.	37 yrs. on 2-6-1950	Casale (Italy) 1955
55	Miss EDELTRAUT FULDA (Mrs. Haidinger) of Wien (Austria)	Addison's disease.	34 yrs. on 12-8-1950	Wien (Austria) 1955
56	Mr. PAUL PELLEGRIN of Toulon	Post-operative fistula following a liver abscess.	52 yrs. on 3-10-1950	Frejus-Toulon 1953
57	Brother LÉO SCHWAGER of Fribourg (Switzerland)	Multiple sclerosis for 5 years.	28 yrs. on 30-4-1952	Lausanne-G.-F. 1960
58	Mrs. ALICE COUTEAULT (nee Gourdon) of Bouille-Loretz	Multiple sclerosis for 3 years.	34 yrs. on 15-5-1952	Poitiers 1956
59	Miss MARIE BIGOT of La Richardais	Arachnoiditis of the posterior fossa (blindness, deafness, hemiplegia).	31 yrs. on 8-10-1953 10-10-1954	Rennes 1956
60	Miss GINETTE NOUVEL (nee Fabre) of Carmaux	Budd-Chiari disease (supra-hepatic venous thrombosis).	26 yrs. on 23-9-1954	Albi 1963
61	Miss ELISA ALOI (nee Varacalli) of Patti (Italy)	Tuberculous osteo-arthritis with fistulae at numerous sites on the right lower limb.	27 yrs. on 5-6-1958	Messina (Italy) 1965
62	Miss JULIETTE TAMBURINI of Marseille	Femoral osteoperiostitis with fistulae, epistaxis, for 10 years.	22 yrs. on 17-7-1959	Marseille 1965
63	Mr. VITTORIO MICHELI of Scurelle (Italy)	Sarcoma of pelvis.	23 yrs. on 1-6-1963	Trento (Italy) 1976
64	Mr. SERGE PERRIN of Lion d'Angers	Recurring organic hemiplegia, with ocular lesions, due to cerebral circulatory defects.	41 yrs. on 1-5-1970	Angers 1978

APPENDIX IV

BRIEF ACCOUNTS OF SIX MODERN MIRACLES
(*Published with the special permission of the Bishop
of Tarbes and Lourdes, and the Medical Bureau
of Lourdes*)

No. 54 (1955) Mr. Evasio Ganora of Italy

Cured of Hodgkin's disease 31 May 1950, at 37 years of age.
Previous illnesses: None known.
Present illness: December 1949, anorexia and asthenia.

January 1950, development of a remittent fever, ranging from
40°C. (104°F.) to 37°C. (97°F.) accompanied by heavy
sweats. A Widal test was slightly positive, in dilution 1/80. His
fever was unaltered by penicillin, and on 23 January his liver
edge was palpable below the right costal margin and felt hard
and painless. His spleen was enlarged two finger breadths below
the left costal margin. Lymph glands normal.

Repeat Widal: negative.
Blood cultures: negative.
Haemoglobin: 75%.
Red cell count: 4,300,000/cmm. Colour index 0.9.
White cell count: 1,400/cmm.
  Neutrophils: 54%.
  Lymphocytes: 30%.
  Monocytes: 14%.
  Eosinophils: 2%.

Marrow examination within normal limits, perhaps a slight
increase in eosinophils.

Sedimentation rate raised (76 mm./hour).
Chest X-ray: pleural thickening at the right base.

Progress was downhill, with no response to intensive antibiotic treatment. He developed skin itch, and accompanying the
constant leucopenia was a relative lymphocytosis and eosino-
philia.

On 10 February 1950, a hard, mobile, painless and bean-sized
lump was noted in his right axilla, and this was biopsied on
16 February. Dr. Fittibaldi was able to exclude tuberculosis on
his examination, and sought the opinion of Professor Storti of
Pavia University, who made a diagnosis of Hodgkin's disease,
with all classical features present.

The patient was given two courses of deep X-ray therapy to
axilla and spleen and blood transfusion but he continued to deteriorate and he was thought to have only a short time to live.

He came to Lourdes on 31 May 1950. On immersion in the
water he felt a great warmth course through his body, and he

was immediately able to walk back to the hospital, and began to perform the duties of a stretcher bearer.

When he was examined at the Medical Bureau his fever had gone, his liver, spleen and glands were no longer palpable. He went back to hard work as a farm labourer, and in 1953 his own doctor testified to his continued good health.

In 1954, full examination at the Medical Bureau revealed no abnormality. In 1955, the International Medical Committee in Paris (Prof. Sendrail of Toulouse and twenty-five doctors) testified to his recovery.

The original histological specimens have been repeatedly and thoroughly reviewed, and the diagnosis of Hodgkin's disease is not denied.

On 31 May 1955, cure was declared miraculous by an Ecclesiastic judgement.

No. 58 (1956) Mrs. Alice Couteault of France

Born 1917. Lives in Le Puy Notre-Dame, (Deux-Sevres), France.

Diagnosis: Disseminated sclerosis.

Previous medical history: 1938: Phlebitis after confinement.

                           1950: Salpingectomy.

Present illness: Onset in July 1949; asthenia with evening temperature to 38.5°C. (101°F.); pain in right sacro-iliac region; spastic gait noticeable. As the symptoms became worse she was examined by a doctor from Thouars, who diagnosed "disseminated sclerosis." In January 1950 this diagnosis was confirmed by Dr. Beauchant of Poitiers, based on her ataxic gait, and exaggerated knee and ankle jerks. By February 1950 she had ankle and patellar clonus, a spastic gait and accentuation of her fever.

In February, March and April her condition worsened, with loss of weight, blisters on the soles of her feet, incoordination and intention tremor, making eating and dressing difficult. She developed speech, visual and sphincter disturbances.

Haemoglobin: 90%. Colour index: 1.0.

Red cell count: 4,256,000/c.mm.

White cell count: 4,400/c.mm.

Wassermann, Kahn tests negative.

Cerebrospinal fluid: albumin 20 mgm. %.

                    sugar 55 mgm. %.

                    chlorides 700 mgm. %.

History of her cure: During the afternoon procession on 16 May 1952, when the Blessed Sacrament was presented to the sick, she suddenly felt she had to get up from her bed, and when she returned to the hospital she was able to walk. Next day she was seen by the doctors in the Medical Bureau of

Lourdes and they found that she walked normally; there were no contractures, no patellar clonus, the knee jerks were normal pupillary reflexes, but corneal reflexes were absent; there was slight vertical nystagmus.

Three days later (on 19 May 1952) on her return home, her own practitioner found that her gait and reflexes were normal, and she had no pain or fever.

Madame Couteault was examined again at Lourdes on 5 May 1953, when six doctors testified that she had no trouble with speech, her plantar responses were flexor, her muscle power was normal, tendon reflexes were slightly exaggerated, and her abdominal reflexes were present. There was a slight degree of vertical nystagmus.

She was re-examined in May 1954, and again in May 1955, when fourteen doctors testified that all nystagmus and cerebellar signs had disappeared and there were no pyramidal signs. She was leading a normal active life, quite symptomless, and had regained weight. In August 1955, Professor Thiebaut, of the International Medical Committee in Paris, certified that he found no evidence of clinical disease, and that her recovery had been maintained for four years.

At Lourdes on 14 May 1964, Madame Couteault was found to be in excellent health and no general or neurological abnormality could be demonstrated.

The cure was declared miraculous by the Ecclesiastic authorities on 16 July 1956.

No. 59 (1956) Miss Marie Bigot of France

Born 1923. Living in La Richardais, (Ille-et-Vilaine), France.
Previous medical history: Recurrent skin infections since 10 years of age. Appendicectomy 1933.
Present illness: She had had poor eyesight for years but deterioration began in 1951, and Dr. Sevegrand, in St. Malo, stated that her visual acuity was 3/10, her fundi were normal, retinae faintly pale, ocular tension normal, visual fields normal.

On 3 April 1951 she developed right frontal headaches, and her temperature rose to 39°C. (102°F.). She failed to respond to penicillin and became semicomatose, even with the addition of streptomycin and aureomycin.

On 18 April 1951 she was examined by Dr. Ferey, neurosurgeon, who found hyperexcitability of the reflexes in arms and legs, hypermetria and adiadochokinesis on the right side, diminished stereognosis and position sense with normal response to touch, pain and temperature. There was hypoaesthesia of the right cornea and diminished hearing in the right ear. There was a tendency to fall to the right.

Cerebrospinal fluid:
Cells 0.6.
Albumin 28 mgm. %.
No organisms seen.
X-ray of sinuses and mastoids: normal.
Wassermann negative.

On 29 April an occipital craniotomy was performed by Dr. Ferey. On opening the dura mater, cerebrospinal fluid ran out under pressure; the fifth, seventh, eighth and eleventh cranial nerves were seen, surrounded by adhesions, which were freed.

Surgical diagnosis: Posterior fossa adhesive arachnoiditis, and Professor Thiebaut later made a diagnosis of an accompanying encephalomyelitis.

Post-operatively, no improvement in her vision, and she needed support while walking, because of weakness of the whole of her right side.

In the following months her disabilities increased, and in July 1951 Dr. Sevegrand found paralysis of the right arm and right leg, with visual acuity 1/10 on the right, 2/10 on the left. Right ear deaf. Dr. Ferey thought a tumour mass had formed due to a localization of infection, but he did not prescribe any new treatment.

Dr. Guilherm, psychiatrist at Rennes, did not make a precise diagnosis, but stated there was "a functional overlay on an organic basis."

In August 1952 Mademoiselle Bigot could walk only with the support of one person, and a walking stick in the left hand. Her sight got worse so that she experienced difficulty even in recognizing members of her own family. Suddenly one day she felt a "tearing" sensation in her head and Dr. Sevegrand stated that she had become blind and deaf with accompanying generalized spasms and respiratory distress. He expected a fatal outcome, and sent for a priest who administered Extreme Unction.

For a month her condition remained so, and even when she could get up her blindness did not allow her to distinguish night from day, her deafness was complete, and her right foot was twisted into equinovarus. She began to study Braille.

History of her cure: October 1952: First visit to Lourdes, with no change in her physical condition.

October 1953: On her second visit, she lost her hemiplegia during the procession of the Blessed Sacrament, after feeling a terrible cramp in her right foot. She was able to fold her rosary in her right hand. However, both eyes were still blind, with bilateral gross papilloedema, and she was still deaf.

October 1954: She returned to Lourdes primarily to have the recovery from her hemiplegia verified at the Medical Bureau. After the Blessing of the Sick, she suddenly heard a noise, and then the crowd singing. Next day she returned home by train and regained her vision quite suddenly on the way. Dr. Sevegrand was able to state that her visual acuity was 10/10 in both eyes. Her recovery has been maintained ever since.

The cure was declared miraculous by an Ecclesiastical judgement with Cardinal Roques presiding, on 15 August 1956.

No. 61 (1965) Miss Elisa Aloi of Italy

Born 15 September 1930 at Patti. Now Mrs. Vacaralli. Vil Giulo Cesare Policoro 750 25, Provencia Matera (Italia).
Past history: Nothing specific relating to present illness.
Family history: Both parents died of T.B. Two brother in good health.
Present illness: In 1948 developed swelling of the right knee. Tuberculosis Arthritis diagnosed. Subsequently had numerous aspirations and incisions of recurrent abscesses as well as curettage during period of 6 months. At same time developed recurring similar lesions of right elbow and thigh. The first episode lasted 18–20 months. Several types of treatment were used including incisions of the abscesses, drainage and antiseptic irrigations, excisions of sinuses, immobilization and, of course, antibiotic therapy of various kinds for varying durations and both locally and generally in various combinations.

Thereafter, from the age of 19 to 26 she spent long periods in four or five different hospitals and about fifty surgical interventions were carried out during this time. There was no question that the diagnosis was that of Tuberculosis associated with secondary infection. Her general condition varied over the years depending on the care given, and available living conditions; her weight varied from 45–55 kg.

In 1957 on 19 March she was admitted to hospital in Case del Sole and stayed there for 14 months. Her general condition was poor with fever, muscular wasting, a deformed left thigh with two sinuses, externally rotationed, and abducted. Whilst in hospital innumerable abscesses appeared in the first three months, sometimes accompanied by considerable fever, and were treated by drainage.

In June 1957 she made her first pilgrimage to Lourdes and nothing unusual happened.

In December 1957 she developed septic arthritis of the left knee.

In February 1958 she was somewhat improved but by April was worse again and was admitted to Messina Hospital in May 1958. From this hospital three detailed certificates provided by Professor di Cesare are available. The first gives a detailed clinical description of her condition on admission and contains an enumeration of all the sinuses then present (about a dozen).

Noted to have intermittent fever and considerable anaemia with a red cell count of 2.3 million, also marked muscle wasting and loss of movement of all joints of both lower limbs. The second certificate confirmed the tuberculosis aetiology and the third certificate was to the effect that the patient had never obained any benefit from either the medication or the surgical processes carried out at the various hospitals to which she had been admitted.

In June 1958 she visited Lourdes again arriving with both lower limbs encased in plaster from pelvis to foot. There were at least four sinuses draining on each leg, two by tube. It was impossible to take her to the baths and she asked to be treated by direct application of the water. On the third day after her arrival all purulent discharge had ceased and the patient demanded removal of the plaster. This was refused but the drains were removed and the dressings continued. On the way home the dressings were changed on the train and none were found to be soiled, and all sinuses were closed.

On 11 June, that is seven days after leaving Lourdes, Prof. di Cesare certified that she was completely cured and that he could not believe that it was the same person who had left in such a hopeless state.

On 5 June 1959 the cure was confirmed by the Medical Bureau of Lourdes meeting with eight doctors present and on 4 June 1960, with 14 doctors present when the decision had been unanimous. It was agreed that the illness described in the certificates existed without doubt and that its course had been abruptly modified where previously there had been no tendency to improve. Furthermore this cure had lasted. It was confirmed by the International Committee on 23 April 1961, based on the report of Prof. Salmon.

On 26 May 1965, the cure was declared a miracle by canonical judgement signed by Mgr. Fasola, Archbishop and Archimandrite of Messina.

No. 63 (1976) Mr. Vittorio Micheli of Italy

Born 6 February 1940, from the Province of Trente.

During his military service, this soldier of the Alpine Corps was admitted on 16 April 1962 to the Military Hospital of Verona, suffering from a large mass in the buttock region, limiting the normal range of movement of his left hip, with leg and sciatic pain.

After various unsuccessful therapeutic trials, radiological examination showed a structural alteration of the left iliac bone (osteolysis of the inferior half of the iliac bone and of the acetabular roof, amputation of the two rami of the ischium and

gross osteoporosis of the femoral head), immediately suggestive
of a malignant type of neoplastic lesion.

At the end of May a biopsy was taken. The exposure of the
tumour had to be made beneath the buttock muscles and the
various sections revealed that the specimen under consideration
was a fusiform cell sarcoma.

The sick man was then immobilized in a frame from pelvis
to feet and sent during the month of June to a centre for
radiotherapy.

Four days later he was discharged—without having received
any therapy at all—and readmitted to the Military Hospital at
Trente.

There, during ten months, no specific treatment—medical, surgical or radiotherapeutic—was prescribed, in spite of:

radiological evidence of persistent bony destruction;
progressive loss of all active movement of the left lower
limb;
progressive deterioration.

On 24 May 1963 the patient left for Lourdes, where he was
bathed, in his plaster, several times.

From 1 June his pain disappeared, his appetite returned, an
unexpected improvement in his general state became established, allowing the patient to consider himself cured.

In spite of this, he returned to the Hospital of Trente, where
he remained hospitalized for several more months under observation; although the X-rays had demonstrated, since the month
of August, that the bony reconstruction of the parts destroyed
was progressing steadily.

His general state of health improved daily and made it possible for the ex-invalid to walk again with his left lower limb in
plaster (as a precaution).

Later, in February 1964, examination showed evidence of
asymmetry of the pelvis, with apparent shortening of the left
lower limb, but with raising of the femoral head to the level of
a new acetabular cavity. This residual deformity constitutes a
very precious stigma of the disease—creating no loss of power
or even inconvenience.

On 24 April 1964 Vittorio Micheli was discharged from the
Hospital while awaiting a pension, declared unfit for military
service.

Since then he has resumed his trade, which is particularly arduous, since it is carried out almost constantly on his feet, without interruption. He has also been able once more to make
long excursions in the mountains.

This cure, before being accepted and confirmed for certain

by the Medical Bureau of Lourdes in May 1967, has necessitated:

> an annual confirmation of his state of health;
> systematic radiography of the region of prime concern and to seek metastases;
> as well as confirmation of lesional diagnosis by Professor Henri Payan (Chair of Pathological Anatomy of Marseille University).

At its meeting in May 1969, the International Medical Committee was unwilling to come to a conclusion (in a way, perhaps, too soon); it adjourned its decision (after, however, a favourable vote), acceding to a counter assessment put forward by some of its members.

Relying on Professor Fabre (Chair of Pathological Anatomy of the University of Toulouse) it confirmed, as a whole, the opinion of the previous experts: malignant tumour originating in connective tissue, not osteogenic.

Also, two years later, the report of Professor M.-M. Salmon at the same International Medical Committee of Lourdes, was accepted by unanimous vote (3 May 1971).

Its conclusions declared:

> the illness qualified as "real, certain, incurable";
> the development of this sarcoma "abruptly altered on the occasion of his pilgrimage to Lourdes";
> the cure "effective and lasting";
> finally the fact that "no medical explanation is capable of being given for this cure."

From that time Vittorio Micheli has been seen again several times at Lourdes, where he comes now as a brancardier member of the Hospitality of his Diocese.

Finally, since 1973, a Diocesan Commission, nominated by the Archbishop of Trente and composed of medical men and of experts in canon law, has enquired in its turn into this extraordinary event, in relation to the rules laid down by Benedict XIV.

After having obtained a favourable opinion, on 26 May 1976, Monseigneur Alessandro Gottardi, Archbishop of Trente, solemnly recognized this cure as "an intervention of the power of God, the Creator and Father, and by the intercession of the Immaculate Virgin."

No. 64 (1978) Mr. Serge Perrin of France

Born on 13 February 1929 at Lion d'Angers.

Serge Perrin was married in 1964 and has three children. He worked as an accountant in a local firm.

In infancy he suffered from chronic otitis media of the left ear, with loss of hearing. When sixteen, he had some "side effects" more severe than usual after sunstroke.

Although he enjoyed good health up to 35 years of age, he had a bad family history of hypertension, vascular accidents and obesity.

In February 1964 he woke up with a very severe headache, and quickly developed difficulty in walking, impairment of speech and made many mistakes in his work.

After returning home, his own doctor, Dr. E. Sourice, found that he had a right hemiplegia, chiefly affecting his lower limb.

Confirmation of his condition was requested first from a neurologist, then from a neurosurgeon, Professor Pecker (Professor of Neuro-Surgery at Rennes). Professor Pecker undertook a series of investigations to determine the cause of such a serious illness.

No cause was found, and as his disablement was regressing, there was no reason to make further tests. He was prescribed vaso-dilator drugs, and three months after the onset of his illness, he was fit to return to work.

During the next five years he led a normal life without any setbacks. Then as suddenly as in 1964, on 2 December 1968, he developed:

> a similar clinical picture (but without any regression this time),
> a similar course of medical investigation.

In February 1969 S. Perrin visited Professor Pecker again. Further arteriograms of the carotid arteries were more definite. They revealed clearly a "left carotid artery thrombosis" confirming the neurological signs. Unfortunately, no improvement was perceptible, neither spontaneously, nor after treatment with drugs.

In April 1969 another consultation took place at Rennes. This revealed:

> "Bilateral insufficiency of the cerebral circulation."
> "Significant changes in the visual acuity, and the fields of vision."

The doctors let it be understood that all medication proved useless. From April–May 1968 he left for Lourdes, from whence he returned obviously more courageous, but in the same state.

For a whole year the situation was this:

> Increasing invalidity (officially relegated to the 3rd category, incapable of work or of looking after himself, from October 1969).

Deterioration of the senses (almost blind and gross diminution of the visual fields).

"Cerebral attacks" of ever increasing frequency.

Treatment was of no avail. His morale had reached its lowest
ebb.

Despite all, he returned to Lourdes at the end of April 1970,
"to please his family." The outward journey and stay in
Lourdes were most trying at times.

On the last day, 1 May, at the end of the Anointing of the
Sick, he experienced some sensation, felt even in his feet.

Some hours later he realized that he had recovered his vision
completely, and could walk again without the use of sticks.

This happened as he was about to leave Lourdes, which
prevented him from being examined at the Medical Bureau. So
it was at his home that the investigations of his cure took place.

First his medical officer and all the team of pilgrimage
doctors examined him. Then Prof. Pecker and Dr. Drevillon
(ophthalmologist) carried out appropriate tests; each in turn
confirmed that there was no trace of his former disability. His
cerebral circulation returned to normal, which explained the
disappearance of his motor and sensory lesions, the absence of
further "cerebral attacks" and the recovery of his vision. After
another carotid arteriogram was done, it was observed that it
was "impossible to affirm that in 1969 a thrombosis had been
present, the evidence of obstruction could have been due to a
spasm," due to an error in technique.

However, Prof. Pecker did not consider this of vital importance, and he wrote on 30 May: "The remarkable feature of
this cure remains quite astounding—even if the arteriography is
not conclusive, I take the view that this sudden cure is most unusual, after an ischaemic cerebral lesion."

From 1 May 1970 his health remained excellent. Before the
end of the year his category of total disability was altered.

He came back to Lourdes four times in the next two years.
On 4 May 1972 the Medical Bureau admitted that this lesion of
"stenosis (or thrombosis) first in the left carotid artery, then of
both," was cured "in a complete, instantaneous and lasting
fashion" and that there was good reason "to declare this cure
as established and certain." Therefore, it judged it proper to put
forward the dossier for consideration by the International Medical Committee of Lourdes.

Before this could happen, the facts were presented to the
Diocesan Medical Commission (nominated by Mgr. Mazerat,
Bishop of Angers), who, after examining them in November
1973, came to the same conclusion.

Finally, the I.M.C.L. in October 1976, after hearing the two
reports of Prof. Mouren (consultant neurologist at Marseille)

and of Dr. Bartoli (ophthalmologist of Troyes), agreed unanimously that "Monsieur S. Perrin presented as a case of recurring organic hemiplegia, with ocular lesions, due to cerebral circulatory defects, without it being possible to define accurately the nature and the site of the vascular lesions.

"This cure, without any effective treatment, by its instantaneity, and the absence of any sequelae, and which has remained stationary for 6 years, can be considered as established in a quite extraordinary way from a medical aspect."

The Members of the International Medical Committee agreed unanimously with this verdict.

The Diocesan Canonical Commission, nominated by the new bishop, began the ecclesiastical scrutiny in November 1977. After a thorough investigation, it upheld the favourable verdict.

As a result, on 17 June 1978, Mgr. Orchampt, Bishop of Angers, pronounced this cure as "humanly inexplicable." He recognized the "miraculous character," and invited Christians to see in this sign an act of the merciful love of the Lord.

APPENDIX V

THE COMPLETE MEDICAL DOSSIER ON THE CURE
OF MR. VITTORIO MICHELI
(Published with the special permission of the Bishop of Tarbes and Lourdes, and the Medical Bureau of Lourdes)

Report by Prof. Michel-Marie Salmon

The report consists of several sections (1):

Statement of the documents of the dossier which requires analytical study so that we may consider it bit by bit.
Summary of facts in order to form an all round view of the evolution of Micheli's illness.
Diagnostic discussion.
The problem of the eventual cure.
Replies to susceptible questions likely to be asked on the subject of the Micheli case.

I. Documents

These are indexed in chronological order (2). These documents were reproduced entirely or partly in Bulletin No. 145–146 of the International Medical Association of Lourdes.

1. *16 April 1962:* A detailed case history (3) drawn up by

the Surgical Unit of the Military Hospital in Verona included full family particulars of the patient, his antecedents, the story of his illness, his state of health on entering the Army, results of paraclinic examinations, an account of an anatomo-pathological examination signed by Dr. Natucci who on 4 June 1962 concluded the diagnosis of "sarcoma of the fusiform cells" without stating the precise origin of the tumour. However, the definite diagnosis made by the surgeon is "osteo-sarcoma of the left ilium" (4).

2. *5 August 1962:* The report of the Military Hospital at Trente which completes the above.

3. *12 May 1964:* The report of the Citta di Levico Hospital at Levico, Trente, signed by Dr. Brandoliani, giving a resumé of the facts of the case from 16-4-62 to 12-5-64. The diagnosis of osteo-sarcoma of the left iliac spine appears to be confirmed.

4. *14 May 1964:* A document issued by the Citta di Levico Hospital signed by Dr. Frizzera based on the medical history of Micheli confirming the diagnosis of sarcoma of the pelvis (5) and approved by the doctors at the Trente Hospital, the Verona Hospital, the Borgo Centre for Tumours, the Radiology Unit of Levico Hospital, etc.

Dr. Frizzera stresses the inexorable development of the tumour, the immediate cessation of this development on the pilgrimage to Lourdes, the disappearance of all pain, the improvement in general health, appetite, etc. The radiological improvement with reconstruction of the bones during the period from November 1963 to February 1964.

5. A series of notes some of which are signed by Dr. Paulo Sauve, Orthopaedie and Traumatology Specialist at the St. Michel Clinic in Rome, mentioning treatments with Pentadyn and Exodan (an Italian medicament similar to French Endoxan) (6).

6. *4 and 30 November:* Two letters from Dr. Archambault of St. Aignan (Loire-et-Cher) confirming that any medicines that might have been given could well have been antimitotic which appear to be inadequate in cancer cases "which strengthens the actions of the Blessed Virgin." In the second letter Dr. Archambault insists on "restitutio ad integrum" and after some remarks adds "it is for the specialists to discuss and settle. But all the same the Blessed Virgin has performed a wonderful deed!"

7. *2 November 1964:* A letter from the Roche laboratories addressed to Dr. Archambault; Pentadyn is a psychotonic, Exodan is used in the treatment of cancer.

8. *7 January 1965 and 18 April 1969:* Two detailed accounts by Prof. Henri Payan, Professor of Pathological Anatomy at the Marseille Faculty of Medicine, who studied the histological

specimens in the Verona Hospital. I quote herewith Dr. Payan's report:

"At the request of Prof. Salmon.

"Specimen 2641/62 of Institute of Pathological Anatomy, Verona Hospital.

"*Bone specimens:* Two samples were examined.

"The first has a massive tumour formation, thick developed in layers. These cells consist of a nucleus of irregular shape, round or angular, slightly chromatie, finely spotted and dotted with a voluminous nucleus. These elements are formed in the centre of a fine fibrillary web and are mitosistic. The tissue is threaded with fine capillaries combined with some oedema and dissociation of hemorrhagie and necrosic elements. In the perilesional area a certain number of hyperplastic capillaries can be observed. On the periphery the tumour extends into the striate muscle causing hypertrophy and destruction.

"The second sample shows that neoplastic levels are in contact with osteoid areas (or bone if there has already been decalcification); these areas are massive in the centre of the medullary spaces; they denote serious cytological changes.

"Conclusion: From a morphological point of view certain aspects could suggest the possibility of a diagnosis of angiosarcoma owing to the pitting of the area of the lesions which could indicate vascular cavities. In fact in the absence of any sanguine infiltration at their levels these indications must be interpreted to my mind as a sarcoma. In view of the presence of an abundant reticular formation it could be considered reticulosarcoma (7). In any case taking into account the usual radiography explanations this tumour shows the characteristics of a manifest malignant neoformation developed in both the bone tissue and in the marrow, in particular in the striate muscles which are attacked direct (8).

"Readings of the micro-photographs (9):

"(a) Massive monomorphous cellular formations characterize the tumour.

"(b) Under stronger magnification the development of neoplastic cells is observed at the centre of a fine fibrillary network and the characteristics of the elements result in a reduced cytoplasm, an irregular shaped nucleus, atypical with angular contours; fine capillaries run through the tissue.

"(c) Neoplastic formations visible at the junction of an osseous space.

"(d) Extension of the tumour into the marrow with penetration into the muscle between the detached and hydrotrophic fibres."

9. *10 February 1965:* Two papers by Drs. Frizzera and Brandolani describing Micheli's condition at this time: "Gen-

eral condition flourishing, mobility of the left hip satisfactory although limited, shortening of left leg 5 cm., reconstruction of left ilium and neocotyle with raising of the head of the femur."

10. *10 and 14 July 1965:* An interrogation (10) to define the circumstances of the cure by the Citta di Levico Hospital. This memorandum confirms that Micheli, who came to Lourdes on a stretcher in 1963, felt his pain subsiding without sedatives or opiates and as from June was able to walk unaided. At first he had crutches, then two sticks; the leg movements were still abnormal, the plaster was strengthened and his appetite improved. In November 1963 X-rays did not show radiological cure but he was able to walk easily and without pain. Micheli could not say if the leg had returned to normal before February 1964 he only realized he was cured on 24 February 1964 when, after the plaster was removed, he discovered that this time he felt he was able to walk, and it was only through precaution that he was left in bed for a further week with his apparatus. As soon as he received permission from the doctor-in-charge he got up and walked.

11. *20 May 1966:* An observation taken by Dr. Frizzera at Levico Hospital: "actually Micheli is walking well. He came to Lourdes on a stretcher in May 1963, and on his return to Italy the pain abated and from the month of June he walked wearing his apparatus." Dr. Frizzera always stresses that Micheli only realized his cure on 24 February 1964, when the plaster was removed. Actually the mobility of the hip remains satisfactory and Micheli works in a standing position.

12. *26 March 1967:* A certificate signed by Dr. Frizzera recalling interesting and significant medical symptoms. Before his Military Service Micheli had suffered from nephritis and polyps in the nose in 1958 which were cured completely. Dr. Frizzera also stresses the fact that Micheli works 8–10 hours a day standing at a textile machine and has never been absent from work on account of his "leg."

13. *2 May 1967:* Dr. Frizzera confirms Micheli's good state of health. Rate of sedimentation normal; a radiograph taken by Dr. Brandolani on 26 April 1967, in the Levico Hospital, is excellent.

14. *10 October 1967:* Dr. Pierini, head of the Radiology Unit at the Military Hospital in Florence and Director of the private radiology unit in Viareggio, affirms that in 38 years of medical practice he has never had occasion to verify a similar reconstruction of articular coxa-femoral bone elements with the complete disappearance of neoplastic infiltration of the marrow. This opinion is also expressed by Prof. Franchi, Doctor-in-charge of the Radiology Unit of the Civil Hospital in La Spezzia.

15. *21 April 1969:* Dr. Claudio Romanese, Specialist in Orthopaedic and Traumatic Surgery, 380 38 Tereso (Trente) writes: "I the undersigned certify that I was Assistant in the Surgical Unit in the Trente Military Hospital from 1960 to 1964. Thus I attended Micheli during his stay in the hospital; this soldier never underwent X-ray treatment nor cytostatic medicines."

16. *23 April 1969:* The results of laboratory tests made at the Levico Casa di Cura. Blood tests: rate of sedimentation 5 to first hour, 10 to second hour, Katz indications 5; anti-staphylolysin rate 50 units; azotemia 0.27; glycemia 0.90; phosphatasemic acid 2 units; phosphatasemic alkali 9 units; hematin 4,700,000; leucotyles 4,700 normal formula. Urine test: nothing to signify. Therefore biological tests entirely normal.

17. *13 October 1969:* A histological statement by Prof. Fabre, Holder of the Chair of Pathological Anatomy at the Faculty of Toulouse (11), who sent us the following letter:

"Dear Colleague,

"Some specimens concerning the Micheli case were passed to me by Valdiguie which were examined not only by myself but also by several members of my department, some of whom are believers others are atheists, and I give you general impression.

"The findings of the microscopic examination did not differ from those of the clinic and in each case it appears to concern a malignant tumour, which is the original diagnosis. The problem became much more difficult when it came to the precise category in which this neoplasm should be placed for two reasons, first the indifferent technique employed prevents a cystological identification, and secondly tumours developed at the expense of tissues of considerable plasticity are often polymorphous.

"Originally Payan diagnosed reticulo-sarcoma. I think it would be difficult to go further and say that it concerns a malignant tumour of conjunctive origin and non-osteogenic.

"I beg you to forgive the delay in replying to you, these specimens arrived at the time of the examinations.

"I hope you can discuss my findings, and remain."

                                    (Sgd) Prof. Jacques Fabre.

"P.S.—Please give Payan my best wishes."

18. *27 November 1969:* The conclusions of Prof. Henri Payan, to whom we communicated Prof. Fabre's opinion. These conclusions will be given in full in the diagnostic discussions.

19. *Radiological Dossier* (12):

(*a*) *1 August 1962* (*in plaster*): The greater part of the left iliac bone is destroyed and the cotyloid and 2/3rd of the lower iliac spine have disappeared; the pubis, the ischium, the two ilio lines, the ischiopubics and the iliac crest cannot be recognized. The upper extremity of the femur has maintained its normal shape but is osteoporotic; it is juxtaposed with the iliac bone since the cotyle has completely disappeared; its elevation is very limited. In mezzotint in the complete stereotype the outline of the marrow can be seen which is very hypertrophied and in which can be found the sunken upper extremity of the femur. Following the outline of the tumour one realizes that it is enormous.

(b) *13 May 1964 (plaster removed)*: The iliac bone is reconstructed, a neo-cotyle has formed about 3 cm. from the old one; its outlines are clear, opaque, complete, the cotyloid fossa is very extended in the direction of the large trochanter. The iliac spine is well calcified, the sub-cotyloid area of the iliac bone is hypertrophied and shows polycyclic aspects. Excellent interline, the head of the femur well articulated in a neo-cotyle. No trace of the tumour can be found.

(c) *10 February 1965:* The X-ray is similar to the previous one, the coxo-femoral articulation is in fact perfectly restored with excellent interline; the general calcification appears to be even better than in the May 1964 stereotypes.

(d) *22 June 1968:* The iliac bone remains well calcified its outline equally well deleniated; one finds the neo-cotyle married up exactly with the head of the femur; the hip is perfectly articulated and the interline is clear; the whole bone structure is normally opaque. One observes two small iliac spaces that are hypercondensed.

(e) *4 April 1969:* There is practically no modification of the radiographs established on the stereotypes of 1964, 1965, 1968 as to the anatomic morphology, the structure and the calcification. The outlines of the neo-cotyle are those of a normal cotyle but displaced near the top, the head of the cotyledon is thick, perfectly opaque, its outer extension which resembles a truss that could have been constructed by a surgeon is massive, solid, enveloping. The head of the femur is surrounded on all sides by this cotyloid ridge and any eventual displacement is impossible. The articular interline is well formed and is also the same as the opposite hip. The transversals are even more apparent at the level of the neck and head of the femur and in the sub-cotyloid area of the iliac bone. One particular point—the sub-cotyloid area is clearly enlarged and nearly twice as thick as the bone area on the opposite side so that the lower part of the articular interline appears to be stumpy and less apparent in fact, we believe, than the superposition of the radiographic shadows which mask the outline of the interline. The centre of the thickened area shows slight clarity surrounded by a light opaque border and projects a small protuberance towards the pelvic cavity. These morphological "imperfections" do not in any way mar the solidity of the osteo-articular system of the hip and are in line with the radiological scars which we will speak of in the course of the discussion (see infra).

(f) *23 April 1969:* Thoracic radiograph taken at the Levico Case di Cura; pulmonary field normal transparency, no pleuro-parenchymatic lesions; hemidiaphragms mobile; costal diaphramatic sinus free. Heart and aorta morphologically normal.

II. The Facts of the Case (13)

Vittorio Micheli, 22 years of age at the time of his Military Service, was admitted to Verona Military Hospital on 16 April 1962 for pain at the level of the left ischium which had started in the previous March. An examination showed neoformation of an indeterminate character in the area of the left ilium, shortening of the left leg, limitation of mobility of the left hip, Lasegue positive of the two sides, patella reflexes exaggerated. Treatment: A.C.T.H., vitamins B1 and B12; no improvement. Rate of sedimentation on 17 April 1962, 42 (first hour). Radiography on 22 May 1962 (i.e. over one month after hospitalization) showed osteolysis of the iliac bone involving the lower iliac spine and the ridge of the cotyle; this picture evoked the diagnosis of a sarcoma type of malignant tumour. Urine test: negative. Blood test: red corpuscles 4,960,000, white corpuscles 3,400, leucocyte formula round about normal.

The condition of the patient grew progressively worse.

29 May 1962: Biopsy under general anaesthesia. An incision at the level of the nate above and behind the cotyloid cavity; the superior gluteal muscles were passed, the inferior gluteal was partly destroyed and replaced by a non-encapsulated neoplasm. The osseous iliac surface was sprinkled with "vegetation" irregular, mamelonated, friable, not encapsulated; many new bone fragments. Histological report (Prof. Natucci): The inferior gluteal is invaded by fusiform cells of a sarcoma characterized by an abundant proliferation of elongated rounded cellular elements with strongly atypical nucleus.

The cellular elements are distributed in clusters set in different directions. The fundamental substance is infiltrated by marked oedema resulting at times in vacuoleous phenomena. At certain points small cellular infiltrations are apparent. An examination of bone fragments discloses "trabula necrosis."

22 June 1962: Micheli is transferred to the Trente Military Hospital. Pain increased in the pelvic region and in the left leg. Large pelvi-paedic plaster.

18 July 1962: Radiography: Nearly complete destruction of the left hemi-pelvis, only part of the ilio-pubio line and the superior third of the iliac spine remain; osteoporosis of the femur.

1 August 1962: The patient transferred to the Borgo di Val-
sugana Centre for Tumours with the object of receiving cobalt
treatment. Three days later he left this establishment as the
Medical Corps seemed to have decided that it would contradict
with treatments by X-rays. General condition very poor; pallid
appearance, muscular hypotonia, enlargement of cardiac
shadow, extra-systoles, blood pressure 10/7. Abdominal and
thoracic examination negative. Diagnosis: osteo-sarcoma of the
left hemi-pelvis (14).

5 August 1962: The sick man returns to the Trente Military
Hospital in pelvi-paedic plaster and remains there until 23
April 1964. During this time numerous radiographs were taken
and in September and October Pentadyn, Butazolidin Polibron,
laxatives (for persistent constipation) and vitamins were prescribed.

13 November 1962: New stereotypes show an increase in the
process of destruction of the left hemi-pelvis with dislocation of
the head of the femur which amounts to 7 cm. Nevertheless the
patient can walk with his plaster apparatus. Here it is noted
that through 9 November until 10 December Micheli has an attack of profuse catarrhal bronchitis with fever, expectoration,
large bubbling rales. This bronchitis was treated with antibi-
otics.

12 January 1963: Condition the same, pain slightly less, the
plaster removed. Radiography: the femur has lost all connection with the pelvis and is completely dislocated. A fresh plaster
applied 19 February 1963. During the early part of 1963
Micheli is treated with various medicaments, Ticinal, Trin-
evrine, Myoglicine, etc.

1 April 1963: The pain increases at the level of the left hip
with radiation towards the knee.

24 May 1963: Plaster removed and replaced by a stronger
one because the patient wanted to go to Lourdes on pilgrimage.
Whilst changing the plaster there was a new examination; the
left hip very deformed, globulous; the left leg has the aspect of
a "dummy" and is joined to the pelvis by a few sheaves of
marrow on palpation no bone elements can be detected but
only a shapeless mass of doughy consistency (15). The patient
unable to make the least movement with the lower left limb
which appears to be "inert."

24 May–6 June 1963: Pilgrimage to Lourdes and return to
Trente.

30 June 1963: General condition much improved, sudden arrest of growth of the tumour (Dr. Frizzera).

14 July 1963: Repairs to plaster. Radiograph check-up: no
marked changes. During the following weeks the improvement

continues, Micheli steadily gains weight and is able to walk without pain.

Sharp gastric attack and intestinal upsets which appear to continue until October; various medicines administered (charcoal, citrosodin, anti-spasmodics, etc.).

8 November 1963: Pain in the hip and knee consistent with climatological conditions. Radiography: no apparent change. At the end of November all pain disappears and there is considerable gain in weight.

5 January 1964: Able to walk again in plaster without crutches and without pain.

18 February 1964: Plaster removed, able to walk easily and freely. The left hip has dislocated appearance; articular movements restored; flexion 18°, abduction 45°, shortening of the left leg 3 cm., atrophy of the thigh 7 cm. Rate of sedimentation 6 for the first hour, exercises performed by the patient in bed. Radiography: (19-2-64): remarkable reconstruction of the bony tissues of the pelvis which had been completely destroyed, a new cavity has formed at the femoral head situated 4 cm. above the former one (16).

24 April 1964: Micheli returns home "cured." Report of the Trente Military Hospital on the date of his departure includes the following: "Soldier returned to his family by special permission, awaiting pension as unfit for military service."

12 May 1964: Check-up visit by Dr. Frizzera (Levico Hospital) who states: "Condition flourishing, able to walk without stick, without pain, with slight limp; left lower limb external light rotation 20°, flexion 15°. Clinically the articular configuration is normal and the articular mobility of the hip is extensive, flexion 45°, abduction 40°, rotations cancel the shortening of 3 cm. of the leg, moderate stiffening of the left knee, flexion 90°. Foot slightly varus with normal movements; a little oedema of the inferior third of the leg and foot; atrophy of the thigh 3 cm. Thoraco-abdominal examination negative.

The Medical Bureau of Lourdes has received regular news of Micheli's progress (see documents); in February and May 1965, July 1967. All these certificates and reports are sent by Dr. Frizzera who has followed Micheli's case at first hand and Dr. Brandolani who confirms his excellent state of health.

In the affected parts: The palpation of the left ilio-pubic line shows the presence of a gross mass the size of a pigeon's egg, smooth, hard, attached to the bone; the mobility of the hip, although partly reduced, is most satisfactory. Micheli can walk without a stick without pain and jump and run. The muscular atrophy of the thigh has regressed progressively and is only 2 cm.

General health: Micheli says he feels very well; he married in

1967, works daily in a textiles factory on a machine and drives a car; his work has never been interrupted.

22 June 1968: Another check-up with radiography at the Levico Hospital. Dr. Frizzera has written to Dr. Olivieri confirming that Micheli is very well; he has never lost a day at work, he wears an orthopaedic shoe to compensate for the shortening of the leg, takes walks in the mountains, walks up stairs; during his leisure hours he works out of doors, plays ball with his neighbours; he barely limps.

The radiographs taken in June 1968 and April 1969 (see documents) show one iliac bone slightly enlarged, well condensed, coxo-femoral articulation well covered by a neocotyle, good interline, excellent calcification of the bone structure which has formed two small hyper-condensed iliac spaces.

23 April 1969: Clinical examination by Dr. Frizzera: General condition flourishing. Weight 81 kgs., height 1 m. 76. Examination of the neck and thoracic organs is negative. Blood pressure 14/9. Abdomen supple and indolorous; spleen and liver non-palpable and normal. Left hemi-pelvis; an irregularity is noted in the ilio-pubic line of osteocartilagenous consistency; the ischio-pubic is normal. The greater trochanter is 3 cm. above normal compared with the right side. Hip movements; flexion 90° external and internal rotations nearly complete; abduction limited one-third, adduction two-thirds, knee normal; foot slight equino-varus. No atrophy of the lower left limb.

Summary: Micheli suffered from a malignant tumour in the area of the left hip with encroachment of the nate and consequent destruction of the greater part of the iliac bone and pathological dislocation (17) of the hip. This tumour was a sarcoma which completely disappeared and the destroyed bone was reconstructed. The patient was closely attended for 8 years.

Before making any conclusions it would be as well to discuss most carefully the known facts reported in the written evidence of our colleagues Drs. Frizzera, Brandolani, Pierini, Franchi, Romanese (18) whose certificates are established conscientiously and scientifically.

III. Discussion

Foreword:

The precise *spirit of this discussion.*

In general we will adopt the view that has guided us since publishing our report on the "Extraordinary Cures at Lourdes" at the International Mariological Congress in 1958 (19), a view that conforms with that of our eminent and much regretted colleague, Prof. Thiebaut (20).

In particular we will discuss specialized medicine and surgery during 40 years in the field of orthopaedic surgery; also anat-

omy and histology since in the course of our careers we have
been occupied as much with morphology as with surgery.

During more than 40 years we have observed and treated
many hundreds of cases of osseous tumours of all kinds. We
will use simple clinical language discarding all more or less fac-
titious science and will at all times stress any faint contradictions
in order to enable doctors or others, clergy or laymen, to consider them for themselves. We will expound our knowledge
with sincerity. Our aim is to give such information to the lis-
tener or reader as to leave him free to accept or reject our arguments and conclusions.

We are assured of the collaboration of highly qualified anatomo-pathologists, Profs. Payan (Marseille) and Fabre (Toulouse), whose national and international reputations are universally recognized and who studied the histological specimens
with members of their teams, both believers and unbelievers,
who gave their opinions in a complete spirit of moral and
scientific loyalty.

We heartily thank our colleagues who did not stint their time
or trouble. We ourselves had a number of conferences at various times with Dr. Payan.

Some Remarks:

Careful reading of the dossier and the statement of facts help
in the detection of errors, contradictions and gaps. This is
hardly surprising. The observations were made in different Italian hospitals and all heads of departments appreciate the
difficulties encountered in publishing medical documents. It must
also be taken into account that the terms used in medical observations vary according to different teaching and training.

Errors are minimal and of no interest. They are merely variations in certain dates of not more than 3 or 4 days, mistakes
in the names of towns or villages, slight differences in the mea-
surements of the shortening of the left leg, etc. (21).

Contradictions: The worst one apparently concerns the thera-
peutics that were actually applied. In document No. 5 the pre-
scribing of Exodan, which is an antimototic, is mentioned (22).
Dr. Romanese, Specialist in Orthopaedic Surgery (document
No. 15) on the other hand peremptorily affirms that Micheli
never underwent X-ray treatment nor cytostatic (antimototic)
medicines. We must choose between these diverse opinions the
one that is categorical and authentic. Nevertheless, according to
the report that appeared in the I.M.A.L. bulletin Micheli had
taken "sedatives" which proves that the patient suffered violent
pain.

Gaps: These concern the paraclinical examinations and treatment.

In the "dossier" there are no radiographs of the complete bone structure, no tomographs (23) of the tumour, no arteriographs or phlebographs (24), no medullagram (25), of hormone dosage. In France we (doctors or surgeons) have a tendency (frequently annoying) to repeat examinations. These arbitrary examinations are chiefly of corroborative value. In Micheli's case this was not done. This is no way a reflection on our Italian colleagues; every institute has its own way of envisaging diagnostic problems. In any case sufficient and necessary action was taken; for instance, the biopsy, the results and verification of which are irrefutable.

The Treatment: No treatment considered to be curative was applied. In France—and in our school of thought in particular—we are inclined, perhaps wrongly, to "stake our all" and to overstep the limits of possibility and sometimes of reason. Why did our Italian colleagues abstain? In view of the size and considerable encroachment of the tumour did it appear to them to be beyond all therapeutic resources? Did they decide to spare the patient necessary suffering? One fact emerges; according to the interrogation on Micheli on 14 July 1965, the sick man received "sedatives and opiates" before his pilgrimage to Lourdes and these medicaments ceased as soon as he returned to Italy.

It is necessary to make these preliminary remarks in order to avoid eventual criticism; but actually they do not influence in any way the solution of the problem of the Micheli case. As in all difficult problems, it is necessary to consider the general essential context.

Our opinion will touch on certain bibliographical references. We have gone through all recent literature dealing with alleged spontaneous cures of cancers, in particular the very fine articles by Fauvet and his collaborators (26) as well as the American work (this appeared in 1966) entitled: *The Spontaneous Regression of Cancer* by Everson and Cole in which is given all the cases of "spontaneous regression" of cancers known at that date in world literature. Eight observations of osseous cancers are reported in chapter 8. It must be noted that all had received surgical or radiotherapeutic treatment. The word "spontaneous" used in these cures is therefore not applicable. We will return to this.

Diagnostic Discussion
We will make use of the evidence, documents, certificates, radiographs and anatomo-pathological examinations placed at our disposal.

(a) Clinical Diagnosis:

In April 1962 Micheli was discovered to have a neoformation of the left nate and hip which had appeared spontaneously without traumatism. From the beginning of the affection this large neoformation "of doughy consistency" (27) developed and increased rapidly in size. Our colleagues, the Italian doctors, surgeons and radiologists, were struck by the size of this tumour, the soft outline of which appeared in mezzotint in the first stereotype, the absence of its precise limits, the encroachment on the marrow, the accelerated rate of sedimentation without any sign of infection, and pronounced the clinical diagnosis of cancerous tumour of the "sarcoma" type. After studying the purport of the observations our colleagues did not consider any other diagnosis (see infra).

(b) Radiological Diagnosis:

Successive stereotypes (1962 and 1963) disclosed a destructive neoformation of the greater part of the left iliac bone with "osteolysis," a complete dissolution as it were of the entire bone and complete disappearance of the entire cotyloid cavity (28) without any sign of delimitation and without any indication of reconstruction. The osteoporosis of the femur which some radiographs appeared to show is an osteoporosis of immobilization and quite different from osteolysis.

These clinical pictures did not give any reason for considering the possibility of an infectious origin of an osteosis of some sort either para-thyroid or other (traumatic for example), not of so-called "essential" osteolysis, the pathogeny of which is unknown. It could not be a benign tumour as the outline would have been limited, nor a tumour of the giant cells in view of the absence of dividing grooves, nor an aneurysmal cyst of the bones because of the clinical characteristics of this neoformation.

However, if the radiographic results gave rise to the almost certain diagnosis of malignant neoformation it could only be confirmed scientifically (29) by the anatomo-pathological results.

(c) Anatomo-Pathological Diagnosis:

The histological specimens were examined many times by Profs. Payan and Fabre and their teams (30).

The anatomo-pathological diagnosis posed two problems, namely:

1. *Was it a malignant tumour?* The histological characteristics, the absence of capsule, the presence of mitoses, atypical cells, the encroachment on the muscles and the destruction

of the tissues did not leave any doubt. At the outset metastases of an early cancer of visceral or other origin had to be eliminated.

A giant cells tumour of unusual aspect and rapid development could have been considered; such tumours have occasionally been included in the category of malignant tumours. According to Dr. Payan, however, the histological specimens that were examined could not possibly have evoked such a diagnosis; neither could a malignant reticulosis be considered. The circumstances of the case leave no doubt; in actual fact it is a sarcoma–a cancer developed at the expense of the conjunctive tissue. French and Italian anatomo-pathologists—fifteen altogether with their collaborators—were all unanimous, including the unbelievers, who knew the circumstances of the cure. This international unanimity is so rare as to be outstanding.

2. *What type of sarcoma was it?* In the Italian hospitals there was talk successively of osteo-sarcoma (31), of sarcoma of the fusiform cells (32) and also of reticulo-sarcoma (33). In the main these diagnoses did not contradict one another (34). By definition a sarcoma is of conjunctive origin wheresoever it may be situated in any part of the conjunctive tissue concerned. It only affects histological changes forming in that part of the anatomy at whose expense the tumour has developed (bones, aponeurosis, different fibrous tissues) (35).

This is indisputable. Meanwhile, in accordance with the wishes of our colleagues and the decision made at the time of the meeting of the Committee in May 1968, we asked Dr. Payan to draw up a further report which he sent us on 27 November 1969, and which we quote in full as follows:

"Sir and dear Master,

"Here are the comments which may be made in response to the findings of the examination of specimen 2461/62 by the Institute of Pathological Anatomy at the Verona Hospital. From the morphological point of view analysis of this document enables two firm conclusions to be drawn: the malignity of the lesion and its sarcoma character. This type of malignant tumour can never be confirmed with absolute certainty. If in the absence of all osteogenic or osteolytic inflexion the idea of osteosarcoma can be eliminated then various interpretations might be considered which might envisage the possibility of an immature sarcoma, a reticulo-sarcoma or an angio-sarcoma. It appears to be difficult to go even further in the interpretation of the pictures owing to the technical conditions used in their production and in the absence of complementary colour and I concur with Prof. Fabre's conclusion, i.e. that it concerns a 'tu-

mour of malignant conjunctive origin and is non-osteogenic'
(36).
"Yours sincerely."

We compare this opinion with that of Prof. Natucci who on
examining the biopsy does not mention "osteo-sarcoma" but
"sarcoma of the fusiform cells" (see documents). We will not
add anything to Dr. Payan's categorical findings but in principle
we ask the following subsidiary question as to the origin of this
sarcoma. Some of the Italian documents mention a sarcoma
that has developed at the expense of the inferior gluteal muscle.
This is an error of locality for in a reverse example we would
have a case of myo-sarcoma; but no account has established
this diagnosis. Besides malignant tumours of the muscles are
exceptional. In order to discover the origin of the tumour the
clinical findings, radiographs and anatomo-pathological results
must be compared.

According to the radiographic stereotypes: in view of the extreme osteolysis of the iliac bone, the disappearance of the cotyle and the size of the tumour it is obvious that this is a sarcoma that has developed at the level of the iliac bone and
which has then invaded the neighbouring bone marrow. Moreover the histological records at the Verona Hospital mention
"vegetation" at the level of the osseous frame which points to
an osseous origin.

Nevertheless, as Drs. Fabre and Payan have emphasized, it is
impossible at the anatomo-pathological level to prove the osseous origin of this tumour owing to the fact that not with-
standing the previous deductions this could concern the bone
structure or only the neighbouring bone marrow that has been
invaded. Our object must be to recognize that this query is of
minor interest because the diagnosis is clear; it is a case of a
sarcoma type of malignant tumour. This is the main factor.

This sarcoma is considered to be an inexorable growth. We
will discuss this point later in connection with so-called "spontaneous" cancer cures. Now after Micheli's anamnesis it appears that this growth was "fulgurant"; he was hospitalized on
16 April 1962, the pain started in March and on 22 May the
greater part of the iliac bone was already destroyed.

IV. The Problem of the Cure
This is linked to two considerations:

(a) *Was treatment applied with a view to a cure?*
The reply is in the negative. There was no surgical intervention nor treatment by physics, antimitotics or cortoids. At
one time there was a question of cobalt therapy and certain
parts of the dossier mention a medicament of the Endoxan type

(antimitotic). But, as Dr. Romanese's certificate peremptorily affirms, no curative treatment of any kind whatsoever was applied. We must believe Dr. Romanese's evidence (37). It appears that Micheli's condition was considered too serious to attempt anything of this kind. A plaster was applied as a precaution to relieve the pain and prevent harmful movements. But a sarcoma has never been cured by immobilization in plaster.

Briefly, according to a study of the context of the dossier which the doctors and surgeons who treated Micheli addressed to the Borgo Centre for Tumours, he was unlikely to last for more than 3 days.

(b) What is understood by the term "cured"?

Fauvet refers to Littré: "A *cure* is the termination of an illness by the return of anatomic elements (tissues, etc.) to their normal characteristics and thereby determining the complete cessation of functional disorders which regain their normal functions."

"Remission: temporary diminution of the symptoms of an illness."

"Regression: after phenomenal development the tumour atrophies, is reabsorbed and decomposes" (38).

In Micheli's case it appears that the word "cure" must be applied: the "anatomic elements" returned to their normal or functional disorders which regained their normal functions. This must be specified exactly.

Is the cure really effective in regard to the clinical, anatomical and radiographic results?

Clinical: The examination on 23 April 1969 reveals a flourishing state of health, a slight limp, no pain, normal walk. Extended hip movements, flexion 90°, rotations normal, only the abduction and adduction are slightly limited; the muscular atrophy has disappeared. Palpation shows an irregularity in the osteo-cartilaginous consistency at the level of the ilio-pubic line. These epiphenomena come under the heading of "scars" which we will go into presently. Briefly, during the past 8 years Micheli has not suffered from any pathological trouble or metastases; he lives a normal family and social life, works at an arduous job standing, walks in the mountains and plays games.

Radiological: A remarkable reconstruction of the iliac bone and the cotyloid cavity has taken place. The stereotypes made in 1964, 1965, 1968, 1969 confirm categorically and without doubt that an unforeseen and even overwhelming bone reconstruction has taken place of a type unknown in the annals of world medicine. We ourselves during a university and hospital career of over 45 years, spent largely in the study of tumours and neoplasms of all kinds of the bone structure and having ourselves treated hundreds of such cases, have never encountered a single spontaneous bone reconstruction of such a nature.

But what is also remarkable is the permanence of this reconstruction; no modifications have appeared for 5 years and the radiographs remain identical in all the stereotypes. This permanence in the bone structure is equally overwhelming in regard to the anatomy, the radiology, the clinical and the general pathology; also, why not say it, from the point of view of medical philosophy and the Absolute.

It is true that the reconstructed cotyloid cavity has formed at a slightly higher level than usual; this epiphenomenon also comes under the heading of "residual scars" (see infra).

We, as well as the orthopaedic surgeon, insist on the actual configuration of the coxo-femoral; it could be said that Micheli had undergone an intervention of the arthoplastic type (39), the moulding of the bone surface is perfect, the articular interline is hardly diminished in comparison with the opposite side, and the uniformity of the bony ilio-femoral system is solid. If a surgical operation of the arthoplastic type had been performed it would not have had such a satisfactory result.

What is the date of the Cure?

According to the historical context the evidence of our Italian colleagues states that it is from the date of the pilgrimage to Lourdes that Micheli's condition improved so radically. The straightforward certificates are convincing. During 1962 his general and particular state of health steadily became worse. In the first half of 1965 there was no sign of improvement. Just before the departure for Lourdes (at the end of May) the region of the hip was globulous, deformed; the left leg was "inert," the destruction of the bone was considerable, the femur was "disarticulate" because of the dissolving and disappearance of the cotyle; the thigh was only attached to the bone by a few sheaves of bone marrow. It was from the date of the journey to Lourdes in June that a "sudden improvement" was observed (Dr. Frizzera).

One fact is of the greatest importance to us (40); the *absence of convalescence*. Micheli regained his appetite immediately; from being prone on a stretcher in a precarious state when he arrived at Lourdes he was able to walk with his apparatus a month later (41). We have never seen such a transformation from a sarcoma tumour *without any curative treatment*. At Lourdes the development of the tumour ceased. The immobilization in plaster prevented the detection of the precise moment that the hip regained mobility. It is obviously regrettable that the plaster was not removed and radiographs taken immediately upon Micheli's return from Lourdes. The reason for this is without doubt that this case was still considered to be very serious. We can understand the psychological attitude of our Italian colleagues who probably doubted the cure and did not want to expose the sick man to unnecessary risks. It was only in 1964 that a new stereotype was made and this shows the exact morphology noted in the 1969 stereotypes.

What was the intrinsic nature of the cure?

Let us go over it again: bones consist of two types of elements; a "framework" (cells and fibrils), a *biologically conjunctive living substance* and *mineral salts* having no life of their own merely being excess material which gives the bone structure solidity and resistance. In the case of a malignant bone tumour *only the conjunctive substance is attacked* and it is at its expense that the cancerous neoplastic cells proliferate and develop *active neo-plastic elements.*

The *mineral salts* are merely inert and submit passively to the fluctuations of the tumoral expansion. It is the *passive elements* that sometimes "encrust" certain parts of the cancer as in cases of osteogenic osteo-sarcoma (42); sometimes, on the other hand, they "evade" the cancer as in cases of osteolytic sarcomas (like Micheli). In the first case radiography reveals calcareous opacity more or less clear; in the second the stereotypes do not show an opaque picture.

What happens at the time of a cure to an osseous sarcoma?

The living conjunctive cancerous elements cease to proliferate and then degenerate; the tumour disappears. This is the *crucial period.* It is only later that the mineral salts—by a process of "calcic mutation" (Leriche)—are mobilized and "recalled" to the level of the bone originally affected. This "mineral recall" is an epiphenomenon which only has indirect relation with the *biological cure* of a tumour. A bone sarcoma can be "intrinsically cured" when "extrinsically" the radiograph of the bone structure does not show immediate modification; it takes time for the bone to recalcify. If an immediate calcic reconstruction were observed the phenomenon would be too "forceful." Thus the "biological" (in the exact sense of the word) state of Micheli developed in two stages: the *first* the disappearance of the sarcoma, and *second* recalcification. The following arguments support this opinion; the light shadow of the tumour had disappeared in the stereotypes taken in 1964 owing to the recalcification and the head of the femur had returned to its normal position and descended nearly 4 cm. after the disappearance of the tumour.

Has the cure been maintained?

Three years ago President Olivieri asked us to present Micheli's dossier because the classic "carcinoma period" of 5 years had expired. We preferred to wait longer. Actually 8 years have passed since he came on pilgrimage to Lourdes and *Micheli's cure has remained totally effective* without the least recurrence.

There is no doubt that it is possible to see later relapses of sarcoma, usually in cases of sarcoma of the marrow and not of the bone structure. Never as far back as we can remember have we observed a relapse of a bone sarcoma after 8 years.

There remains the question of *late metastases of cancers*. A great deal has been written on this subject. Pathogenic hypotheses abound. Does it concern authentic metastases developed at the expense of certain neoplastic cells emboled in the blood or lymphatic vessels which after a long period of quiescence (43) proliferate under unknown influences and result in a tumour which is discovered at a clinical or radiographic examination? Or is it a matter of *new tumours* of the same type as the original tumour but without relationship with it? This new tumour with the same characteristics as the original one by reason of its position, possible virus infection and hormonal secretions. This problem of metastases or new independent neoformations is far from being settled. For our part (44), we have never observed bone sarcoma metastases after 8 years.

Is the cure perfect? Do "scars" or residual "marks" of the illness still exist?

We must understand one another on this point. Certainly there is not "restitutio ad integrum" in as much as the cotyle is not reconstructed in its usual place. Nevertheless we stress for the third time that from the *morphological anatomy point of view the actual articulation is similar to normal articulation.* As regards the functions, there is no handicap, no pain, Micheli works regularly at a job that has to be carried out standing up, leads a normal social life, goes for walks in the mountains, etc. In short only "scars" persist which are found in all cures whatever their nature and characteristics. They are *biological or anatomical "marks" apparent or unnoticeable* which we again insist without qualification do not detract from the intrinsic quality of the *essence of the cure.*

When a fistula is "cured" it is replaced by a scar; when a wound is healed a scar remains. These marks are found equally in the bone marrow as in the bone structure. In Micheli's case the presence of light *radiological scars* does not conflict with the cure nor its "quality."

Certainly the word "perfect" would not apply. In Medicine there is never a completely "perfect" cure in the sense that no biological or anatomic-clinical traces of the original malady exist. We insisted on this point in our report at the International Mariological Congress in 1958.

In our opinion, the marks or scars authenticate the previous existence of the illness and in the present case of the tumour.

In another world, we tell ourselves philosophically, the absence of all "marks" or "scars" would be in the nature of "coercion" incompatible with the nature of man whose fundamental prerogative is that of possessing the freedom of acceptance or refusal.

Is the cure medically explicable?

The reply to this question is the "basis" of the task entrusted to us (45) and before making it we must query medical records —do comparable cases to Micheli's exist or not?

Numerous articles and other works have been devoted to the problems of *cures or spontaneous regressions of cancers;* we have reread Fauvet's articles and Everson's book (46). In most of the observations reported they do not come across the factor *"spontaneous"* by reason of the fact that there has been therapeutic treatment (surgery, radiotherapy, etc.).

Several cases dealt with *regression of metastases* when the original tumour was removed; others concerned intercurrent phenomena resembling a serious infection such as erysipelas. A serious infection can effectively promote the destruction of an eventual cancerous virus, provided the virus origin of cancerous tumours is admitted.

From another point of view certain malignant tumours such as *sympathies* (47) can undergo maturation or be exposed to ischemia and then regression occurs and the tumour disappears. This is never the case where osseous sarcomas are concerned. Here is an example that is often quoted—a study by Nelson in 1962; a girl aged 9 was seen in 1950 with an enormous retroperitoneal tumour and a biopsy revealed sarcoma (?) of nervous origin or a fibro-sarcoma. There was no treatment. Ten years later she was completely cured. This case does not really come within the scope of our investigation; there was no bone damage, the diagnosis was indefinite and certain retroperitoneal tumours do regress spontaneously.

If one extracts from these articles the observations made after treatment had been given the presence of intercurrent infections is noted and the cases of spontaneous cures of cancers are exceptional and inexplicable.

In Everson's book four cases of interesting observations are given:

Nelson's report, already mentioned.

A report by Dobson and Dickey (1956) concerning a child aged 5 months seen in 1943 who had an enormous tumour at the apex of the thigh and right flank, which, according to radiographs, had encroached on the iliac bone and femur. It is difficult to judge from the reports and stereotypes reproduced if the tumour was of osseous origin or not. A biopsy revealed *fibro-sarcoma*. This tumour regressed spontaneously and there is no medical explanation.

A study by Penner (1947); a child aged 2½ months with a tumour on the lower part of the left thigh with encroachment on the femur. A biopsy revealed *myosarcoma*. There was no treatment and at the age of 5½ years a complete cure.

It is to be noted that these last two cases dealt with young children in whom the development of neoplasms is often repulsed.

An observation by Levin (1955): a young woman aged 29 seen in 1952 suffering from a most deadly tumour on the upper extremity of the left humerus. A biopsy revealed a *"possible osteogenic sarcoma"* not excluding a possible diagnosis of *"giant cells malignant tumour."* Any curative treatment was refused and she was immobilized in plaster. Radiographs taken in 1955–56 revealed a complete cure with certain "anomalies" in the area of the humerus. This "spontaneous" cure is one of the rare authentic ones.

Whatever it was, it was after reading this report that in Micheli's case we continued to discuss the hypothesis of a *tumour of the giant cells,* the diagnosis of which is sometimes difficult. All the anatomo-pathologists in Profs. Fabre and Payan's teams were explicit—in this case it was impossible to envisage the possibility of a tumour of the giant cells.

As an additional safeguard we have searched carefully through our medical dossiers and must state that during 40 years' practice we have not found one single case of *spontaneous cure of a sarcoma.*

Our opinion is therefore categorical: no medical explanation can be found for Micheli's cure. This is confirmed by the views of our colleagues Pierini and Franchi *who have never experienced a similar reconstruction of the bone elements of the coxo-femoral articulation combined with the total disappearance of neoplastic infiltration of the bone marrow* (48).

We have questioned a large number of orthopaedic surgeons, particularly those who specialize in malignant bone tumours. All have replied, as we do ourselves, that in the course of long careers *they have never encountered "spontaneous cures" of malignant bone tumours.* One of them, highly qualified and prominent in national and international medical circles, replied in writing to our query "that if a bone cancer was cured without treatment it was because of a diagnostic error." Such a reply is to say the least astonishing; in effect it refused to have confidence in the competence of our anatomo-pathological colleagues and, what was more serious, refused to credit the histological examinations! Therefore why perform biopsies? Why have recourse to the microscope? Such equivocable behaviour has a retrograde effect by a century at least and could "ring the knell" of anatomo-pathological medicine which is the only criterion.

Actually, according to the clinical documents, histological specimens which were examined again and again dozens of times, the radiographs and the microphotographs, no possible diagnostic error could have been made. All the diagnostic, clinical, radiological and anatomo-pathological elements agreed.

Definitely a *medical explanation of the cure of the sarcoma from which Micheli suffered* was sought and none could be found:

> Micheli did not undergo any specific treatment.
> Micheli did not suffer from any susceptible intercurrent infection that might have had any influence on the evolution of the cancer.
> Micheli was able to walk again one month after his return from Lourdes.
> A completely destroyed articulation was spontaneously reconstructed without any surgical intervention.
> The lower limb which was useless became sound.
> The prognosis is indisputable: that the patient is alive and in a flourishing state of health 8 years after his return from Lourdes.

In the dossier files at the Medical Bureau of Lourdes the following is asked (question No. 3): *was the development of the malady suddenly modified whilst there was no tendency towards an improvement?* The reply is in the affirmative; it was after Micheli's return from pilgrimage to Lourdes that his condition was transformed.

Conclusions

Firstly, perhaps I may be allowed to offer a few assorted reflections:

A colleague whom we consulted on Micheli's case replied "It is a staggering fact." The concise word "fact" is apt; medicine is a *"training of verification"*; first we observe and we try to "explain" afterwards.

We must judge the "facts" with *moderation, consideration, good sense, simplicity and medical humility,* the humility of a Carrel, a Pasteur. We must guard against the "sin against the spirit" which attempts through arrogance *always* to seek an explanation. When a doctor does not find a valid explanation he must assume a spiritual humane attitude and accept in all good faith, *loyally and impartially,* that the case is "inexplicable." Believers and unbelievers must let the facts speak for themselves—so that the believer does not see *extraordinary cures* everywhere—and the unbeliever does not take refuge in *useless negation or scepticism.*

Briefly, when confronted by an *extraordinary cure* we doctors must be *morally certain;* the illness *existed,* the cure is *effective,* no *medical reasoning* can explain this cure.

We propose the following conclusions:

Micheli's illness was real, certain, incurable.
The evolution of the sarcoma Micheli was suffering from was suddenly modified although there was no sign of any improvement when he went on pilgrimage to Lourdes.
The cure is effective.
No medical explanation of this cure can be given.

Michel-Marie Salmon,
Professor of Anatomy,
Surgeon-in-Chief of Hospitals,
Professor of Child Clinical and Orthopaedic Surgery,
National Correspondent Member of the Academy of Surgery and of the Academy of Medicine of France.

NOTES

1. This report is drawn up in such form and style as to be understood either by doctors or others whether French or foreigners. Certain notes give some explanations intended to enlighten the uninitiated. The text contains some repetitions intended to facilitate the understanding of ideas which are often barren.
2. We sincerely thank Dr. Olivieri who has translated the documents written in Italian.
3. The case history is the document containing the clinical and para-clinical statements, the diagnosis and treatment.
4. Osteo-sarcoma is a cancerous tumour of the bones which is listed with general sarcomas. Sarcoma is a tumour which evolves and develops at the expense of the connective tissues. The bones are constituted essentially of connective webs encrusted with calcerous salts (see infra discussion) which give the bone structure its frame and its resistance. Sarcoma prevents epithelization; cancers of tissues of an epithelial nature (membrane, glands, etc.).
5. Dr. Frizzera wrote "sarcoma" and not "osteo-sarcoma."
6. Actually no anti-mitotic was administered to Micheli (see infra).
7. A reticulo-sarcoma can develop in the bone tissue or in the

extra-bone tissues (lymphatic ganglions, aponeurotic ten-
dons).

8. We draw attention to this "invasion," this "penetration" of
tumour cells in the adjacent tissues; an invasion which is
one of the primary characteristics of cancer (note by
writer).

9. Micro-photographs enclosed with Prof. Payan's report have
been passed on to the members of the I.M.C.

10. Appeared in I.M.A.L. Bulletin No. 145–146, page 25.

11. In a search for greater objectivity and truth the International Medical Committee at its meeting in May 1969
asked for an additional confirmation of the diagnosis of
malignant tumour.

12. The main stereotypes have been reproduced on paper and
sent to members of the I.M.C.L. They are given at the end
of this report.

13. There is general agreement on the observations made in the
various establishments where Micheli was hospitalized; one
can only detect a few errors in the transcription of the
names of towns and in the summing up of certain details.

14. We will return in due course to the diagnosis of osteo-sarcoma.

15. These are the same terms as those used in the report that
appeared in the I.M.A.L. Bulletin, p. 23 (see supra).

16. These are the words used in the radiological report.

17. A pathological dislocation is the "displacement" of a joint
due to the destruction through illness of the articular bone
elements; it is opposite of traumatic dislocation due to an
accident.

18. Documents Nos. 11, 12, 13, 14, 15.

19. The edition "Academia Mariana Internationalis," Vol. XII,
pp. 206–245. Via Merulana 124, Rome, 1960.

20. The remarkable conference of Prof. Thiebaut in I.M.A.L.
Bulletin Nos. 145–146, pp. 3–13, 1969.

21. We have often asked some of our qualified collaborators to
measure the length of a similar limb, but the figure obtained was not identical.

22. A product which impedes in an elective fashion the development of cancerous cells and sometimes even destroys
them. In actual fact in the course of our career we have
never observed any result in malignant conjunctive sarcoma
tumours of the bone structure.

23. Tomographs; series of radiographic shots.

24. Radiography of the arterial system and veins after injection
of a product opaque to X-rays into the vessels.

25. Microscopic study of the cells of the bone marrow clinically healthy, the marrow being removed with a special

trocar. The medullagram shows if there is invasion of the bones at a distance from the tumour (microscopic metastases).

26. In the Practitioners Review T. XIV dated 11-4-64 and T.X. No. 22 dated 1-9-68 under the title "The Cures and Spontaneous Regressions of Cancers." These articles admit to 170 "spontaneous" cures in the first and 24 in the second. Later we will discuss again the value of the term "spontaneous."

27. Terms reproduced in the I.M.A.L. Bulletin (p. 23) already cited.

28. Cotyloid cavity or cotyle; cavity of the iliac bone which encases the femoral head.

29. We use this term out of courtesy for our foreign colleagues. In medicine we do not like the word "science" in the mathematical sense (see our report to the International Mariological Congress at Lourdes, 1958).

30. Members of the public are sometimes astonished at the multiplicity of microscopic tests. They should know that histological diagnosis of a benign or malignant tumour is often difficult. It is for this reason in the interests of truth that we have done all we can to anticipate eventual criticisms and objections.

31. Developed at the expense of the bone structure with abnormal bone reconstruction.

32. Developed at the expense of the conjunctive bone marrow.

33. Developing at the expense of the bone structure as well as the bone marrow.

34. To reassure the reader who is not a doctor we point out that histological variations are only possible in the affected area, monomorphous, polymorphous cells.

35. The fundamental living part of the bone consists of conjunctive tissue, the mineral salts are excess elements without life (we recall this purposely for the benefit of the "profane" in Medicine).

36. Non-osteogenic signifies that no development of bony tissue exists and thus is not an osteo-sarcoma in the traditional sense (see infra).

37. We cannot enumerate the various treatments prescribed for the pulmonary trouble, the constipation and general state; these without doubt could not have any effect on cancer.

38. The following remark can be made: without qualification, according to Littré, in the case of a tumour the regression is certainly a "cure." It is for reason without doubt that in their book Everson and Cole use the term "regression."

39. Intervention consistent with reconstruction of an articulation.

40. See our report on the Mariological Congress, p. 232.
41. Document No. 11; observation by Dr. Frizzera.
42. Which apparently comes more or less from the bone struc-
    ture.
43. Medical term meaning: repose, sleep.
44. I make excuses for referring once again to this experience
    of 40 years.
45. This was written by an expert in a report requested by the
    magistrates on a Tribunal or a Court of Appeal.
46. Loco citato.
47. Benign or malignant tumours developed at the expense of
    sympathetic nervous systems or suprarenal glands.
48. Document No. 14. Prof. Pierini is head of the Radiology
    Unit at the Military Hospitals in Florence and Prof. Fran-
    chi is doctor-in-charge of the Radiology Unit at the Civil
    Hospital at La Spezzia.

❦ Index ❦

Barèges, 28
Barrère, 149–50
Barrière, Henri, 210
Barthecoy, M., 113
Bartrès, 24, 71, 130, 179
Basques, 108, 156
Bath, Somerset, 145, 147
baths, 118–22, 138, 142–48
Bayonne, 39
Béarnais *patois,* 35
Beauchamp, Comte de, 148
Beck, Countess Bianca de, 80
Beckett, St. Thomas, 42, 43
Belgium, 39, 80, 210, 217, 218, 219
Belley, 82
Benedict XIV, Pope, 197
Benson, Arthur, 125
Benson, Mgr. Robert, 125
Le Béout, 142
Berlin, 155
Bernadette of Lourdes, St., 81, 130–31; background, 23–25; visions, 25–33, 88, 185–86; asthma cure, 36–37, 76; Father Peyramale's support for, 37, 38–39; and the Miraculous Medal, 96; books about, 102; objections to souvenir trade, 102–3; dislike of statue in Grotto, 116, 166; ill-health, 131, 170; joins Sisters of Nevers, 166–67, 170; preservation of her corpse, 170–73, 174–76
Bernardines, 167
Bétharram, 34, 93, 131, 179
Biarritz, 32
Bigorre, 35, 40, 42, 72, 77, 131, 148
Bigorre, Count of, 40

Bigot, Marie, 215, 227, 230–32
Bigourdan dialect, 24, 29, 35, 72
Billet, Dom Bernard, 102, 186
Bire, Marie, 125, 225
Blessed Sacrament procession, 122–23, 132–33, 193, 215, 216
Blois, Bishop of, 213
Boclande, Mabel de, 63
Boissarie, Dr., 157
Bolivia, 39
Bologna, 63
Bonaventura, Sister, 88
Bouhort, Justin, 200, 222
Bordeaux, 41, 63, 69
Bordes, Father, 82, 139
Boulevard de la Grotte, 68
Bouley, Berthe, 213
Boulogne, 56, 135
Bourges, 129
Bourisp, 34
Bouriette family, 113
Bouriette, Louis, 113, 222
Bouyssonnie, M., 79
brancardiers, 118, 119–20, 140–41, 145
Brazil, 39, 217, 219
British Caledonian, 188
British Rail, 47, 59
Brophy, Michael J., 88
Buglose, 34
Burgundy, 168
Buscail, Jean, 113

Caesar, Julius, 75
Café Français, 88
Calvet, Melanie, 101
Camden Council, 55
Canada, 39, 217, 219
candles, 153–55

Printed in the United States
by Baker & Taylor Publisher Services